What Would Madison Do?

The Political Journey Progressives and Conservatives
Must Make Together

Stephen Erickson

ISBN:1546549838
ISBN-13:978-1546549833

TO TIMOTHY, JONAS & THOMAS,
AND FUTURE GENERATIONS OF
U.S. CITIZENS

"Stephen Erickson has written an important and powerful book about uniting citizens on Left and Right to reform America's corrupted political system. Filled with characters, drama, success and failure, it reads like a great novel. But in this case, it's all true."

— Peter Schweizer, bestselling author of *Clinton Cash*, *Extortion* and *Throw Them All Out*, and President of the Government Accountability Institute.

"Progressives need to read this book. We need to understand that we are missing opportunities to improve our democratic systems because we are not talking to each other."

— Joan Blades, Co-founder, MoveOn.org and Founder, Living Room Conversations

*"As I read Stephen Erickson's book, I am awed by its honesty... **What would Madison do?** is a must read for citizens who want to take up the mantle of change, because its sobering account ensures that we who demand change are muscled-up for the fight to save our democracy."*

— Arnie Arnesen, progressive media personality, former Democratic New Hampshire state legislator, candidate for governor and congress, and Fellow at Harvard University's Kennedy School.

*"At a time in the United States' history when extreme partisan politics have become a dangerous new norm, it is refreshing to explore ideas that both the left and the right can equally embrace. Stephen Erickson has made a valiant argument for common sense reforms that would tame the beast that Americans abhor, namely, special interests with their vice-like grip on our elected representatives. **What Would Madison Do?** should serve as **THE** springboard for united action to help save our republic."*

— Colleen Conley, Founder, Rhode Island Tea Party, and Managing Editor, RightAlerts.com

Contents

Introduction: Our Unalienable Right to Reform

On a brilliant and hopeful June day in 2014, I rendezvoused on the Portland, Maine, waterfront to share a pizza with one of the vice presidents of Common Cause, the nation's largest progressive political reform organization. We were following up on a meeting in Washington with a leading and well-connected conservative reformer earlier in that same spring.

What we were planning was something potentially extraordinary and unprecedented in American politics: prominent and powerful progressive and conservative leaders – thinkers, reformers, media professionals, financiers and maybe even some politicians on the Left *and* Right – would sit down together to explore an alliance to fundamentally clean up America's corrupted and dysfunctional political system.

Among other measures, we proposed a popular Left-Right alliance to 1) get the corrupting influence of money out of elections and legislation, 2) encourage citizen government instead of political careerism through a system of term limits, and 3) promote fair elections without special advantages for incumbent politicians, the very wealthy or particular political parties. It was the beginning of a process that could unite the country to finally check the selfish interests that have come to dominate our government. And change everything.

◇◇◇

Can there be any doubt that we Americans have lost faith in our political system? According to Gallup, only around 20% of Americans trust their government in Washington "to do what is right."

The 20% figure tends to match the dismal public approval level for Congress, which has been scraping bottom at historic lows.[1]

On the eve of the 2016 election, public opinion surveys revealed unprecedented popular disapproval for both the Democrat and Republican nominees for president, Hillary Clinton and Donald Trump.

Much is often said by elites about the average citizen's lack of understanding and sophistication when it comes to politics and public policy, but the public opinion data reflects common sense. Ordinary folks get it. Our system is not producing good political leadership. As a result, government is failing us. For at least forty years, it has failed us in too many ways to mention but here are some of the lowlights:

For two whole generations, the middle class has been struggling while poverty levels have remained constant. Only high-income people are making any progress.

For citizens concerned about our annual federal budget deficits and the government's looming financial commitments, the rising sea of red ink is relentless and irresponsible. Entitlement programs – Medicare, Medicaid, and Social Security – go unreformed, even though they are on track to bankrupt the nation.

For those concerned about human-made climate change, the government does nothing meaningful to reduce carbon emissions.

The United States experienced two financial debacles during the past 40 years: the S&L crisis, which came to a head in the 1980s, and the banking crisis of 2008, which together cost the economy trillions and trillions of dollars. No one was ever punished for the 2008 crisis. Banking corporations are still too-big-to-fail; in fact, they are bigger than ever.

Meanwhile the Federal Reserve continues to experiment with the economy by indefinitely keeping interest rates at historically low levels. Some call this reckless as well as a big subsidy for the rich.

Issues associated with illegal immigration never get fixed.

The Affordable Care Act is not what anybody really wanted and has not yet controlled costs.

Though the Cold War was successfully brought to a close, the United States was blindsided on 9/11 and then blundered into Iraq. We spent thousands of lives and billions of dollars creating a power vacuum in the Middle East into which have stepped 1) Iran, a sponsor of terrorism with nuclear ambitions, and 2) ISIS, a political / religious movement as cruel and as evil as any the world as ever seen. Ultimately this tragedy is America's failure and our collective responsibility.

As if not satisfied with the terrible mistake in Iraq, the United States went on to topple the government in Libya and create another terrorist safe haven there.

There is more dysfunction here that we can reasonably blame on one political party or the other. Both Republicans and Democrats have controlled the government at various times, yet no one outside of the system is happy with the result.

What's gone wrong? What would James Madison do?

What should "we the people" do now?

These are the essential questions I seek to answer.

This book has three major threads that run throughout its course. First it is framed by my personal story of trying to unite leaders on the Left and Right for political reform. Second, in so doing, I spotlight the political obstacles standing in the way of creating a united bipartisan reform movement, which is the first critical step toward fixing the system. Third, I weave in James Madison, who I believe has much to teach us about what has gone wrong and what we can do about it. With Madison's guidance, I suggest a way forward.

◊◊◊

I hope what I have to say about James Madison will stand up under scholarly scrutiny, but this is not an academic book and it's not even primarily about Madison, though he's important. It's about us, we the people of the United States, and what we must do *together*.

Progressives[i] and conservatives are divided on the proper size and role of government, and many other issues. These differences may or may not be reconcilable, but it's important to recognize that those who benefit from the system – politicians, political parties, partisan media, and everyone who sustains and enriches himself or herself from the status quo – have a vested interest in keeping us apart. Right now they have us just where they want us: at each other's throats. Hateful and mindless partisanship is the status quo's best friend.

Progressives may struggle with parts of the book. Hang in there with me. I think you will cheer my conclusions in the last two chapters.

I also ask conservatives scornful of "campaign finance

---

[i] For the sake of convenience, I use the label "progressive" synonymously with "liberal" and "Left" to indicate the left side of America's political spectrum.

reform" to reconsider. A political system in which law-makers may accept money and other benefits from the same interests they regulate is inherently corrupt.

When it comes to fixing our corrupted political system, we need to turn off the talking heads and start listening to each other for a change. Therefore, for tactical reasons, I have written this book with a specific target audience in mind: political activists and informed voters on *both* the Left and Right. There are different messages here for each side of the political spectrum, alongside a plea for populist unity. If we want our democracy/republic back, then populist conservatives and progressives must unite in a provisional alliance to reform our corrupted American political system. I believe I know how we can make it happen.

I am a conservative who speaks from experience. In 1993, I abandoned work on a doctorate in American history at the College of William and Mary to take a job as Resident Scholar at US Term Limits. (This was around the time of the Supreme Court decision, *US Term Limits v. Thornton.*) I published articles about James Madison, term limits and election reform for the Heritage Foundation and Cato Institute. When the term limits movement ended in the Supreme Court, I deliberately chose not to stay in Washington, even though politics and public policy have always been my primary interest. I knew at the time that I did not want to become part of the Washington establishment.

I moved to New Hampshire, where I made a life but never found a calling. Still obsessed with politics and what I perceived as the corruption of the nation's founding vision, I set out in 2010 to "save America." Of course I never expected to save America myself, but I thought maybe I could begin to bring together the leaders who could.

As you will see, I have spent years herding political cats. Most either refused to be corralled or wandered off. The good news is that we Americans, collectively, know what needs to be done. I believe you'll find that my experience, with guidance from James Madison, shows us the way forward.

◊◊◊

Some, mostly progressives, might wonder why Madison matters. On the other side, others, mostly conservatives, might wonder whether it's right to change the system that he and his fellow founding fathers created.

James Madison is appropriately considered the "father of the Constitution" for the role he played before, during and after the convention that drafted the Constitution in Philadelphia in 1787. Madison was a key figure in organizing the convention and making it a momentous event. While many of Madison's contemporaries thought the Articles of Confederation might be revised, Madison planned to recreate the entire framework of the government from the ground up and make it a truly federal system rather than a mere association of individual states, which is what it essentially was under the Articles. [2]

Prior to the convention Madison led his Virginia delegation in drafting the "Virginia Plan," which was the rough working draft for the Constitution itself. During the convention Madison was among the most active debaters. He didn't get his way on many points but was always in the fray. Madison's notes, taken at the convention, are the gathering's most comprehensive.

After the convention Madison became famously known as co-author of *The Federalist Papers*: eighty-five essays, out of which he penned at least twenty-nine. The essays were written to promote the Constitution to the American people and persuade them to ratify it in state conventions.

Progressives may argue that Madison's extremely wealthy white slave-owning status disqualifies him as an authority on popular government. Several points need to be made in response. First, any leading thinker of the 18th century had to be wealthy enough to have leisure time to buy books, read, and perhaps attend college. Madison graduated from Princeton (called the College of New Jersey at the time). Throughout his life, Madison received bundles and trunks of books in the mail from various places. Back then, books were precious and expensive items.

The slave labor system, for its part, was a significant and unhappy feature of the world that English colonists, especially Southerners, were born into. Madison, Jefferson and Washington hoped and expected that the awful system would disappear. Each of these three founders took at least some meaningful step against slavery. In 1785 Madison spoke out in the Virginia Assembly in favor a bill introduced by Jefferson that would have gradually abolished slavery in Virginia. A French observer remarked of Madison, "A young man (who) astonishes by his eloquence, his wisdom and his genius has the humanity and *courage* (for such a proposition requires no small share of courage) to propose a general emancipation of the slaves."[3]

Yes, in theory Madison, Jefferson and Washington all could have been stronger abolitionists, but who among us in the 21st century can honestly say that, born into their circumstances, we would have done more? Would we have cloistered ourselves in our room all day as Madison did, reading books to improve our minds so as to better serve our country? Or would we have played cards, raced horses, feasted and drunk brandy like much of the other Virginia gentry? It's too easy to judge and condemn from a position of political correctness over two hundred years later.

Madison is worth studying for his learning and his genius. To understand what he hoped to accomplish for the American republic in his time is to see the way forward to reform the system in ours.

Some say that we should never alter the Constitution, because it's the wisest form of government ever conceived by humankind. I have heard a number of evangelical Christians even describe the Constitution as "divinely inspired."

I find the notion of a "divinely inspired" Constitution a little bizarre. This puts the Constitution alongside the Bible as a sacred text. The Constitution is not some idol to be worshipped. It is a political document and the product of many political compromises. The founders themselves certainly recognized the Constitution for what it was and, importantly, expected that it would be amended as circumstances warranted. They would be alarmed at the notion of a "living Constitution" that "evolves" by power grabs, usurpations, and surrenders of legitimate legislative authority, but they intentionally gave succeeding generations processes for deliberatively and legally amending the highest law of the land.

Since the Constitution is a political document, it sometimes reflects the politics behind it rather than the spirit that animated the American founding. For that spirit, we can turn to James Madison.

◇◇◇

On June 8, 1789, Congressman James Madison rose to offer a preamble to the first amendments to the Constitution, beginning a process that would become our Bill of Rights. This preamble was never included in any official document except for the *Annals of Congress*, but its relevance for us makes it worth repeating.

Madison wished to remind his fellow citizens then and for all time that . . .

> . . . *all power is originally vested in, and consequently derived from, the people. That Government is instituted and ought to be exercised for the benefit of the people; which consists in the enjoyment of life and liberty,*

> *with the right of acquiring and using property, and generally of pursuing and obtaining happiness and safety.* **That the people have an indubitable, unalienable, and indefeasible right to reform or change their Government, whenever it be found adverse or inadequate to the purposes of its institution.**

Is this now such a time? If so, how do we proceed? Again, what would Madison do?

.

1: Political Vice #11

In the cold of January 25, 1787, three companies of rebel militia, numbering more than 2,400 men, began converging on the federal arsenal at Springfield, Massachusetts, where several cannon, numerous muskets with bayonets, and ample powder were stored. All three rebel companies were led by veteran soldiers of the Revolution. One was Daniel Shays, whose name this rebellion would take.

Major General William Sheppard of Westfield and a militia of 1,200 men still loyal to the government of Massachusetts arrived at the arsenal first and deployed the cannon.

Unfortunately for the rebels, one of their three companies halted its march due to a failure of communication. The other two trudged forward through the four-foot-deep snow toward the well-defended arsenal. At the vanguard were 400 "old soldiers" eight deep, clutching their muskets.

These were Sheppard's neighbors and fellow veterans of the Revolutionary War; he did not want to use force against them. Likewise, the rebels had no personal grievance against the militia men defending the arsenal. While each side acted in the purest of fervently-held principles, we will see that they were in fact pawns in a corrupt political game being played in the distant capital.

Sheppard ordered the cannon to be fired over the heads of the plodding militia, to scare them off. But the cannon's roar had the opposite effect. Now the rebels, enraged, came on at the quickstep. Sheppard ordered the cannons charged with grapeshot and lowered to "waistband height." Concealed artillery on the advancing rebels' flank unloaded. Four men dropped dead and many more were wounded, staining the pristine snow a bloody crimson. The rebels who remained standing reversed themselves in a hasty retreat.

After eight long and ultimately successful years of war against the British for liberty, popular government, and independence, how had it come to this?

James Madison followed the events in Massachusetts as best he could from New York, where he sat as a member of Congress under the Articles of Confederation during that same winter. And Madison was deeply worried. It was the latest and most dangerous example suggesting that self-government in America was not working. Madison saw irresponsibility, chaos, and narrow-minded behavior all around him. Enlightened political leadership was nowhere to be found. Foreign debts, incurred to fight the war, went unpaid. Foreign treaties entered into by the Continental Congress were ignored or violated by individual states. Some states, most notoriously Rhode Island, issued paper currency to alleviate debt, unleashing a fury of inflation. Other states, like New York, set up trade barriers with their neighboring states. Every interest in the young nation seemed to be selfishly serving itself, without regard for the common good. Massachusetts was the worst. Whole counties in that state defied their government, and by midwinter, the blood was spilled. The hard-fought values of the American Revolution seemed to be immediately rotting away. [4]

◊◊◊

Everyone knows what the American Revolution was for: liberty and self-government, of course. Less well understood is what the Revolution was against, which was *corruption*.

By the 1770s, the colonists had perceived that "the balance of the [English] Constitution had been thrown off by a gluttonous ministry usurping the prerogatives of the crown and systematically corrupting the independence of the [English House of] Commons," writes historian Bernard Bailyn.[5] With the English parliament bought and paid for, the colonists smelled the stench of civil decay wafting across the Atlantic and believed that they were its next victims. Through taxes, newly enforced commercial regulations, the beginnings of an imperial bureaucracy in America, and the movement of some trials from local courts to Admiralty courts, the colonists concluded that their self-government was under attack.

In America, as in Britain, the more cronies the Crown could hire, the more revenue it could raise, which enabled the hiring of more corrupt officials until the entire British Empire became a tyranny, with a class of rich and powerful men at the center robbing the rights and resources of the people as a whole. From the colonists' point of view, the cancer originating back in England had to be stopped at the water's edge.[6]

American colonists did not develop this theory of political decay all by themselves. The idea that Britain was terribly, perhaps hopelessly, corrupt was commonplace in London. The English presses ran furiously to proclaim the news that the British political system had become a fetid swamp. There was no need for some colonial crank to rant about the fallen English Constitution when the great parliamentary leader, William Pitt, who would later argue for forceful suppression of the rebellious American colonies, lamented "the notorious decay of the internal vigor of the constitution" and urged electoral reforms to "stop the rapid progress of corruption." English pamphlets and newspapers were stuffed aboard ships trading with America, circulated, and juicy bits reprinted for widespread consumption throughout the colonies.

The American concern about spreading corruption more broadly reflected a harsh judgement on the degeneracy of Britons themselves. Charles Carroll of Maryland, a signer of the Declaration of Independence, expressed the feelings of many. "I despair of seeing the constitution [the English one] recover its former vigor" wrote Carroll. He concluded that "vast influence of the crown, the luxury of the great, and the depravity of the common people are unsurmountable." Everyone in the mother country was grasping and self-serving, it seems, and such men were running the British Empire for their own selfish ends.[7]

The War for Independence was in some ways a test of the American character. Did Americans possess sufficient civic virtue to prevail? Were their institutions strong enough, and where new institutions were needed, would they be up to task?

Though the military victory was won, the war had been financially exhausting. The states and the Continental Congress had all borrowed large sums of money to fund it. They issued IOUs to be redeemed upon the independence of the United States. Unfortunately, as is typical in postwar periods, the economy contracted and fell into deep recession, if not depression. Pent-up demand for English and other foreign manufactured goods siphoned hard currency out of the economy. Depressed economic times, combined with weak and inexperienced governments, caused the postponement of debt repayments.

Holders of securities naturally wondered if they would ever be paid off. Most former soldiers of the Continental line, who had been compensated in such notes, couldn't wait. Having been away from their farms fighting the war, they needed cash to rebuild, so nearly all of them sold their securities to speculators at deep discounts. For example, Massachusetts notes issued in 1778 immediately traded at one-fourth of their value and by 1781 had sunk to one-fortieth of their original worth. When state governments finally got around to begin paying off the notes, most took into consideration their depreciation and the fact that the notes were no longer in the hands of the original recipients and buyers. The Continental Congress redeemed some of its notes at a ratio of forty to one and the state of Virginia at one thousand to one. But not so Massachusetts, which extraordinarily decided to redeem its securities at a ratio of one to one, and even pay interest on top of that. Herein lies the true cause of post-revolutionary insurgency in Massachusetts that became known as "Shays' Rebellion."

Contrary to what has been taught in schools for a generation or more, "Shays' Rebellion" was not about poor indebted farmers oppressed by a rapacious class of capitalist merchants. In the words of historian Leonard Richards, who has corrected the old quasi-Marxist explanation, it was caused by the state government "and its attempt to enrich the few at the expense of the many." Here again, corruption would rear its rotten head, and the results would shock the young nation.[8]

The Massachusetts Constitution was adopted in the dead of winter, 1780, one of the coldest and harshest that state has ever seen. The only means of getting around was by snowshoe. From the remoter towns, there was simply no realistic way to get to Boston to the ratifying convention. The constitution was approved by a bare quorum and contained unprecedented property requirements for office holding and for voting.

When the new government convened, at least 40% of its members either held some of the depreciated securities or had close relatives who did. Since 80% of the notes were in the hands of speculators, few if any of these legislators would have been the original owners. Most had likely bought the securities on the cheap at small fractions of their original worth. If they were typical speculators, they might have engaged in market timing and involved themselves in land speculating; buying cheap state-owned land was one of the few things the depreciated notes were good for. The wealthy speculators of the merchant and landowning class were the Wall Street bankers of their time and place.

From the point of view of many citizens in Massachusetts, their government had been captured by a pack of greedy parasites. Securities redeemed at a ratio of one to one would be a huge bonanza for those left holding the notes.

Poll taxes to pay off the securities went up five to six times and were to be paid in hard currency, of which there was precious little in the economy. The middle-class farmers of Massachusetts were stunned. Town after town humbly petitioned the legislature for relief. Under British rule they had never been required to pay anything close to the amount now demanded of them. The proposed taxes that sparked the Revolution were nothing by comparison.

Some of the taxed citizens were soldiers of the Massachusetts line, who had stuck it out with General Washington through terrible battles and awful winters, often without proper clothing and equipment that the states and the Continental Congress had failed to provide. Now their own government was taxing them for larger sums than they had received for the almost worthless notes that they had been forced to sell near the end of the war. It was too much to bear.

Between August and December of 1786, whole communities in the form of militia forcibly shut six courts in the Massachusetts backcountry. The courts were the only instrument of state control in rural areas, and with their costly fees, were themselves a source of grievance. The rebels called themselves "regulators," like similar movements in the Carolinas in which backcountry planters and farmers forcibly resisted corrupt mercantile interests located on the coast.

Boston-based political and financial interests were thrown into a state of alarm. An army was raised and paid for, mostly by the speculators, who loaned the government the necessary funds. Under General Benjamin Lincoln, who had accepted Lord Cornwallis' sword at Yorktown, the army of 2000 began marching from Boston. They were supposed to be joined by 1200 and 600 additional men from the central and western parts of the state, but only 1000 showed up.

News of the force heading their way prompted Daniel Shays and his fellow regulators to attack the Springfield arsenal. When he arrived, Lincoln found that the entire backcountry was hostile and his own troops' hearts weren't in it; widespread desertions were reported. He would have to move quickly. After a night march through a blizzard, he surprised the sleeping rebels in a snowy dawn at tiny Pelham, Massachusetts. Lincoln's army, too exhausted and uncoordinated to capture the rebels, sent them fleeing in all directions. Many soon turned north, over the border to the completely sovereign state of Vermont, where they would find sanctuary under the government of Ethan Allen, who himself had led a rebellion against the great land barons of New York.

Twice the Massachusetts regulators made critical blunders, once in their uncoordinated attack at Springfield and again when they let their guard down at Pelham. But what if either of these events had gone differently? Had they successfully seized the powder, artillery, and other weapons at Springfield, it was said they intended "to march directly to Boston, plunder it, and then to *destroy the nest of devils, who by their influence, make the Court*[ii] *enact what they please*, burn it, and lay the town of Boston in ashes."[9]

[ii] "Court" is an old term used here to refer to the Massachusetts legislature.

◊◊◊

Events in Massachusetts represented everything that James Madison feared most and were fresh in his mind as he sat bored by the feckless speechifying all around him in Congress. America couldn't risk any more Shays' Rebellions. Madison had worked hard to organize an upcoming convention, scheduled to meet in Philadelphia in May, that he hoped would completely restructure the federal government and give it the strength to put down dangerous rebellions, but also he hoped to discourage unjust lawmaking of the sort that caused the rebellion in the first place.

To organize his thoughts, Madison decided to pass the time in Congress by categorizing the many failures of American government. Pen in hand as the politicians all around him bloviated, Madison jotted down a list under the heading, "Vices of the Political System of the United States."[10] He counted twelve of them. Vices one through three related to the states' tendency to ignore the federal government. Vices four and five were about the states' disharmony with each other. Vices six and seven dealt with the confederated government's lack of coercive powers and its inability to guarantee security. Number eight was that the confederated government lacked legitimacy because it was a creation of the states and not the people directly. Vices nine, ten and twelve were about state laws: there were too many laws, they contradicted each other and they often went unenforced. All the vices listed by Madison were fairly specific — that is, all except number eleven, which was a political essay unto itself. He referred to this vice as the "injustice of state laws."[11]

"Injustice?" Here was a vice far more general than all the others. In fact, the "injustice" Madison described was the root cause of all the other vices.

To modern ears, the choice of the word "injustice" seems a little off the mark. We tend to think of "injustice" in the context of courts of law, or lack thereof, and the punishment of the innocent. But Madison uses the term here in association with lawmaking, legislators, and the laws themselves. It was a deliberate choice of words because Madison believed that legislators should be disinterested, fair-minded, rational, farsighted and wise rather than biased, impetuous, narrow-minded, self-interested, self-serving or corrupt. "Representatives" really weren't even supposed to "represent." Rather, he wished them to be impartial judges capable of governing for the broad, common and long-term good of the nation. He wanted legislative bodies to be *judicious*. The choice of the word "injustice" is particularly appropriate considering the context of Shays' Rebellion and the government policies leading up to it.[12]

Under his vice #11, Madison noted that even in republics, the laws created were sometimes not just; they could serve narrow interests at the expense of the common good and sometimes they trampled on the rights of individuals or minority groups. Madison went on to write that unjust laws in a republic had two possible sources. The cause of the injustice, or "evil," to use Madison's word, must either lie "in the representative bodies" or in the people themselves. The evil of injustice in a republic is carried out by "factions," which are described by Madison in *Federalist #10*. The meaning of words changes over time and for us, the word "faction" doesn't really capture what Madison had in mind. Here is Madison's definition:

> *By a faction I understand a number of citizens, whether amounting to a majority or minority of the whole, who are united and actuated by some common impulse of passion, or of interest, averse to the rights of other citizens, or to the permanent and aggregate interests of the community.*[13]

Madison's definition of "faction" is nearly a perfect match for a term we use all the time in relation to politics: *special interests*. He goes on to discuss ideological and religious interests, which he considered dangerous enough. "But the most common and durable source of faction," writes Madison, "has been the various and unequal distribution of property."

> *A landed interest, a manufacturing interest, a mercantile interest, a monied interest, with many lesser interests, grow up of necessity in civilized nations, and divide them into different classes, actuated by different sentiments and views. The regulation of these various and interfering interests forms the principal task of modern legislation, and involves the spirit of party and faction in the necessary and ordinary operations of government.*

What Madison said over two centuries and a quarter ago is as true today as it was then; indeed, it is *truer* today. Catering to special interests was, for Madison, a "dangerous vice." Interests, when introduced into government councils and into legislation, cause "instability, injustice and confusion" and are "the mortal diseases under which popular governments have everywhere perished."

Madison pointed out that there was nothing to be done about interests in free society. "Liberty is to faction (or interests), what air is to fire" explained Madison in *Federalist #10*. One can't snuff out special interests without destroying individual liberty including the freedom of association and free speech. Madison concludes that the "causes of faction (or interests) cannot be removed; and that relief is only sought in the means of controlling its *effects*" (Madison's emphasis). [14]

Interests exist both in society and in the halls of government. Of these two places, the interests that exist in society were the most dangerous. How could these interests possibly be controlled without the heavy hand of government? What would keep them from capturing the government and using it for selfish ends?

In a republic, a self-interested minority would normally get outvoted by a majority, which in theory would make minority factions less dangerous to the public good. But what if the selfish interest formed a majority with designs to oppress a minority? Then what?

Madison, like many of the founders, read deeply into history. He studied all the great political theorists going back to ancient Greece and studied all the republics that had ever existed. Lately he had been particularly interested in confederated republics, whose situations were most analogous to that of the United States. The historical record was not promising. Most of them died young, and on these Madison performed political autopsies in an attempt to learn what killed them. Conventional wisdom had it that a republic could only exist in a small country, like a Greek city-state. Otherwise, a powerful authoritarian central government was necessary to hold a large nation together. But after reading the work of the famous Scottish philosopher, David Hume, Madison began to ask himself if this conventional wisdom made sense.

As Madison thought about the problem of interests and their tendency to capture government, he had a revelation. If you put three men in a room, with the first two of the same interest in opposition to the third, the third man will most likely be given a bad deal. The same is true if two hundred out of three hundred citizens share a common interest, or two thousand out of three thousand. The majorities in these cases were unlikely to restrain themselves. But, thought Madison, what if the sphere kept expanding, to tens and hundreds of thousands of citizens? As the republic got bigger, interests would multiply. The more interests, the less likely one of them would be large enough to form a majority.

In a small democracy, like an ancient Greek city-state, one selfish interest easily formed a majority and became oppressive. The problem was only somewhat alleviated in a republic as large as a single American state. But in a truly United States, a very large republic, which had never been tried before in the history of republics, interests could potentially check interests, with none obtaining the majority necessary to capture the government. Maybe the United States didn't have to go the way of all those short-lived republics Madison read about. Maybe its first defense was its potential size, assuming the United States could form a more powerful union. Here Madison made a unique contribution to republican theory in his argument for the advantages of a large republic over a small one.[15]

Madison recognized that the second place in which self-interests damage the common good is within the government itself. And of course, voices in the government would often naturally and unfortunately represent the self-interests competing in society at large. To control the effects of selfish or special interests on government, Madison believed in the necessity of a system that was later described as one of "checks and balances." Through contrasting powers, means of election, and terms in office, the various branches of government would check each other to prevent the capture of government by corrupting self-interests. Hopefully, only the common interest would be strong and durable enough to survive the entire legislative process.

◊◊◊

The federalists, who narrowly convinced the young American nation to adopt the Constitution, showed no sympathy for the Massachusetts rebels. There was no point watering down the message they wished to deliver. The choice was outlined starkly. Americans could either follow the example of the selfless George Washington in calling for a stronger central government capable of maintaining peace, order and liberty, or they could keep the current chaotic system and risk regular upheavals by violent factions, led by wild-eyed, self-centered insurgents like Daniel Shays, against the people's own governments.

In fact, this is not exactly how Madison viewed things. When he penned his Political Vice #11: "The Injustice of State Laws," he clearly had in mind the "monied interest" that had come to control the government of Massachusetts. While he did not support the rebellion, he understood its cause.

Years later, after the adoption of the Constitution, Madison served in Congress when Secretary of the Treasury Alexander Hamilton proposed a three-point program to finally address the nation's Revolutionary War debt. Hamilton advocated 1) immediately paying off the debt owed to foreign nations, 2) assuming unpaid state debts and 3) redeeming all the outstanding Continental notes at full face value and with interest.

As a Congressman, Madison fully supported the first measure; repaying the nation's foreign creditors was a matter of national honor and necessary to establish America's financial credit in the world.

The second proposition was more problematic since some states, notably Massachusetts and South Carolina, retained large debts while other states had paid theirs off. Madison proposed that it would be fairer to compensate states with and without debt equally. This would cost more, but it would serve the cause of justice.

Then, when it came to Hamilton's third proposition, which represented a situation perfectly analogous to the one in Massachusetts that had caused Shays' Rebellion, Madison balked. As in Massachusetts, most of the Continental and remaining state notes were not held by their original owners but were in the hands of speculators who had bought them on the cheap. Here Madison came up with a creative alternative. He suggested that the notes be redeemed to their current holders at the highest market price they had achieved since the war ended, minus the balance of the face value amount, which would be paid back to the patriotic citizen who, in time of war, had loaned the government money, or to the original soldier who was paid in these notes as compensation for serving his country. Madison's proposal was a model of reasonable compromise and justice.

◊◊◊

At the time of the Revolution, it was widely understood that for a republic to survive, the people must possess a high degree of "civic virtue." They must be willing to resist selfish impulses, act justly, and sometimes make great sacrifices for the common good. Madison was doubtful that people could ever possess enough civic virtue to hold a free society together. Factions might capture the government and become oppressive, which is why the frame of government and its mechanisms were so important.

But in Massachusetts, in the aftermath of Shays' Rebellion, the people demonstrated their virtue. First, though several rebels were hanged and others like Shays himself lost property and were compelled to live in exile, most were pardoned upon signing an oath of loyalty to the state. Moreover, the speculator interest was swept from government in the next election. Payments on the Massachusetts notes ceased and taxes were slashed. Though their leaders would not share in the victory, the rebel forces ultimately won.

On the subject of Madison's proposal in Congress to divide the payments of debts between current speculator note holders and the original note holders, the measure was not adopted. It was argued that the administrative challenges, including tracking down the original note holders, were too burdensome. Madison thought it should be tried anyway, because, as he wrote in *Federalist #51*, "Justice is the end [or purpose] of government."[16]

Madison's dissent signaled the end of his partnership with Hamilton, who thought the United States should imitate many of the financial and political practices of Great Britain, practices that Madison viewed as unjust and corrupt.

As treasury secretary, Hamilton proposed a National Bank that would both promote the economic development of the nation and tie the financial interests of the wealthiest gentlemen throughout the states to the federal government. The quasi-public National Bank would receive federal taxes, hold federal funds, be a source for short-term federal loans, and a little bit like our modern Federal Reserve, serve as a bankers' bank and regulate smaller private banks. The government would own one-fifth of the National Bank and the rest would be financed through private investment in the form of one-fourth hard currency and three-fourths government notes. With an initial investment of $500,000 in real money, the bank would offer the nation $10 million in ready credit and insure a supply of cash for a growing economy. From a financial point of view, Hamilton's banking plan has always been considered brilliant, and it was.

At his first opportunity, Congressman Madison rose to oppose it. He would speak against Hamilton's bank proposal on the House floor for an entire day. Madison, with unusual passion, argued that the bank was unconstitutional; the powers granted to the federal government were enumerated and the creation of a national bank was not among them. They had discussed at the Constitutional Convention whether the federal government would have the authority to charter corporations (which at this time were always partially public and monopolistic enterprises) and decided against it. The banking bill, said Madison, was a "usurpation" and a dangerous precedent that would set the federal government on a course that would destroy the limits that the Constitution had placed on federal power. The federalists had specifically promised that the Constitution's sweeping language, like the "necessary and proper" clause, would be read narrowly; now they were on the verge of violating that promise, decried Madison. If the Congress could create a bank out of the "necessary and proper" clause, then what were the limits on congressional authority under the Constitution? Moreover, the bank would benefit the moneyed and commercial interests of the nation; those gentleman speculators who were about to receive a windfall for the redemption of their Continental and state notes were now invited to invest those same securities into the bank and drive their government-backed profits still higher.

Madison lost the argument, but the bank's charter expired in 1811, which should have been fortuitous since he was president at this time. He now had the authority to undo the bank's "usurpation" of power and violation of the Constitution. But, surprisingly, Madison's own secretary of the treasury, Albert Gallatin, argued for renewing its charter. It turns out the bank was useful, particularly with war looming. Congress, however, felt differently and narrowly failed to renew the bank's charter. During 1816, in a bewildering reversal of Madison's initial fierce opposition to the bank, his administration chartered the Second National Bank of the United States.

How could this be? It's possible that Madison simply had a change of heart. Maybe he came to see how the bank benefitted the economy and the nation's finances. But how did a national bank suddenly become constitutional in Madison's eyes? Did having the political control over the bank in his own hands make a difference? Did Madison prove by his own example the corrupting nature of power? He was human, after all. If so, it is an important lesson. Perhaps even the wise and ethical James Madison might have allowed power to color his perspective. If it could happen to him, it could happen to any leader, which underscores the wisdom of Madison's founding vision that the United States be a nation of laws enforced by a rigorous system of checks and balances. As it turned out, the Second Bank of the United States was put under the direction of a political hack, William Jones, and became a cesspool of corruption.[17]

Madison's flip-flop on the National Bank is a point of emphasis in Jay Cost's fine book, *A Republic No More: Big Government and the Rise of Political Corruption.* His thesis is that the Constitution created a federal government of very limited enumerated powers, but once those limits were broken, government power and political corruption increased correspondingly. One result is that our Constitution leaves us today ill-equipped to resist the kind of corruption enabled by a federal government vastly richer and more powerful than anything ever imagined by the founders when they drafted the Constitution.

The story of the rising tide of corruption and domination by interests in American government is a long one, but a number of milestones stand out. The introduction of the "spoils system" in the age of Andrew Jackson placed government jobs in the hands of political operatives. At its core, the spoils system was a corrupt bargain between political hacks who wanted civil service jobs, and politicians who wanted to be elected.

Meanwhile, as the years passed and the party system thrived, the commercial interests of the Northeast remained one of the nation's most powerful factions. Tariffs to protect Northeastern industries from foreign competition were particularly controversial in the South and West. To farmers and planters in these regions, the tariffs seemed unjust.

The most dangerous faction by far, however, was the slaveholding interest of the South. Slavery was not just. It was not just to African-American slaves, obviously, and it was not just to white workers who might potentially have to compete against slave labor in the territories. Madison and Jefferson had expected that the slave labor system would disappear, but the slave interest was intent on perpetuating and expanding the system into the West. The result of course, was the nation's worst nightmare and its bloodiest clash between factions in the Civil War.

The Civil War, and the Reconstruction that followed, enlarged the role of the federal government and offered abundant opportunities for selfish interests. The Republican Party, which was dominant in this era, in the words of Jay Cost, "constructed massive and unstoppable statewide machines that raided the public treasury merely for its own perpetuation."[18]

In theory, the Civil Service Act of 1883 was an improvement over the old patronage system, but members of Congress retained powers that furthered their own reelections, including the authority to distribute benefits to campaign donors and constituents.

The time of the robber barons was a heyday for crony capitalism, when the largest corporations were able to dominate the government. Using Madisonian arguments, the progressives successfully pushed back, but their reforms came with a bigger role for government – and new, different and still greater opportunities for corruption.

With the arrival of the New Deal, big business was invited to climb into bed with government in order to supposedly rationalize and harmonize economic activity under the National Industrial Recovery Act. The chief beneficiaries turned out to be large corporate interests and the politicians who gave them their expanded powers and privileges.

The New Deal set the stage for the political mobilization of interests on a grand scale. Up through the Great Society of the 1960s and on to the present, interests set up house in Washington to pressure government for favorable treatment. From pharmaceutical companies to abortion clinics, the oil industry to solar panel manufacturers, trial lawyers to agribusiness, and the American Association of Retired Persons (AARP) to the National Rifle Association (NRA), special interests began to throw their weight around. Some interests are more likable than others, depending on one's point of view. We can argue about which interests are good or benign, and which are malevolent. The big picture, however, is undeniable. Government has come to serve the sum total of a multitude of interests. But is this massive conglomeration of narrow interests synonymous with the common good or the national interest? James Madison would say no.

Recall that James Madison believed that government based on justice could be protected from special interests in a large republic because no single interest would ever become powerful enough to form a majority at the expense of the common good. But Madison and his fellow founding fathers could not foresee modernity. They did not count on the rise of an immensely rich and complex society and economy – and powerful government to match – that lay over the time horizon. The Age of Enlightenment in which Madison lived, with its keen interest in the acquisition and dissemination of knowledge, set the stage for the incredible technological leap that was coming. In terms of technology, the era of the American founding was closer to the Middle Ages than it is to our time. Technology and the accompanying social changes would advance more in the next two hundred years than in the past two thousand. Industrialization, transportation, communications, immigration, finance, medicine, military technology, information technology, political participation and social values would all be revolutionized far beyond the founders' wildest imaginations.

One response to so much change was the growth of government to help manage it all. Government has grown from less than 7% of GDP at the beginning of the 20th century to 20% in 2015 (it's been higher in time of war and recession), all while the GDP itself has increased exponentially. Not only did government gain gargantuan spending power, it also gained immense regulatory power. The opportunity for selfish interests to feed off such money and power is today almost limitless.

Madison had struggled to erect defensive barriers in the Constitution against selfish interests. Today countless interests have their way with the government by banding together through lobbyists and lavishing campaign contributions on incumbent politicians. There is no longer the need for any particular interest to win a majority in order to capture the government, as Madison expected. Rather, merely inserting a line or two in an omnibus spending bill or quashing a particular regulation is all that is required for an interest to thrive. As we will see, successful interests that prefer not to play the game may have campaign contributions extorted out of them anyway by self-interested career politicians who threaten them with legislative punishment. Indeed, selfish political interests are the linchpins of the whole system. The defenses against special interests put in place at the time of the founding have been completely overwhelmed by modern society and government as thousands upon thousands of special interests now feed at the trough of power together. Today, virtually all of the incentives that drive the American political system are self-interested and short-sighted rather than judicious. Madison's vision for a just American republic capable of serving our common and national interest has been flipped completely upside down.

We now find ourselves far down an unintended road. Again and again, Americans found that they wanted a stronger national government than the one provided by the framers of the Constitution. Ambiguous-sounding clauses cracked open and the breaches were exploited. Precedent built upon precedent, solidifying gains in federal authority. Anti-federalists were proved correct that the powers of the federal government would inevitably bust out of the frame of the Constitution.

Progressives who favor a "living Constitution" have no problem with this reality. Conservatives lament the violations of the original intent of the founders and argue that any necessary changes should only have occurred through the deliberative amendment process provided for in the Constitution itself. It's an important discussion, but not one that is essential for our purposes.

Principled progressives and principled conservatives are never going to agree on the proper size and role of government, but we can agree that *principles* and not *interests* should drive public policies. We can agree that Madison was correct in his desire to frame a government that would resist selfish interests and legislate justly for the broad and long-term good of the nation and its citizens. And we should find the wisdom and civic virtue to work and fix our corrupted political system *together*.

2: Vices of the System, Twenty-First Century Style

In 2010, before putting on my Superman cape and beginning my quest to "save America," I tried to channel my inner James Madison (surely we all have an incredibly wise, aristocratic, slaveholding founding father in us somewhere). I kept thinking about how everything that was or was not happening in the American political system ran contrary to Madison's vision for judicious government. Two then-recent examples of public policy malfeasance embodied almost everything that is wrong the system.

The first was the financial crisis that erupted to the surface in 2008 and the subsequent legislative response in the form of the *Dodd-Frank Wall Street Reform and Consumer Protection Act*. The second was the *Affordable Care Act,* a.k.a. "Obamacare." With this second example, I risk sailing into partisan waters. I ask progressives who support the law to bear with me.[19]

On November 12, 1999, President Clinton, smiling his familiar and almost permanent smile, sat at a table surrounded by lawmakers and other officials, including Republican Senator Phil Gramm (R-TX). The occasion was the signing of Gramm-Leach-Bliley, formally called *The Financial Services Modernization Act*, a new law with the sole purpose of putting the final nail in the coffin of an old law: the *Glass-Steagall Act*.[20]

The *Glass-Steagall Act* had been around since 1933 and was designed to promote stability in the banking sector. Among its purposes was to separate safer traditional banking activities from riskier activities involving the buying and selling of securities. As the Great Depression made clear, bank failures can bring down the whole economy.

The principles behind the *Glass-Steagall Act* had been under pressure for years, and often in ways that were under the public radar. For example, a Cleveland Federal Reserve official named Walker Todd was reviewing some legislation passed in 1991 called *The FDIC Improvement Act*, when he was astonished to discover some provocative language that had been added to the legislation without a committee hearing or any review or advance notice at all. It essentially said that investment banks and insurance companies were to be treated the same as FDIC-insured banks in the event of some sort of financial collapse. The language had been inserted by Democrat Senator Chris Dodd of Connecticut, a state heavily dependent on the insurance industry. Did this language leave the taxpayers on the hook for potentially billions and billions of dollars should big insurance and securities companies act irresponsibly? It sure looked that way. Tellingly, Todd's superiors at the Fed tried to keep him from publishing his findings and he was given a reprimand for raising the issue.[21]

By 1999 word was out on the street – Wall Street, that is – that the government simply would not allow a large bank to fail because of the possible impact that failure might have on the entire banking system. The Fed had already bailed out a big hedge fund, Long Term Capital. If the government would intervene to save a hedge fund, it would certainly intervene to save a big bank. The killing of *Glass-Steagall* was not so much the cause of the financial crisis, but rather, a confirmation that financial institutions were all potential candidates for government bailouts should they get into trouble. Banks could now grow their securities and insurance businesses, get larger, and take much riskier bets than they otherwise might have, knowing that the taxpayers would not let them fail.

In economics, this is what's known as a "moral hazard." A safety net placed under financial institutions can encourage reckless behavior. Banks came to resemble casinos. The money that would be made and lost would be staggering and unprecedented. It was a system of private profit at public risk. Or, as the big banks might have said to the taxpayers: "Heads I win, tails you lose."

Republicans take their free-market beliefs seriously. Why didn't they perceive that the American banking system was not a pure free-market enterprise? Why didn't Phil Gramm, an economist no less, and the other Republicans behind the repeal of *Glass-Steagall* appreciate that they were exposing the public to substantial economic risk that might entail even bigger government in the form of massive taxpayer-financed bailouts?

Campaign donations can be perspective-altering. Wall Street is among the most generous of political campaign donors. From 1989 to 2008, according to the Center for Responsive Politics, the financial services sector invested $2.2 billion in direct campaign contributions to federal politicians and spent $3.5 billion on lobbying – more than any other special interest during the same period. [22]

Also, lobbyists hired by Wall Street firms, as well as a whole range of American industries and labor, have established key relationships with elected officials over the course of many years and re-elections, often effectively putting members of Congress in information bubbles. A kind of "groupthink" takes over, which is the most charitable characterization of what happened in the case of the banking collapse of 2008. More darkly, it's possible that our elected officials were (and still are) simply and crudely *bought*. The motivation doesn't really matter; the result is the same.

It's one thing for pro-business Republicans and Federal Reserve bankers to be taken in by other bankers, but Democrats are supposed to be ideologically suspicious of big business. Democrats would surely not be so easily captured by Wall Street, would they? Yes, they would, as Senator Dodd's single-handed expansion of the corporate safety net, above, suggests. And it was another Democrat, Bill Clinton, who signed the repeal of *Glass-Steagall*. Clinton was perhaps listening to his secretary of the treasury, Robert Rubin, who had spent twenty-six years successfully leading Goldman Sachs, America's most prestigious investment bank at the time. Just after the signing of the repeal, Rubin would leave Washington to become vice chairman of Citigroup. In their illuminating book, *Reckless Endangerment,* which I draw from extensively here, authors Gretchen Morgenson and Joshua Rosner write that "Over the following decade Rubin pocketed more than one hundred million dollars as the bank sank deeper and deeper into a risky morass of its own design."[23]

For all those big banks to fail, they required something risky to trade. That "something" was subprime mortgages.

President Clinton and members of Congress from both parties were keen on expanding home ownership. The Clinton administration organized a coalition of banks, securities firms, builders and Realtors into a partnership that planned to move American home ownership from 64% of the population in 1994 to 70% by the year 2000. To achieve this goal, banks, at the encouragement of the government, would have to lower borrowing standards. A parade of loose lending practices followed that ended in subprime mortgages.

The financial crisis might not have happened if it were not for Fannie Mae and its sister government-sponsored enterprise (GSE), Freddie Mac, which purchased mortgages from lending institutions across the country. For the government to have to play this role at all suggests that it would buy loans that no one else wanted. Fannie Mae, in particular, would be at the vanguard of the degradation of lending standards as well as a pioneer in packaging mortgages into securities.

Fannie Mae, like *Glass-Steagall*, was a Depression-era creation. Its mission was always to make home buying easier for low-income Americans. Fannie Mae received government support and was supposed to be regulated like a government agency, but it has shareholders and it compensated its executives like a big Wall Street firm. Under the direction of James A. "Jim" Johnson, Fannie Mae would become the largest financial institution in the world.

Fannie Mae's mission was to promote home ownership, but one of Johnson's first decisions when he took over was to base the company's executive compensation on growth and profits. Johnson's own take while running Fannie Mae, from 1991 through 1998, was $180 million, with a nice $900,000 annual pension on top of that. Toward the end of his tenure, the company would resort to accounting fraud in order to maintain the illusion of growth and the reality of executive bonuses. Accountants at Goldman Sachs taught accountants at Fannie Mae how to cook the books (Johnson was given a seat on the Goldman board, for which he eventually received another cool $500,000 per year).

For most of his tenure, though, Johnson did not have to rely on fraud to get paid. He was able to maintain blistering growth by degrading lending standards and keeping Congress in his back pocket. Because of Fannie Mae and its congressional supporters, buyers of homes no longer needed to put the traditional 20% down to obtain a mortgage. They could put down 5%, or even next to nothing. A good credit score, obtained instantaneously, would be enough in many cases – no tax returns or pay stubs required. In time, even the home buyers' credit history became mostly unimportant. In the 1990s, with the "dotcom" bubble showering cash down on the economy, risk seemed a thing of the past.

Still, every now and then a lone member of Congress or a regulator somewhere would reconsider that antiquated notion of risk and question the taxpayers' exposure to it. Every now and then a genuine anti-poverty housing organization would notice the uptick in predatory lending, made possible through loose lending standards, and make a public complaint.

But Democrats in Congress, who like Republicans take their ideology seriously, betrayed their own values by letting the most vulnerable get trampled in the housing mania. Critics who questioned Johnson's business model hadn't a chance. Between 1989 and 2009, Fannie Mae would invest $100 million in lobbying and campaign contributions. Fannie Mae not only had an army of lobbyists, but it actually *paid other lobbyists* not to lobby against it, according to Morgenson and Rosner.

Jim Johnson's Fannie Mae also manipulated the political process through its legally charitable Fannie Mae Foundation, which allowed it to give generously to housing organizations or corrupt anti-poverty groups like ACORN that could be bought, which in turn could be called on to mobilize faux-grassroots campaigns and lobby on Fannie Mae's behalf. The foundation set up field offices in key congressional districts. High-profile politicians, like Senator Ted Kennedy (D-MA) and House Speaker Newt Gingrich (R-GA), were pleased to soak up the press generated by Fannie Mae at their local offices. (In the 2012 Republican primary campaign it would come out that Gingrich was later paid $1.6 to $1.8 million by Freddie Mac as, in Gingrich's words, "an historian.") Congressional staff and family members were hired to work in Fannie Mae field offices. An aide to Senator Bob Bennett (R-UT) ran one office and an aide to Senator Tom Daschle (D-SD) ran another. Hundreds of local political leaders could be mobilized to call their members of Congress at the drop of a hat in support of easy lending standards. The Fannie Mae Foundation poured so much money into academic research that it bought off virtually all the academics in the housing area. The rare critic of Fannie Mae was branded as anti-housing and ground into powder.

Fannie Mae and private banks engaged in an awkward embrace. On the one hand they needed each other. Fannie Mae could not legally generate its own mortgages. Its charter only permitted it to buy mortgages on the open market. Fannie Mae needed a constant and growing supply of mortgages to purchase in order to keep growing itself. Private lenders at the point of sale, for their part, increasingly wanted a place to unload their risky mortgages, and they appreciated Fannie's willingness to buy them. But Wall Street also looked enviously upon Fannie Mae's growth, resented its government-backed advantages, and in time would increasingly compete with the GSEs by selling their own mortgage pools and passing them off like hot potatoes.

To help maintain Fannie Mae's advantages against private competitors, Jim Johnson courted Angelo Mozilo, the head of Countrywide Financial, the largest private mortgage lender in the country. He offered Mozilo's Countrywide a special discount on fees taken per mortgage purchased in exchange for Countrywide's business. No one seems to have asked the question of whether it was proper for a government-backed entity to favor one private financial institution over another, but in the late 1990s Fannie Mae and Countrywide grew together. Mozilo learned to emulate Johnson's tactics by announcing low-income housing partnerships and cozying up to members of Congress. Mozilo created a special VIP lending program for the people who were useful to him. He personally approved these loans, which became known as "the friends of Angelo program." Jim Johnson personally received several such loans, worth a total of more than $10 million. Of course, politicians got "Friends of Angelo" loans too, including Senate Banking Committee Chairman Christopher Dodd (D-CT), Kent Conrad (D-SD) and Barbara Boxer (D-CA). Naturally they also happened to be friends of Jim Johnson's, and that was no coincidence.

By 1999 Johnson had turned Fannie Mae over to his protégé, Harold Raines. Johnson's departure was well-timed. In the early 2000s, during a less friendly Republican regime, the GSEs would come under increased scrutiny, and audits would disclose the crooked books. But before all was said and done and the GSEs put into conservatorship, Fannie Mae would end up holding half of all the subprime mortgages issued — with the taxpayer holding the tab.

In the meantime, privatization of Fannie's corrupt practices was well under way. With interest rates low, investors were hungry for high-yielding securities. Big banks poured vast sums of money into buying up subprime mortgages, creating a mortgage-backed securities market that included riskier and riskier products.

It didn't matter how dubious the mortgage was if the rating agencies, such as Moody's and Standard & Poor's, continued to stamp trashy securities full of toxic loans with glowing AAA or AA ratings. The ratings agencies were actually paid by the GSEs and the private banks to do their bidding. The more mortgages the agencies rated, the more money they made. Where was the incentive to be honest? And where was the incentive to be overly concerned about risks when there was so much money to be made now — with the promise of government bailouts as a backstop should something go wrong?

Of course, a lot went wrong. When interest rates began to tick up in 2004, the adjustable-rate-mortgage time bombs began ticking as the sums required to make mortgage payments increased, sometimes beyond a home owner's ability to pay. Even so, Wall Street remained desperate to find more junk to securitize and sell, so still more risky mortgage products appeared: for example, "interest only" loans and "negative amortization loans," in which consumers could put off making whole payments and have the balance wrapped back into the loans.

Democratic politicians like President Clinton and Chairman of the House Financial Services Committee Barney Frank had hopped on Jim Johnson's train to expand home ownership by altering traditional lending standards. But poor and working class people paid the biggest price of all for the corrupt practices of Wall Street and Washington, beginning long before the crisis hit the front pages. Atlanta attorney and activist William Brennan shouted out warnings for the better part of a decade as he watched unscrupulous lenders charge usury rates, sometimes in the double digits, and strip the hard-earned equity out of poor people's homes. Philadelphia activist attorney Irv Ackelsberg declared in 2001 that in the inner-city predatory lending was the "crack cocaine" of housing finance. It was "a poison sucking the life out of our communities" and "hard to fight because people are making so much money."[24] In Atlanta, by 2009, there were 4000 to 7000 housing foreclosures per month, mostly in African-American inner-city neighborhoods.[25]

Meanwhile, Rep. John LaFalce (D-NY) and Paul Sarbanes (D-MD) wrote bills to rein in predatory lending. They even had the backing of the chair of the House Banking Committee, Jim Leach (R-IA), who had been one of the sponsors of the *Glass-Steagall* repeal. But these bills had so little overall support that they never came up for votes in committee. They were "never really in play," said one banking industry lobbyist. "The industry could and would have blocked [those proposals], but we didn't really have to."[26]

After the bubble burst in 2008, President George W. Bush's secretary of the treasury, Hank Paulson, would create the architecture for all of the big bank bailouts, including the $700 billion Troubled Asset Relief Program (TARP), later reduced to $475 billion. As Paulson worked to bail out big banks, he also worked with his friends. He had spent a career at Goldman Sachs, and he was one of four recent treasury secretaries plucked from Wall Street.

The damage done as a result of the financial crisis is incalculable, but some have tried to assess the cost. As one analysis pointed out, "myriad factors are involved, including such things as the toll of unemployment and lost wages, losses in the stock market and corporate earnings, declining home values, the depletion of retirement savings, and decreased consumer spending." Looked at from the higher level of lost GDP, however, economists have calculated the cost of the crisis at $12.8 trillion. At least the TARP funds have been mostly paid back.[27]

In 2008 Barack Obama swept into the White House with a promise to end the gross mismanagement and corruption that led to the financial crisis. At a campaign stop he had said of the housing and financial debacle, "Instead of establishing a 21st-century regulatory frame-work, we simply dismantled the old one aided by a legal but corrupt bargain in which campaign money all too often shaped policy and watered down oversight." It was true enough.[28]

However, when it came time for the new Democrat-controlled Congress to write and pass the much-needed fixes to prevent another financial crisis, congressional Democrats relied on the usual seniority system for leadership. The law that would emerge and be signed by the new president was *Dodd-Frank*, identified by two names as responsible for the financial crisis as anyone. Senator Dodd had personally seen to it that FDIC insurance was expanded to cover insurance companies and firms dealing in securities. Frank had been Fannie Mae's most vociferous congressional cheerleader and defender. Both Dodd and

Frank had accepted personal favors from the industries they were supposed to regulate.

On April 13, 2009, the ranking Republican on the Senate Banking Committee, Judd Gregg (R-NH), took to the floor to warn of "populist" approaches to banking reform. He needn't have worried too much. He reviewed all the legitimate causes of the crisis, except those centered on Wall Street. He said that reform should be about "Main Street," but even today Main Street banking has structural disadvantages compared to the big banks. Upon retirement from Congress, Mr. Gregg took a job at Goldman Sachs. Since then, banks on "Main Street" have been swallowed up by big banks at an alarming rate.

Perhaps it's not surprising that, just a few years after the passage of *Dodd-Frank*, the big banks were bigger than ever, and "too big to fail" is still the unstated policy of the federal government toward large financial institutions. The moral hazard is alive, well, and along with the nation's big financial institutions, ready for the next big bailout.

Christopher Dodd and Barney Frank both retired from Congress. Dodd, who had helped put a safety net under big banks and insurance companies, became a de facto lobbyist (though not technically) for the Motion Picture Association. During the fiscal cliff fight of 2013, as politicians fought to control the flow of the federal government's red ink to at least some limited extent, Dodd did his job by securing tax breaks for Hollywood. In that same bill, Goldman Sachs would get a fat subsidy for the building of its new Manhattan headquarters. Again, this was a bill that was supposed to be about fiscal discipline.

President Obama, for his part, had accepted $42 million from the finance, insurance and housing sectors for his 2008 election campaign, and he appointed Tim Geithner as Secretary of the Treasury. Geithner, a protégé of Robert Rubin, had served as president of the important New York Fed from 2003 to 2008, on the eve of the crisis. The New York Fed, in particular, was supposed to monitor Wall Street but Geithner, like many others, failed to act or warn of the banking system's instability during his time there. In fact, he worked to lower capital requirements for banks. The inspector general for the Troubled Asset Relief Program (TARP), Neil Barofsky, in his book *Bailout*, charges Geithner with unnecessarily favoring big banks with relief money and shortchanging distressed home owners during his tenure as treasury secretary.[29]

In the current political system, as in the financial crisis, no one is held accountable. Little changed in Congress as a result of the 2008 election, immediately after the crisis. The same old group of politicians was re-elected, including 94% of all House incumbents and 83% of all incumbent US Senators. Meanwhile, public approval of Congress was scraping bottom near record lows at 18%. Collective irresponsibility almost never translates into individual accountability. Incumbent advantages and the partisan blame game keep almost everyone in power no matter how poor the public policy. Whatever the calamity, it's always someone else's fault.

In the case of the financial industry and Fannie Mae, not one person went to jail. Not one. Progressive journalist Matt Taibbi, writing for *Rolling Stone,* places the lack of accountability squarely on the Obama administration and specifically on Attorney General Eric Holder, "the best defense lawyer Wall Street ever had," who let "one banker after another skate on monstrous cases of fraud, tax evasion, market manipulation, money laundering, bribery and other offenses." Taibbi concludes that Holder's lack of law enforcement when it came to the big financial interests "preserved Democratic Party relationships with big-dollar donors, kept the client base at Holder's old firm nice and fat, made the influential rich immeasurably richer and allowed Eric Holder himself to crash-land into a giant pile of money upon resignation (as attorney general)." Holder is now back at his old Wall Street law firm, Covington & Burling. His old office had been kept empty for him. It's as if he never left.[30]

It's probably safe to say that the Affordable Care Act, a.k.a. "Obamacare," isn't what anybody really wanted when it comes to reforming America's health care system. Republican opposition in Congress was unanimous when the law passed and is still strong today. Many Democrats, for their part, would prefer a single payer system.[31]

What can and should be said about Obamacare is that it is providing generally good health insurance to people who previously could not afford it. The questions are, how much was American healthcare really "reformed," at what cost, and what does the story of Obamacare tell us about our political system?

For those who follow politics, the spectacle of the Affordable Care Act's passage is scorched in memory. Since no Republican would support the bill, Senate Majority leader Harry Reid had to make crazy deals for obstinate Democratic senators from Nebraska and Louisiana, dubbed the "Cornhusker kickback" and the "Louisiana Purchase," respectively. They arranged for their two states to receive special goodies unavailable to the other forty-eight states. Fortunately, under the media spotlight, these porkish inequities were stripped from the final bill.

It was a bill that few if any members of Congress bothered to read. It was, after all, 906 pages, which is actually not especially atypical for modern legislation. Nancy Pelosi would famously say that sometimes one had to "pass the bill so you can find out what's in it."

To the original 906-page bill would be added 9,625 pages of regulation, which would lead to an estimated *1,492,000 hours* of paperwork.

Lobbyists from the health insurance, pharmaceutical and hospital industries were at the table when the bill was written. Billy Tauzin, the big pharma lobbyist and former

Republican senator from Louisiana, liked to say, "if you are not at the table then you are going to be on the menu."[32] The quote suggests an essential dynamic in the relationship between interests, especially corporate interests, and elected officials. Schmooze and pay the politicians to get what you want, which feels like a form of bribery. But fail to schmooze and pay the politicians and risk getting punished through adverse regulations or taxes, which feels like extortion.

The pharmaceutical industry, a.k.a. "big pharma," did OK. In the law's final version, it would still not have to negotiate drug pricing with its biggest customer, the federal government, but it would fund an expensive ad campaign in support of the Affordable Care Act. The juicy contract for big pharma's ad campaign in support of the act would go to a company founded by David Axelrod just before he took the position of senior adviser to the president.

The trial lawyers have been feasting on the American medical system for decades; they had never left the table. There would be no tort reform.

The insurance companies were issued an invitation they could not refuse. Their margins were narrow, people hate them, and they felt vulnerable. They left the feeding frenzy satisfied. Their profits, though not large by corporate standards, at least seemed guaranteed along with a government-sponsored market expansion.

The medical device makers were not at the smorgasbord, so they got taxed, but in the end their lobbyists did damage control and reduced the original amount. They showed up at the door late and snatched a doggy bag.

The launch of the Healthcare.gov web site was, of course, an abysmal flop that cost the taxpayers at least $319 million before it had to be almost completely re-engineered.

President Obama also made over thirty unilateral changes to the law. Many say that such changes are illegal because it is the legislative branch's role to make or change law. The president declined to go to Congress for the changes, obviously because Congress was at least partly in the hands of Republicans, who were elected to overturn the law.

But the most damaging aspect of the Affordable Care Act may have nothing to do with special-interest giveaways, wasteful spending, or executive overreach. The choice of Obamacare itself as the best approach to fixing America's inequitable and ridiculously expensive healthcare system is probably the biggest failure of all.

In January 2010, a still fresh and optimistic-sounding President Obama took to the podium in the House of Representatives to deliver the State of the Union. When he got to healthcare reform he promised, "Our approach would preserve the right of Americans who have insurance to keep their doctor and their plan." Of course, this was not necessarily true and the president, who is smart and was deeply informed throughout the process, surely knew that he was not speaking the truth. (As it turned out, I could not keep my doctor under Obamacare.) He would utter this untruth again and again.

The president also said that his plan would "reduce costs and premiums for millions of families and businesses." It was true in that government subsidies would make it much easier for many families to buy health insurance, but nothing meaningful would be done to control the cost of healthcare overall. Rather than fundamentally reforming the system, Obamacare would expand healthcare and cause the healthcare sector to consume a still-greater chunk of the nation's gross domestic product, far more than any other country in the world. Real cost controls were more hope than change.

The President went on to acknowledge the rising opposition to the plan that he and the Democratic leadership in the Congress were coalescing around. He added something that must have sounded like throw-away lines to many:

> *But if anyone from either party has a better ap-*
> *proach that will bring down premiums, bring*
> *down the deficit, cover the uninsured, strength-*
> *en Medicare for seniors, and stop insurance*
> *company abuses, let me know. (Applause.) Let*
> *me know. Let me know. (Applause.) I'm eager*
> *to see it.*

If, amid the applause, a television camera had panned over to Ron Wyden, the Democratic senator from Oregon, and closed in on either of his ears, it's probable that a small plume of black smoke would have been seen pouring out. Wyden, like an overachieving high school student who made everyone else look bad, was the nerd that the Democratic establishment had stuffed into a locker. Wyden *had* a better approach to healthcare reform.

It is widely understood that the fatal flaw in America's healthcare system was planted during World War II at a time of wage and price controls. To reward employees when wages could not be raised, businesses were permitted to offer tax-free health benefits to their workers. This policy led to the current system of employer-supplied healthcare, a system unique – and uniquely costly – among industrialized nations. It is, in effect, a subsidy for expensive healthcare. Offering a fancy healthcare plan is cheaper for the corporation than offering the equivalent in higher salaries, which are subject to taxes. The insured employees, largely disconnected from healthcare costs, have little or no incentive to shop around for the best healthcare value. The result is a porous, irrational and outrageously expensive healthcare system.

Wyden proposed to restructure the system to make it universal, market-driven and consumer-centric. Under his plan, businesses would lose their tax deductions for employee healthcare and would be required to offer workers the cash equivalent of what the employer would otherwise spend insuring the individual employee. Under a universal mandate, every American would be required to buy health insurance. Those migrating out of corporate plans would be left holding a wad of cash in hand with which to do so. Those who could not afford health insurance would be subsidized through tax credits and revenue generated by ending the healthcare tax breaks for businesses. Like Obamacare, the plan would be universal and would not discriminate against people with pre-existing conditions. Unlike Obamacare, it could offer consumers a broad range of choices and promote market competition based on value. Importantly, unlike Obama-care, Wyden's plan, the Wyden-Bennett Bill, had Republican support. Bennett was the Republican senator from Utah. The bill had six Republican and six Democratic sponsors.

Ezra Klein, a prominent progressive policy wonk writing for *The American Prospect* in 2008 said, "What's remarkable, though, is that Wyden and Bennett, working together, have come up with a bill that is more far-reaching, and more fundamentally transformative to our health system, than anything offered by the presidential candidates."[33]

In his bill, Wyden essentially wedded the Democrats' desire for universal healthcare with the Republican desire for market competition and consumer choice. It was universal, bipartisan and would have been cost-neutral two years after implementation according to the director of the Congressional Budget Office, Peter Orszag, who would later become President Obama's director of management and budget.

Wyden's approach held out the promise of a transformed, universal and more cost-effective healthcare system, which in turn could be the key to transforming the nation's big medical entitlement programs, Medicaid and Medicare. To reform these programs, using the same consumer-centric model, Wyden partnered with Republican congressman and future House Speaker Paul Ryan. To-gether they came up with a plan that would allow future Medicare recipients to either choose Medicare or take ad-vantage of the new approach; the assumption is that sen-iors would appreciate choice and cost savings and would voluntarily migrate away from the old Medicare system.

To be sure, there is lots of room for debate within Wy-den's model. Democrats will always want more regulations and safeguards, and Republicans more consumer choices and fewer regulations. But by working with Bennett and Ryan successfully, Wyden has shown that these differences can be bridged. Wyden has found Madisonian wisdom on healthcare, the political sweet spot that can serve the broad and long-term good of the nation.

So why did Wyden's approach to healthcare reform fail?

One reason is that some big businesses balked at giving up their generous tax breaks.

Another is that unions did not want to give up the lav-ish healthcare plans they had negotiated with their employ-ers.

Ideologically, many progressives will be satisfied with nothing less than a single payer system. These folks op-pose Wyden. And many conservatives will never accept a universal mandate. Still, one suspects that a super-majority of the American people in the center would be happy if bipartisan leaders like Wyden and Ryan had the support in Congress to fix our healthcare system, rather than settle for reforms that are not real reform at all.

Probably the biggest obstacle in the way is self-interested partisan politics. Powerful political disincentives exist that prevent Republicans and Democrats from coop-erating in Congress. If one side is characterized as "evil, selfish and stupid" by the other, which happens all the time in politics, then it becomes very hard to work togeth-er. Everybody is insulted, and why would you cooperate with a party that you are simultaneously characterizing as ignorant and malevolent? Such co-operation would undermine the all-important political messaging.

A perfect example appeared in the run-up to the 2012 election. A Democratic-leaning group produced a video of a man closely resembling Republican Paul Ryan pushing an old woman in a wheelchair off a cliff. This is what all Republicans do, no? Why on earth would anyone work with a man out to murder Granny? Democratic political operatives were furious at Wyden for muddying the message by partnering with Ryan on Medicare reform and making the 2012 Republican vice presidential candidate look like he could possibly be a reasonable and decent human being.

Based largely on the nation's political experience during the financial crisis and the passage of the Affordable Care Act, we can make our own list of "the Vices of the Political System of the United States," just as James Madison did over two-and-a-quarter centuries ago during the nation's founding. Here is what it might look like:

VICES OF THE POLTICAL SYSTEM OF THE UNITED STATES TODAY

Special interests make campaign donations to elected officials in a system that closely resembles *bribery.* Wall Street and Fannie Mae maintained a steady flow of campaign cash to elected officials before and after the financial crisis. All the big players in the healthcare sector also fund political campaigns. Big Pharma even funded an ad campaign in favor of the Affordable Care Act.

Special interests make campaign donations to elected officials in a system that closely resembles *extortion.* This is the other side of the coin. Interests are either at the table feasting or they are on the menu. Medical device makers were not at the table during the healthcare debate, and they ended up getting taxed. As will be seen in other examples, elected officials shake down interests for campaign cash.

Elected officials are too partisan. Elected officials won't work with the other side because bipartisanship undermines all-important partisan political messaging. Given the choice between 1) the old healthcare system 2) expanding the old system to cover everyone as in the case of the Affordable Care Act 3) a universal payer system or 4) Senator Wyden's consumer-centered system, Wyden's plan is clearly the policy consensus and bipartisan choice. Yet his plan wasn't even brought to the table.

Elected officials betray their principles. Republicans betray their free-market principles by supporting the "too-big-too-fail" banking system. They also seldom live up to their rhetoric when it comes to reducing government spending. Democrats, by advocating for lower lending standards, allowed predator mortgage companies to take advantage of poor and working people. The Obama Justice Department prosecuted no one for the crimes committed on Wall Street that led to the financial crisis. Generally, elected officials are both too partisan and, at the same time, neglect their most sacred ideological principles; they tend to make the wrong choices in each case.

Elected officials are short-sighted. By lowering lending standards in the 1990s to promote home ownership, Democrats and Republicans in government ignored the long-term consequences of their actions in favor of making less-than-creditworthy voters happy at the time. Elected officials are too focused on the next re-election when they should be legislating for the next generation.

Narrow interests get their way at the expense of the national interest. In the run-up to the financial crisis and during the healthcare debate, there was no sufficiently powerful political voice at the table for the broad and long-term national interest.

Members of Congress are prone to "groupthink." The lack of regulation of Wall Street and the weakening of lending standards was bipartisan malfeasance.

Revolving doors open and shut between government and industry. The Bush and Obama administrations were packed with Wall Street veterans. Eric Holder, Billy Tauzin and Chris Dodd all used their influence in Washington to benefit special interests.

The Executive usurps congressional authority. As a member of the US Senate, President Obama had been a critic of executive overreach, but as president he unilaterally, through executive orders, gave numerous waivers for exceptions out of the Affordable Care Act and made other far-reaching executive decisions without congressional authorization. Members of Congress too willingly surrender their authority for partisan reasons or to avoid taking stands on controversial issues.

The bureaucracy is subject to political manipulation. Political interests prevented federal employees from doing their jobs. A whistleblower who pointed out the danger of language in a bill that offered FDIC backing to non-traditional banking activities was reprimanded and silenced. Practically no one at the Justice Department was tasked with prosecuting white-collar criminals on Wall Street after the financial crisis; career prosecutors were kept from doing their jobs.

The politically connected and their families have unfair advantages. David Axelrod's company got the big pharma media campaign contract. Close friends and family of members of Congress from both parties were hired by Fannie Mae. Members of Congress can personally benefit from insider information relating to government projects.

The wealthy have unfair advantages. Through campaign contributions, exceptionally wealthy citizens can buy access to elected leaders. Candidates who have the ability to self-fund their own campaigns have obvious advantages over those who cannot.

Congressional incumbents have unfair advantages over challengers when running for re-election. Washington groupthink and partisanship are tied to the low turnover in Congress and incumbent advantage. For the purposes of re-election, it does not matter how poorly Congress performs. Re-election rates for incumbents running again for the US House are typically around 95%. Senators are re-elected at a rate of around 85%.

Just as in James Madison's list of vices, all the political

vices listed above have at their core the idea of *injustice*. Each promotes selfish interests at the expense of the common good. Our political system gets fixed only by addressing this or a similar list of political vices.

◇◇◇

I didn't exactly have this list in mind when, back in 2010, I got it into my head to broker a deal between the American Right and Left for political reform. Even if I had, I wasn't realistically going to hand such a list to some influential leaders and say, "Hey, let's do all of this!" and expect anything to happen.

What I knew at the time was that the populist American Left and Right each had, and still have, a political reform that it desperately wants. The Left wants a clean elections system, in which interests, especially big business, can no longer influence elections and legislation with campaign contributions. Such a system would necessarily mean modifying the Supreme Court's *Citizens United* decision and other related rulings. And the Right wants term limits for members of Congress in order to discourage political careerism and instead promote citizen government. As I will argue, a new and clean elections system for the United States, and limiting the tenure of members of Congress, are Madisonian solutions that will address a majority of our political vices.

I also knew that among ordinary folks, neither goal – term limits nor clean campaign finance – was an especially tough sell for either side. Majorities of Democrats have supported congressional term limits for decades, even when Democrats control Congress. Most Republicans understand that permitting lawmakers to take campaign donations from the same interests they regulate is inherently corrupt. Yes, there will be obstacles and devils in the details, but we will never get to the details if we don't sit down together first. My self-appointed job was to get a balanced group of leaders on the Left and Right to the table.

I also thought we could safely add a ban on gerrymandering. No one outside the system appreciates this self-serving practice that promotes uncompetitive elections by allowing politicians and political parties to draw the boundaries of their own congressional districts. Voters should pick their representatives rather than allowing representatives to choose their voters. Adding this reform would make the overall package more attractive to everybody at the popular level.

I recruited a board of directors, we passed by-laws, and we applied for IRS 401c4 tax-exempt recognition. The group created had begun as an online blog dedicated to Left – Right collaboration, CenterMovement.org. (This is when I became familiar with Senator Wyden's work.) After we decided to focus on political reform issues we called ourselves Americans United to Rebuild Democracy but later changed the name of our fledging organization to the Clean Government Alliance. Compared to other reform groups, we were an embryo among dinosaurs.

Organizationally, there is a huge imbalance between the reformist Left and Right. The Left has many organizations and spends millions of dollars trying to get money out of politics. The Right has essentially no reform movement or organizations. If the Left wanted to make a deal with the Right, it's not clear that they would know who to talk to. This is the niche I intended to fill. I would hook up the prominent progressive reformers and their organizations with reform-minded conservatives. But where to begin?

I started locally. As it happened, the most bipartisan reform organization, Americans for Campaign Reform (ACR), was located near me in Concord, NH. Unique among such groups, they had prominent Republicans on their steering committee, including former Senators Warren Rudman and Allan Simpson. I developed a friendly relationship with one of their staffers, Jeff McLean, who liked our three-reform approach. Unfortunately, John Rauh, the founder of ACR, could never be persuaded to support term limits. We had to look elsewhere.

Jeff soon left ACR and agreed to be our vice president, which was very helpful since he knew the ins and outs of the so-called "reform community." Jeff was keen on the Harvard Law professor/reformer Larry Lessig, who had become a kind of "rock star" of political reform. Lessig had also taught law at Stanford and Chicago. Prior to getting involved in political reform, he was known for copyright reform and is the founder of the Center for the Internet and Society. He has won numerous awards and was named one of *Scientific American's* Top Fifty Visionaries. Lessig, though a progressive, had started life as a conservative and had even clerked for the late Supreme Court Justice Antonin Scalia. Now he was openly calling for conservative support, especially among the not-yet-fully-demonized Tea Party, which Lessig accurately recognized as a movement with an anti-corruption element to it. He was pouring tremendous personal energy into his own anti-corruption work, traveling all around the country with a very effective slide show that had gone viral.

Lessig called his group "Root Strikers." At the beginning of his presentation he featured a picture of an immense tree including its underground network of roots. Against this backdrop he would quote Henry David Thoreau: "There are a thousand hacking at the branches of evil to one who is striking at the root."

The imagery is near perfect. We flail away at the many failings of our government that spring from the underlying system that nourishes its endless dysfunctions. My only criticism of Lessig's analogy is that he sees money as the sole root of the problem. But what is this money for? It is for re-election and political power. Without the desire for re-election and political power, money is unimportant. I would argue that the evil root system consists of structures and substructures that go deeper than the corrupting influence of just money in politics. Money is the route (and root) that leads to power.

Jeff and I scored a meeting with Lessig outside a Harvard Square café on a brisk November day in 2010. My first impression of Lessig was that he seemed distracted. I supposed that when you are a busy Harvard law professor this kind of goes with the turf. Still, I was happy for the meeting.

I soon got around to pitching him the essence of our proposed bargain between the Left and Right: clean elections for term limits. Lessig explained that he was not a big fan of term limits, based on the experience with them in California (more on this later), but he could accept term limits as part of a larger deal. I was delighted and promised Lessig that I would do my best to recruit conservative partners for him. I am sure that he did not take me very seriously.

"You don't seem excited," I remarked.

Then he smiled, and replied, "No, what you propose would be great."

Shortly after I got home I somehow acquired the e-mail address of Joan Blades, one of the founders of the progressive activist group MoveOn.org. I wrote her and explained my plan. She thanked me and said that if Lessig was on board then she would help rally MoveOn. Joan would later turn out to be one of the rarest and most admirable citizens I would meet during the course of my work, because she had dedicated a significant part of her life to civil Left-Right dialogue and deliberative democracy, a fact that explains why she responded to me so quickly.

I was feeling optimistic. It seemed that I had already wrapped up the support of some major players on the Left. Could it really be this easy? And who should I reach out to on the Right?

3: "A Perpetual Disqualification to be Re-elected"

When he first decided to run for the US House of Representatives, Dr. Tom Coburn's motivation was to be a different kind of congressman. "What bothered me most," he wrote, "was cowardice in public servants and elected officials who placed their political careers ahead of the best interests of the next generation."

To inoculate against the seduction of power and public office, Coburn pledged to term-limit himself to three terms in the House. He later did the same thing as a senator, limiting himself to no more than two terms. He vowed it would never be about the next re-election for him. He would vote and act on his conscience and not his personal political interests. No one was more opposed to political careerism than Dr. Coburn (he preferred not to be called "Senator") and no one was a more forceful advocate for congressional term limits. His book on his experience in the House, *Breach of Trust*, reads like an ode to term limits, with warnings about the danger of government by profes-sional politicians woven into nearly every page.[34]

There was also no sharper-beaked fiscal hawk than Dr. Coburn, who had had been dubbed "godfather of the Tea Party movement," and when it came to government ex-penditures, he was known on Capitol Hill as "Dr. No." He had gold standard credibility with conservatives but he was also known to work with Democrats. Coburn is prin-cipled but not rigidly ideological. He considers Barack Obama a personal friend, despite their substantial political differences. A regular on FOX News, especially with Greta Van Susteren, and also on MSNBC's Morning Joe, Dr. Coburn was easily one of the top ten most prominent con-servatives in the country. Because of all of the above, I decided that he was the ideal conservative to lead a reform alliance from the Right. I just had to hope that he'd be open to radically re-imagining our system of campaign fi-nance. And that he'd be willing to sit down and talk.

◇◇◇

Tom Coburn was born in Casper, Wyoming, in 1948, the son of an optician who founded Coburn Optical In-dustries, where the young Coburn would serve as manu-facturing manager at the company's Ophthalmic Division in Virginia. No slouch in business, he grew the division from 13 employees in 1970, to 350 employees and cap-tured 35% of the US market. Remarkably, he then decided to become a doctor, graduating from the University of Oklahoma Medical School with honors in 1983. He opened up a medical practice in obstetrics in Tuskegee, OK, where he estimates that he has delivered 4000 babies.

Eleven years later he was running for Congress. Co-burn entered Congress as part of the freshman class of 1994, which was led by Newt Gingrich and famously elect-ed on the "Contract with America," an agenda enumerat-ing specific poll-tested actions a Republican Congress would take in its first one hundred days if it won a majority. More generally, writes Coburn, it was "a commitment to the American people to restore our founding principles of limited government and to address the long-term challenges that are threatening our future prosperity and strength." These challenges were chiefly the national debt – both the existing debt and future financial commitments that the federal government had made in the form of the nation's big and costly entitlement programs: Medicaid, Medicare and Social Security. Then, as now, these programs will bankrupt the federal government unless they are reformed. Addressing our national debt was Coburn's top priority during both of his stints in Congress.

From Coburn's point of view, things started off well enough in the new Republican House of 1995. It looked like they were determined to put the nation's fiscal affairs in order. In May, Congress passed a budget resolution that cut spending in real terms for the first time since 1981. Later that year Congress approved a resolution that would balance the budget in seven years; it would be the first balanced budget since 1969.

Congressional resolutions, however, are only mere promises. The Republicans found that President Clinton refused to sign bills that limited spending, initiating a "government shutdown crisis" of the sort that has now become familiar. To Coburn's dismay, the Republicans caved under the leadership of House Speaker Newt Gingrich. In a now-familiar pattern, the Republicans in Congress and a Democratic president disagreed about how much money the government should spend, but it was Republicans who got blamed for the impasse and the shutdown; they had not the courage of their supposed convictions. Then as now, when the cameras get turned on, Democrats always look like they are confidently doing the right thing, and Republican congressional leaders always look like deer in the headlights.

In 1997, Congress passed another balanced budget resolution. This one had President Clinton's support, but it put off the hard choices to the outlying years, which in Coburn's opinion made the agreement useless. Then, in 1998, the bubbling "dotcom" economy delivered a surprise: a $70 billion budget surplus. This windfall, however, came entirely from an unexpected increase in Social Security revenue. Since Social Security is an underfunded future commitment, any surplus should have been set aside to pay what is owed to future retirees.

Instead, members of Congress looked upon the surprise bundle of cash as a gift that could be spent right away. Much to Coburn's horror, Republican chairmen of the Transportation and Agricultural Committees led the charge to immediately draw on the unexpected Social Security revenues in an orgy of appropriations spending

On the Republicans' overall failure to deal with the federal debt, Coburn concludes that they lacked the political backbone to stand up to special interests and partisan attacks. "Rather than standing on our core principle of reshaping the federal government in an image closer to our founders' intent, we succumbed to the fear of losing control of Congress." And it was Republicans who led an effort "to squander the taxpayer's money on monuments to career politicians and advertisements for their re-election campaigns." Republicans would again fail to address the debt, and in fact make it worse, during the years under President George W. Bush.

But it's not just the budget-cutting priorities of conservatives that suffer from congressional shortsightedness and the mania for power and re-elections. Progressives concerned about human-made climate change are frustrated for the same reasons. In 2009, a pork-laden 1,200-page cap and trade bill, allegedly designed to limit carbon emissions, limped out of the Democrat-controlled House of Representatives. It was full of corporate giveaways and postponed carbon restrictions, putting off the tough medicine that progressives believe is necessary to heal the planet. Some principled progressives couldn't stomach this legislative monstrosity. House member Dennis Kucinich (D-OH) had this to say:

> I oppose H.R. 2454, the American Clean Energy and Security Act of 2009. The reason is simple. It won't address the problem. In fact, it might make the problem worse. It sets targets that are too weak, especially in the short term, and sets about meeting those targets through Enron-style accounting methods. It gives new life to one of the primary sources of the problem that should be on its way out– coal – by giving it record subsidies. And it is rounded out with massive corporate giveaways at taxpayer expense. There is $60 billion for a single technology which may or may not work, but which enables coal power plants to keep warming the planet at least another 20 years. Worse, the bill locks us into a framework that will fail. Science tells us that immediately is not soon enough to begin repairing the planet. Waiting another decade or more will virtually guarantee catastrophic levels of warming. But the bill does not require any greenhouse gas reductions beyond current levels until 2030.

Some might argue that Congress would not produce such an awful bill under a public campaign financing system, and it's true that a number of the interests in the bill that fund campaigns might not get their favors from the government if they had no way to influence politicians with campaign donations.

Some of these interests, however, are regional, like coal

for example. Even with a clean elections system in place, career politicians from coal-producing areas who want to keep their jobs will be very reluctant to undermine an industry on which many of their constituents depend. By contrast, a term-limited member might be more willing to do the right thing for the greater good rather than the selfish thing that furthers a political career.

Then there is the overall tendency in the 2009 Cap and Trade Bill to put off the pain, no matter how necessary. Democrats don't want to be blamed for higher energy costs any more than Republicans want to be blamed for budget cuts. When holding power is what matters most, hard choices are avoided.

The "chronic problem" with Congress, says Tom Coburn, is that the institution is dominated by career politicians who continually sacrifice the long-term interests and vision of the country "at the altar of short-term political expediency." Coburn's understanding of this fatal dynamic in our politics is why he term-limited himself twice, and it's why he was such an ardent supporter of the final item on the Republicans' Contract with America: "congressional term limits."

Unfortunately, the Contract with America had some fine print in it. The Republicans never promised that they would pass a constitutional amendment for term limits; they only promised that they would *hold a vote* on such an amendment. The frustrating episode unfolded around the time I worked at US Term Limits. I had been hired in the run-up to the Supreme Court decision, *US Term Limits v. Thornton,* which had delivered a seemingly fatal blow to the term limits movement, since the court had ruled that states may not impose term limits on their elected representatives and senators in Congress. Now term limits could only come about through a constitutional amendment, which in turn meant that either Congress must vote to term-limit itself or that the states must call a Constitutional Convention, as permitted under Article V of the Constitution, though no such convention has ever been convened in our nation's history. Both paths forward, then, appeared extremely difficult. Still, the 1994 election was held in the shadow of the term limits movement and the Republicans were running on term limits in their Contract with America. If the GOP kept to the spirit of its contract, an amendment for congressional term limits would move on to the states for potential ratification.

The people of all twenty-three states that permitted citizens' initiatives — that is, that allowed citizens to pass laws themselves in referendum — had voted to term-limit their own representatives in Congress. There was disagreement over the appropriate limit for House members. Should it be three terms (six years) or four terms (eight years) or 6 terms (twelve years)? For senators, it was generally agreed that two terms (twelve years) was the proper limit. U.S Term Limits was accused of bullying local organizations into accepting the three-term limit for the US House because they deployed paid signature gatherers, and this way, were usually able to impose the group's preferred three-term limit. While one certainly might question this top-down, money-driven operation, the leadership of US Term Limits was right to be concerned about uniformity in the proposed limits.

When it came time for Republicans to vote on term limits in the House based on their Contract with America, many members voted for the three-term limit, but others voted for different limits. "In the end," says Coburn sadly, the newly elected Republican leadership in Congress "rigged the vote to make sure that every Republican could go on record voting for term limits of some kind while ensuring that no measure received a majority of votes." Republican "leaders were more interested in term limits as a campaign issue than as a real reform."[35]

My unique contribution to the term limits movement of the 1990s was to show how and why James Madison supported re-election restrictions for members of Congress. I published an article for the Heritage Foundation's *Policy Review*, "A Bulwark Against Faction: James Madison's Case for Term Limits," which circulated on Capitol Hill among the friends of term limits and was read into the *Congressional Record* (which is never read by anybody except those mentioned in it).[36] It was a small contribution in the scheme of things, but it was something in which I took pride and provided me with some credibility thirty years later as I sought to broker a grand bargain between reformers on the Left and Right.

Recall that Madison hoped that American legislators would act in the interest of justice — that is, for the whole and long-term good of the country — and not on behalf of narrow interests. In Vice #11 of his "Vices of the Political System of the United States," Madison described the nature of politicians, which would be all-too-familiar to Tom Coburn and many other concerned Americans more than two hundred years later.

Madison pointed out that citizens run for public office out of three motivations, to serve: 1) ambition, 2) personal interests and/or 3) the public good. "Unhappily the two first are proved by experience to be the most prevalent," observed Madison. Elected officials, he said, will industriously pursue their self-interests in the name of the public good. As they continue to serve themselves, they may get re-elected by masking their real objectives. Even the more selfless and well-meaning representatives may get duped by cunning leaders with private agendas, cautioned Madison. He must have given considerable attention to the question of how a constitution might be framed to encourage this third and rarest motivation in politics: service for the "public good."[37]

After jotting down his "Vices of the Political System of the United States" in New York, Madison returned to Virginia to rally the state's political leaders behind his vision for a new United States Constitution to replace the Articles of Confederation. He led his state delegation in creating a draft proposal for the Constitution, which became known as the Virginia Plan.[38] The Virginia Plan unsurprisingly called for a stronger federal government, one with the authority to hold a vast and diverse American republic together, which was a priority at the time. The basic model of the Virginia Plan was not especially original. The bicameral form — a legislature with two houses — dated back to ancient Greece and was reflected in the political structures of Great Britain. Almost all the states also had bicameral legislatures.

Classical political theory understood that lawmaking bodies needed to embrace two essential qualities: *wisdom* and *virtue.* Madison addressed the necessity of encouraging these values in government in *Federalist #57*:

> *The aim of every political constitution is or ought to be first to obtain for rulers Men who possess the most wisdom to discern the most virtue to pursue the common good of the society, and in the next place to take the most effectual precautions for keeping them virtuous whilst they continue to hold their public trust.[39]*

Wisdom obviously required learning, but historically the most educated citizens were found in the aristocracy. Only the privileged had the resources and leisure time to attend college, purchase books, and read. The problem with aristocracy was that it was a fixed class, frequently corrupt, luxury-loving, and self-serving. Virtue was more likely to be found in the body of the people, who, though often lacking education and broad perspective, better appreciated the value of hard work, neighborliness and, especially, sacrifice for the common good. The ideal republic blended the qualities of knowledge and learning, represented in an upper house or senate, and virtue, found in a lower house, reflective of the people. Together they might produce wise and just laws.

One of the challenges for the founding generation in America was to recreate the positive qualities of the traditional upper house without a titled aristocracy, a class repugnant to the values of the Revolution. Madison, in consultation with his fellow Virginians, George Mason, Edmund Randolph and George Washington, proposed that the people directly elect members of the lower house who in turn would elect the upper house, in what he called a "refining" mechanism designed to elevate the most capable and educated leaders with outstanding public reputations.

It was a system of "checks and balances." The narrow-mindedness of more ordinary citizens would be countered by an educated elite found in the Senate. The potential corruption of the Senate, which might turn into an aristocracy, would be checked by the lower house, a reflection of the public virtue found in the people. The innumerable interests found in society would check each other in the large American republic, where an invigorated federal government could thwart interests set on serving themselves at the expense of the whole (As already noted, Madison failed to appreciate the possibility of a government so large that it could serve thousands and thousands of special interests simultaneously at the expense of the whole).

To promote the right sort of incentives in representatives who would hold office, Madison's Virginia Plan called for term limits, or mandatory "rotation" of offices, as the practice was called. Moreover, it would restrict each representative of the lower house to a one-term limit, without the possibility of even one re-election.

Here was a radical idea. A new collection of lawmakers would be drawn from the body of people at every election, which would give the lower house somewhat the quality of a jury, called to office for a short period of time to render judgments on important public matters before returning to their normal lives. It may have seemed the best way to give the lower house the judicious quality desired by Madison and infuse the system with the public virtue most likely to be found in the body of the people.

The notes that Madison took at the Constitutional Convention don't tell us why the founders failed to adopt any form of term limits for either members or Congress or the president. But Madison, during the course of the Convention, tried to create virtual term limits on U.S. senators by suggesting a long nine-year term that could not begin until some ripe age in their lives, so that by the time their first terms were up they would be too old to run for re-election, or in Madison's words, "would render a perpetual disqualification to be re-elected."[40] Since Madison believed that most elected officials seek office out of ambition or self-interest rather than public service, perhaps he reasoned that at the end of life priorities shift. Rather than focus on future prospects of wealth and power, motivations of the aged turn to their own personal legacies. They begin to ask themselves with increasing urgency how they will they be remembered when they are gone.

◊◊◊

The best examples of civic judiciousness in action today are found in the operation of juries. All across the United States ordinary citizens routinely sit in judgment of defendants accused of various crimes, including the most heinous offenses. Jurors are, of course, ordinary people who must be educated on the spot in both the law and the particulars of the case. They must get up to speed quickly on what are often very complex matters involving legal intricacies and complicated situations pertaining to business or technology. They are often sequestered during the trial to ensure that their judgments are not influenced by current public opinion. The juror is frequently asked to uphold the abstraction of "justice" in the face of powerful motivations and passions that implore the juror to act otherwise. In spite of this, the justice system usually gets the jurors to overcome personal biases, feelings and prejudices, see beyond the superficial, apply reason, resist popular pressure, and act for the common good.[41]

Madison wanted legislators to act similarly. The one-term limit proposed for the US House in the Virginia Plan would have created a jury-like body for half of Congress. In *Federalist #10* he pointed out that all lawmakers, who necessarily have interests, act as their own judges and juries in legislative matters, which makes them highly fallible. But one way to control the effects of self-interests on legislators − to make them less fallible and more judicious − is to minimize the incentives that go with the desire for re-election.

Consistent with Tom Coburn's experience in Congress, if a career politician is faced with a choice of either passing legislation that will serve a narrow constituency and help with re-election, or passing legislation that will be good for the long-term interests of the entire country, then the career politician, whose priority is re-election, will likely choose the narrow interest. For a career politician, that re-election is all-important. For the citizen in Congress performing temporary public service, more like that of a juror, the re-election is less important. While there is no guarantee, the term-limited citizen legislator, rather than the career politician, is likely to be more judicious, more farsighted and more inclined to serve the common good rather than the narrow interest. This is the primary − and uniquely Madisonian − benefit of term limits.

A second benefit of term limits, which Madison also surely appreciated, is that forcing turnover in Congress infuses fresh perspectives into government. This is the reason for term limits argued by the ancient Greeks and their English political heirs, who called the practice "rotation" of offices. Modern advocates of deliberative democracy argue somewhat similarly that public wisdom can best be harnessed if, in any decision-making process, the points of view are diverse and decentralized.[42] In other words, the best outcomes will result from a wide universe of perspectives. Many years in office, however, weaken decentralized perspectives and can yield to the groupthink of long-term professional office holders. While ideological differences remain, the shared biases of those people who become part of the permanent Washington establishment can lead to very unwise decision-making, as happened, for example, in the run-up to the financial crisis of 2008, when both Democrat and Republican office holders together made catastrophic blunders.

There are several arguments typically deployed against term limits. First, it is often said that term limits, by forbidding incumbents from periodically running for re-election, restrict voter choice and are, therefore, arbitrary and undemocratic. But a republic is not a strictly majoritarian political system. From the very beginning of American government, limits have been placed on majority rule. Many of these limits are found, of course, in the Bill of Rights. In fact, term limits were part of many early state bills of rights, such as the influential Virginia Declaration of Rights, suggesting that many citizens of the founding generation considered mandatory term limits to be an essential safeguard against tyranny, alongside other enumerated rights designed to protect liberty. After Franklin Delano Roosevelt's unprecedented third and fourth terms in office, the president of the United States was term-limited by the 22nd Amendment, with very few voters feeling put upon that their choice is overly restricted.

Some argue for the need of experienced legislators, which term limits would discourage. But because of the current incentive structure, career politicians learn how to get re-elected; they don't necessarily learn how to govern well. Indeed, in many ways long-standing members of

Congress in the current system have simply stopped governing in favor of the perpetual political campaign. They often don't bother to read lengthy bills like the Affordable Care Act, and they increasingly cede constitutionally-granted legislative authority to the Executive branch or to the bureaucracy. The experience of many years in Congress becomes a liability to the national interest rather than a benefit to the extent that it leads to a focus on endless campaigning, rigid partisanship, insularity and groupthink. As the example of the citizen-juror suggests, ordinary people can get up to speed on fairly complex matters very quickly if they apply themselves without distraction. No one suggests that the president, who is limited to only two terms, is still a novice after his first term is up.

Some contend that term limits empower wily lobbyists, who will prey on novice legislators, but generally the opposite is true. Open Secrets, the gold standard for information about money and politics on the web, argues that of "the ten things voters should know about money-in-politics," #6 is that "donors seek a long-term relationship" with members of Congress. Former lobbyist Jack Abramoff points out that it takes a significant amount of time and money for a lobbyist to establish a fruitful relationship with a politician. And experience at the state level suggests that term limits would destroy substantial lobbyist investment when a legislator is forced to retire.[43]

It is true that legislative staff and various policy think tanks probably become more important under term limits, but such an outcome is not necessarily harmful to the workings of democratic government. Congressional staff and think tanks can reasonably be relied upon to be the repositories of institutional memory and public policy information for members of Congress. They can, like expert witnesses in a court of law, make information available to those who must decide.

The most forceful arguments against term limits relate to the experience with them at the state level, particularly in California. It should be remembered that term limits are not a reform for its own sake, but a device designed to discourage political careerism and make legislatures more jury-like. As such, term limits have indeed failed in California, where they have been deployed as a stand-alone reform in the middle of a career politician's rise to power. California legislative districts are very large — about half the size of a Congressional district — so usually the only people who can expect to win in one of them are either a city or county politician with an existing political base and war chest, or a self-funded private citizen of considerable wealth. In California, therefore, career politicians get term-limited in the middle of their political careers, which only makes them accelerate their fundraising and pandering to narrow interests, in preparation for rising higher on the political ladder. To effectively disrupt political careerism in California and elsewhere, term limits would need to be applied more systematically, with forced breaks in between all kinds of office seeking, and in conjunction with other reforms, including a clean elections system and much smaller legislative districts.

◊◊◊

So James Madison had favored term limits on members of Congress but had not been successful incorporating them into the Constitution. By the last quarter of the twentieth century it became clear that Americans of all political stripes were favoring term limits also. Polling data shows that public support for congressional term limits was already in the 60-65% range during the late 1970s and early 1980s. In the 1990s, approval of term limits increased to between 65% - 70%, which was when the people of the twenty-three states that permit citizens' referenda all voted to enact term limits on their own representatives in Congress. Although the Supreme Court reversed all of these state laws, public opinion in favor of term limits has grown even stronger. Since 2010 support for term limits has been regularly over 70% and has reached as high as 78%.[44]

At the popular level, support for term limits is thoroughly bipartisan. Republicans support term limits most strongly, with margins that can exceed 80%. Democratic support is also unambiguous, with clear majorities for term limits even when both chambers of the Congress are in Democratic control, as was the case in 2010, when 54% of Democrats were in favor. More typically, Democratic support is in the 60-65% range. But career politicians, both Republican and Democrat, are blocking the way. Some elites on the Left also tend to oppose term limits; these are often people with influence and money.

It's also safe to say that progressives in general place more faith in professionalism and are far more concerned about the corrupting influence of money in politics than they are about political careerism. This is why Larry Lessig agreeing to a deal — a clean elections system *and* term limits to be bundled together in a single constitutional amendment — was so important. But how would I, just an ordinary citizen, ever get two prominent and very busy people like Larry Lessig and Senator Tom Coburn in the same room, let alone broker an actual partnership?

Jeff McLean, the former Americans for Campaign Reform staffer who had some experience lobbying on Capitol Hill, reminded me that the key to securing a meeting with a senator was first to establish a relationship with the chief of staff. Jeff and I headed down to Washington in mid-December of 2010 to sound out various prospects on our plan to unite leaders on the Left and Right behind a clean elections system and term limits, with a ban on gerrymandering thrown in. Meeting Coburn's chief of staff, Michael Schwarz, was high on our to-do list. I had e-mailed Schwarz but got no response. Jeff cold-called from outside the Senate office buildings as snow started falling. He got Schwarz on the phone and the chief of staff invited us in.

A thin older man with a quick smile, glasses and gentle

voice, Mike Schwarz was very gracious. As he greeted us, he poked fun at the notion of global warming as the un-seasonable snow fell from the sky, the same way that pro-gressives frequently bewail global warming on any day that it is unusually hot. Mike listened to our proposal and thought it "imaginative." Coburn was immersed in budget-ary matters at the moment, but Mike thought he could raise our proposal with the senator after the first of the year. He shared his boss' disgust with amount of time members of Congress spend fundraising. Thinking as a chief of staff, he wondered aloud which Democratic sena-tor would be most likely to partner with Coburn on our project. Mike mentioned Ron Wyden (D-OR) or perhaps Sherrod Brown (D-OH). I tried to steer him toward Les-sig. We did not want this to be a politician-centered pro-ject. The proposal had to come from outside of the Wash-ington Beltway. Coburn would be the exception because his entire political life was like one great struggle against the self-centered nature of the political class. I kept bring-ing up Larry Lessig as the ideal leader to bring the Ameri-can Left into an alliance.

Later I followed up with Mike, suggesting that Senator Coburn have lunch with Congressman Walter Jones, a Re-publican member of the House Tea Party Caucus and long-time supporter of public campaign financing, includ-ing the *Fair Elections Now Act*.

I had also recently met former Comptroller General of the United States David Walker, who has devoted a big part of his life to warning his fellow citizens about the danger of our federal debt. He's been way out ahead on reform issues because he understands the real impact that our malfunctioning political system has on public policy decision making. Walker may have been the first public figure to call for both congressional term limits and a clean campaign finance system. Not surprisingly, he and Coburn have a lot of mutual respect due to their shared concern about the nation's finances. I followed up with Walker, who offered to lobby Coburn on behalf of our proposal.

Things were looking up as far as I could tell, but months went by with no word from Mike Schwarz. I e-mailed him in March but heard nothing back. Spring turned into summer, when Congress went into its usual recess. I worried that we'd never get our chance to pitch Coburn on our plan. What I most wanted was to broker a dinner between Coburn and Lessig. Intellectual accommodation is built on relationship building. The two leaders needed to get to know and trust each other, and breaking bread together is an especially good way to create a bond between people. The face-to-face contact, spread over a couple of hours, almost guarantees a chance to start a friendship.

But there was no Lessig-Coburn dinner in sight when fall arrived and Congress reconvened. At the end of October, I wrote Mike again, suggesting I come down to DC in early December and talk to Coburn myself if that was possible. I found an excuse to drop Mike another line in November. A whole year had gone by since we first met. At this point I had little to lose. Finally, Mike got back to me. He said he'd ask Senator Coburn to find some time for me during those first few days in December. So I flew to Washington only to find that Coburn was unavailable. Mike seemed embarrassed. Typically, a chief of staff in a senator's office is all-powerful, but with a strong-willed senator like Coburn, who probably acted as his own chief of staff, his was not a typical Senate office. Mike invited me up to the Hill to meet with him, at least. That's when we got to know each other a little.

Michael Schwarz, a product of Irish and Jewish lineage, cut his teeth growing up in the rough-and-tumble politics of Philadelphia. Just where and when he met the senator from Oklahoma, I don't know, but he had been Coburn's chief of staff during his time in the House as well. Mike sympathized when I admitted that the Iraq War, the profligacy of the Republicans during the George W. Bush years, and congressional Republicans who were as corrupt as Democrats, had alienated me from the Republican Party for a time. But of course the subsequent rule by Democrats was bracing; I was back in the GOP fold. Mike was sympathetic to my take on the recent history of the Republican Party. I learned during this meeting that Mike was dying of ALS, or Lou Gehrig's Disease. I was startled to see that the muscles in his hands had deteriorated so much that he could not rip open the paper packet that contained a tea bag; I had to do it for him.

After I returned home Mike sent me Coburn's direct e-mail and that of his scheduler. At last a short meeting was set up for March 13 on a day that Lessig had plans to be in Washington. I had hoped for a dinner meeting, but maybe this was a reasonable first step. Coburn wanted to see if a dinner meeting was worth his time. Lessig and I caught the same flight out of Boston and into Reagan National. The time together allowed me to get to know Lessig better; it started to feel like a partnership.

We were early and occupied ourselves trying to find a copy of Lessig's book at the Union Station bookstore to give to Coburn and we chatted on a bench in one of the lovely parks on Capitol Hill. Finally, we headed over to Coburn's Senate office for the twenty-minute appointment for which I had been waiting over fourteen months. The goal was to walk out of that meeting with the promise of a future dinner date between Lessig and Coburn. Possible financing of the project to unite progressives and conservatives behind comprehensive political reform was starting to line up, if only I could assemble the credible Left-Right partners.

I had never lobbied a member of Congress before and was impressed by the grandeur of a senator's inner office. It was a very large and ornate room, with the door Lessig and I were escorted through at one end and a massive desk at the other, behind which sat Senator Coburn, off in the cavernous distance. Unsmiling, he rose up to greet us. We were directed to some parlor furniture in the middle of the office; an aide was there to take notes. I think Coburn said "good morning," then proceeded to sit down with us and stare at me as if to say, "OK, what is it? I hope you're not here to waste my time."

I knew from Mike that Coburn was frequently angry because of the "charade" (to use Mike's word) that was substituted for governing in Washington. My sense is that much of Coburn's time in Congress is an exercise in anger management. If so, as far as I was concerned, Coburn's was a righteous rage, but still, this particular moment was intimidating. I felt myself stumbling with banalities as I began to talk, but eventually I said what I came to say. I knew that he thought as a doctor and so I remarked how doctors were trained to treat diseases rather than symptoms. The horrible symptoms made manifest in bad government could not be eliminated until we cured the disease, a cancer driven by career politicians who perpetuate themselves in office by taking campaign contributions from the same interests they regulate. The only way we could defeat the system and cure the disease was in a grand alliance of the American people, from Left to Right. We could wed the favorite reform of conservatives, term limits, with the favorite reform of progressives, clean elections, and package them together at the heart of a comprehensive clean government amendment to the US Constitution. We would unite as a people on the Left and Right in a powerful alliance to fix our broken system together.

Coburn began by reflecting that something must be done. Americans were disheartened and angry. He alluded to the recent Occupy Wall Street protests, and emphasized, somewhat ominously, that there was danger from radicalism "on both sides." On clean elections, he imagined a citizen objecting to the notion that he could no longer make campaign contributions. Either Lessig or I responded that it was an inherent conflict of interest for lawmakers to take campaign contributions from the same industries and professions they regulate, and there is simply no way to distinguish or separate campaign donations based purely on principle from those contributions that are really all about influence buying and selling. It was necessary to consider how private money in the public business of lawmaking corrupted legislation.

Lessig was kind and supportive, describing the plan of bundling clean elections with term limits as my "vision." The meeting flew by and before we knew it Coburn was rising to his feet. Our meeting had been a successful audition for a more substantive event. Coburn extended his hand to Lessig and looked him in the eye. "Maybe we should have that dinner," he concluded.

Outside again I called Michael Schwarz. "How did it go?" he asked. I told him that Coburn OK'd the dinner. Mike responded with some kind of corny yet charming anachronistic expletive, like "Hot Dang!" I can't remember exactly, but he was excited. He asked Lessig and me to stop by his office and was disappointed that Larry was already on his way to another appointment. I suggested he meet me outside. All I could think of was that a dying man, rather than being cooped up in an office, should feel the warmth of the sun on his face. So we sat on a bench facing the Capitol Building. I daydreamed about staffing up our Clean Government Alliance and locating it in Washington.

"I think we need to keep our eye on that place," I said to Mike, looking at the Capitol.

"Yes," he said, nodding in agreement.

We shared a quiet, hopeful moment there, sitting on that bench. Hopeful, at least for our country. Mike would pass away within the year. Coburn described Mike as among "the kindest, gentlest people that anyone has ever met." He said that his chief of staff would not only give money and feed the homeless he regularly encountered on the streets of Washington, but he befriended them. He spent time with them. Coburn says that he gave them the "love and dignity that comes from being reminded that we are children of the Creator." Mike was a devout Catholic. He was also active in the pro-life movement. If he had ever run for office himself, he would have been vilified, condemned and defined as part of the "war on women." Such are the times we live in. Mike had made me no guarantees about how Coburn would come down on radical campaign finance reform. Many conservatives are reflexively against "welfare for politicians," as many Republican insiders call public campaign financing. Here were the two great obstacles: vicious self-serving partisanship and knee-jerk ideological groupthink. I had my work cut out for me. I am grateful to Mike for who he was, and for helping me with that work.

4: Political Intoxication and Going Clean

In April of 1777, James Madison, the young revolutionary and scion of Orange County Virginia's most genteel families, stood for re-election to the state's new legislature. Men of Madison's social position, of which there were few, always dominated the local political offices. His re-election was practically assured. The lesser property holders would do as they always did, and dutifully vote for the leading gentlemen from the best families. These ordinary citizens trusted in their better-educated and more refined neighbors. They expected little in return except fidelity to the community's interests. That, and all the food they could eat and all the whiskey they could drink supplied to them by the candidates on Election Day. Once rip-roaring drunk, they were ready to do their civic duty and elect their leaders, as they had done for generations.

Madison thought this system of bribery through food, drink and intoxication on Election Day, ill-suited to the values of a republic. So for this Election Day in 1777 he stayed home and declined to purchase libations for the electorate. To his neighbors, evidently, Madison could come off as a bit of a zealot — cheap and above it all, too. Madison was defeated for re-election that year by a tavern keeper, who was well equipped to serve his would-be constituents. It was the only time Madison ever lost an election; he would never withhold food and drink on Election Day again. Revolutionary idealism had its limits.

Not only did Madison refrain from liquoring-up the electorate in 1777, but he didn't even make a personal appeal to the would-be voters that year. This, too, he considered un-republican. The example shows just how far from reality — especially the future reality — were the republican principles of Madison and other leaders of the founding generation when it came to political campaigning. The founders idealistically expected the leading citizens with the best public reputations to be automatically elected to office; all such men need do was go about their normal business and wait for the electorate to spontaneously carry them into office on their shoulders. As it turned out, elections don't work quite that way.

Madison and his fellow founding fathers also opposed political parties, which they believed would serve themselves at the expense of the nation. Voters were expected to rationally elect the most capable leaders, regardless of associations, cajoling, and manipulation, just as legislators were to coolly judge each issue and argument on its merits, without regard to personal or party interest. It was idealistic to the point of naiveté. No wonder, then, that no provisions in the Constitution relate to political campaigning or campaign finance.

Political parties quickly emerged as a reality in Madison's lifetime and as the 19th century unfolded became a dominant feature in American politics, along with the phenomenon of the political campaign. As previously noted, Andrew Jackson found a creative way to pay for his campaigns, by offering all his principal campaign workers positions in the federal government, especially in the customs service and the post office. Presidents Jefferson and Madison had moved a few Federalists out of office when they came to power, but Jackson's innovation was different not only in scale, but also in intent. It was not just about hiring bureaucrats who were politically loyal; rather, under Jackson the positions were payment for the contributions made by local politicians and political operatives. The hiring of government officials was transactional. Madison would have been aghast.

It only got worse as the 19th century wore on. In addition to the spoils system, campaigns became funded by big business during the first golden age of crony capitalism. Big banks, railroads and other interests bought the government, especially the Senate, where individual senators often ran their own states' political machines. Today some conservatives regret the adoption of the 17th Amendment, which ended the indirect election of senators by state legislatures. They complain that this innovation weakened federalism and the 10th Amendment, which reserves all powers not enumerated in the Constitution to the states, by removing the voices that states had in the federal government. While probably true, the relatively few electors on which US senators relied for their offices were easily bought and the narrow electoral base on which senators stood was an ongoing invitation to corrupt dealings.[45]

Another source of corruption that served the cause of political interests first appeared as early as the time of Madison's presidency, in 1812, when Massachusetts Governor Elbridge Gerry drew state senate district lines to benefit his own political party. One of these districts appeared in a highly irregular shape said to resemble a salamander, and thus the first "gerrymandered" legislative district was hatched. By 1900, the manipulation of legislative districts became extreme, when they were not only drawn into tortured shapes but also sometimes cut into highly unequal population sizes. The manipulations were part of an unsavory understanding between the Republican and Democratic parties. Gerrymandering helped Democrats in the South disenfranchise African-Americans while the practice furthered the Republican disenfranchisement of immigrants in the North by loading them up into tightly-packed urban districts.[46]

Gerrymandering was only the first in a series of corrupt practices designed to make elections less competitive and provide powerful advantages to favored political parties and, later, incumbent politicians. Incumbent members of Congress voted themselves a "franking privilege," which allowed them to send free mailings to constituents. The practice was benign until mass mailings turned it into an essential campaign tool, a tool that is unavailable to challengers.

Beginning with a lone clerk around the turn of the 20th century, congressional staff ballooned in the decades after World War II into dozens of employees who serve, to some extent, as full-time, year-round re-election staff for incumbent politicians. Today field offices where congressional staff perform constituent services regularly boost the images of incumbents among constituents. At election time, congressional staff must technically go on "leave" in order to participate in an incumbent's political campaign, but they are paid so handsomely that often they perform this campaign activity for "free." Challengers, in contrast, must always raise money to pay campaign staff, and they rely extensively on uncompensated volunteers.[47]

With the popular proliferation of televisions after 1950, politicians had potential access to a political weapon far more powerful than any that had come before, but television advertising was and is expensive. By the end of the 20th century incumbents were out-fundraising challengers by an average ratio of five to one. Today, incumbent campaign financing continues to increase every election cycle.[48] The reality is even worse for ordinary citizen challengers than this ratio suggests, since the average includes the politicians working their way up the ladder who have spent time in lower offices building up their political war chests and connections, as well as wealthy self-funders. Accomplished citizens of modest means seldom get elected to Congress. The re-election rate of incumbent members of the US House never falls below 85% and is typically at 95% no matter how much the public disapproves of Congress as a whole. In the 21St century Mr. Smith doesn't go to Washington anymore; all he can do is tweet, blog, and troll on Facebook.

It is said that incumbents spend 30-70% of their time fundraising, a range confirmed by insiders with whom I spoke. A Democratic Congressional Campaign Committee (DCCC) slide, presumably utilized to acculturate freshman members, got leaked to the *Huffington Post.* It recommends that only 20% of a member's time, or two hours per day, be spent on policy work in committees or on the House floor. Four hours per day, the DCCC said, should be spent dialing for campaign dollars on the telephone, one to two hours with constituents, one hour in "strategic outreach" (more politics and fundraising) and one hour "recharge" (all that fundraising and schmoozing is exhausting). Clearly most of a representative's' time is spent running for re-election, and most of that time, fundraising.[49]

With their hands on the wheel of power, incumbents are uniquely positioned to raise campaign cash. Here, progressive and conservative reform wonks have somewhat contrasting opinions about the source of the corruption.

Progressives consistently portray the problem as something close to legalized bribery, in which special interests buy the government. Conservatives are far more likely to point the finger at sitting politicians, who play a game of extortion to extract campaign contributions out of industry by threatening industry with legislation averse to their interests or denying various interests access to power.

As the conservative muckraker Peter Schweizer points out in his book on the subject, *Extortion,* sometimes various bills are introduced again and again, and each time is an opportunity to squeeze campaign cash out of a threatened interest. For example, bills that propose to tax retail sales over the internet have repeatedly come before Congress. Each time sitting politicians use the threat to the industry to raise campaign donations from internet retailers. Some interests who regularly experience the shakedown don't believe that legislation is necessarily the objective of any given proposed law. As Schweizer concludes, "What goes on in Washington's halls of power has less to do with lawmaking than with moneymaking." Larry Lessig makes a similar point about corporate tax breaks, which are never permanent but perpetually subject to renewal, with each renewal an opportunity for political interests to raise more campaign cash.[50]

In 2010, when it became clear that the Republicans were going to take over the House and that John Boehner would become speaker, executives from AT&T sent him twelve campaign donations on a single day – Election Day. Previously, when the Republicans had been in the minority and without significant power, Boehner had received only token support from AT&T. Here was a contribution that looked something like a bribe. Now that Boehner was to have real power, AT&T wished to buy access. Similarly, House Republicans would score forty-seven political donations from AT&T executives after voicing support for a merger with T-Mobile, which the Obama Administration was opposing.

In 2011, a popular bipartisan bill was making its way through the House that would have prevented local governments from taxing cell phone users. It was a win-win for politicians and the telecommunications industry, so this legislation looked like a slam dunk. But for some reason, Boehner held up a vote on the measure. Whatever could that reason be? He was waiting for something. It seems that even popular and uncontroversial legislation wasn't going forward without industry paying a toll. In a two-month span, employees at Verizon and AT&T wrote over two hundred checks totaling $180,000 to members of both parties. Only then did a vote on the bill finally come. Here was a case that looks more like extortion.[51]

I once personally witnessed an attempted extortion by the hands of a member of Congress. Sometime in 1995 I was behind the desk when the phone rang at the Washington, DC office of NAASCO, a San Diego based shipyard that produces ships for the US Navy. I was the "temp" in the small office, which included a lobbyist and a corporate vice president who was a former high-ranking naval officer.

The phone call was from House Minority Leader Dick Gephardt's office. Gephardt's representative informed the NAASCO vice president that the congressman was going to be in the San Diego area in the near future. He said that Gephardt would be happy to stop by the shipyard and discuss any issues management might have on its agenda, in exchange for either $1,000 to be donated to Gephardt's Leadership PAC or $3,000 to be donated to the Democratic National Committee.

A new ship coming out of shipyards like NAASCO's takes a shakedown cruise before entering service. The call from Gephardt's office was a shakedown of a different sort. I typed up the memo. The VP had three options for NAASCO's president. First, simply make the campaign contribution, as they had done with other members of Congress who had approached them similarly. Second, decline Gephardt's "offer." Third, try to scare off Gephardt, the very pro-union Democrat, by reminding him that they had labor trouble at the yard. A thousand dollars paid out by NAASCO, a division of the billion-dollar corporation, General Dynamics, was comparatively nothing. NAASCO is a defense contractor, dependent on government business, competing with a small number of comparable defense contractors. Keeping members of Congress happy was critically important. But maybe giving to Gephardt might have angered the Republicans, who were now in the majority. I would have advised trying to scare him off with the labor issue, which was a clever suggestion. I don't know which option the executives at NAASCO eventually chose.

In another interesting example illustrated by Peter Schweizer in *Extortion*, Hollywood and the music industry have been plagued by the theft of intellectual property almost since the digital age began.[52] Arts and other digital creators have a point; every time a song, a photo, a game or a video is downloaded without permission, its creator is robbed almost as surely as if a thief had shoplifted something from a store. Efforts to stop internet piracy had gone nowhere in 2009 and 2010, but in 2011 the motion picture and recording industries, encouraged by their allies in Congress, decided to make another push with two pieces of legislation, the *Stop Online Piracy Act* (SOPA) and the *Preventing Real Online Threats to Economic Creativity and Theft to Intellectual Property Act* (PIPA). Lobbyists were hired and checks dispensed to members of Congress and the president, which came at an opportune moment since everyone was gearing up for re-election in 2012. President Obama said that he'd "probably" sign these bills if they landed on his desk.

Warning sirens blared in Silicon Valley. The legislation was seen as a grave threat to the open culture of the internet and the profits of companies that operate there. The tech industry was traditionally reluctant to play the political game. But now, did it have a choice?

An arms race ensued, with the titans of Hollywood and Silicon Valley deploying millions of dollars against each other to lobbyists and politicians of both parties. The same politicians could collect from both sides, and sometimes even the same lobbyists did also. Schweizer makes a plausible case that the entire battle was orchestrated by Democratic insiders to raise campaign donations. Political operatives, writes Schweizer, call such an operation a "double milker." Politicians can milk interests on both sides of an issue. President Obama eventually turned against SOPA and PIPA, so the only ones who benefitted in the end were those who are part of the political class.

Schweizer could be wrong. The conflict over internet piracy and intellectual property could just have been another case of conflicting interests duking it out. The president might have simply had a change of heart based on public opposition generated by the internet-based interests. Were two powerful interests each trying to bribe the government to get what they wanted, or were politicians shaking down interests for campaign cash? Was it both?

I once asked Charlie Kolb, who served for ten years as the president of the Committee for Economic Development (CED), which was more prevalent when it came to congressional fundraising. Was it institutionalized bribery, as the progressives believe, or institutionalized extortion, which is what conservatives say is mostly going on? If anyone could answer this question it would be Charlie, who not only ran the nation's most venerable big business organizations but was also a committed reformer who had served on the boards of Common Cause and Americans for Campaign Reform. He is also a Republican who worked in the first Bush Administration. And Charlie didn't have an answer to the question.

It's not hard to imagine why conservatives and progressives have differing views on the "campaign finance as bribery or extortion" question. Progressives are more trusting of government and call on it more to regulate self-interested industries. Conservatives, for their part, are suspicious of government and often see industry as victim to over-regulation. With pre-existing villain–victim narratives, each side is ideologically predisposed toward one argument or another.

One thing is for certain. The money flows to those with power. The party in power can raise campaign money much more easily than the party out of power. Incumbents

can raise campaign money much more easily than challengers, who usually have no power. Congressional committee chairmen can raise more cash from the interests
they oversee in their individual committees than non-
chairmen and non-committee members. And those who
could theoretically change the system – those with political
power – have absolutely no incentive to do so and thereby
undermine their own power.

In fact, it doesn't really matter whether most of the political fundraising looks more like bribery or extortion.
Both dynamics are clearly occurring. We can all agree that
legislation should be considered on its merits and that
campaign money should play no role. We can also agree
that insiders should not be permitted to use their power to
gain advantage over their political opponents and make
American elections fundamentally unfair.

◇◇◇

Americans today can see the big picture. According to a
New York Times study, 81% of Republicans and 84% of
Democrats either believe that our system of campaign finance requires "fundamental changes" or that we need to
"completely rebuild it." Virtually no one thinks it's fine as
it is, while a total of just 13% believe that only minor
changes are necessary.[53]

In 2013, Gallup asked voters if they could support "a
100% government-funded campaign system for federal
elections," with 50% saying they could, 44% saying they
could not, and 6% undecided. The partisan breakdown
consisted of 60% of Democrats and 41% of Republicans
in favor of public funding of political campaigns.[54]

In the minds of many conservatives, anything like
"public campaign finance" will immediately be interpreted
as "welfare for politicians." Undeniably, attracting conservative support for a new clean elections system is the
most challenging piece of any comprehensive clean gov-

ernment solution. But 41% of Republicans for public campaign financing is a substantial base from which to build. And I was finding – at the grassroots level, at least – that conservatives understood the problem and were open to solutions involving public money. Packaging term limits with public campaign financing as part of a deal between conservatives and progressives will certainly help bring conservatives on board.

The University of New Hampshire similarly tested the popularity of public campaign finance by asking respondents to agree or disagree with the following statement: "We need a new system of campaign finance, including public funding." The results among Republicans were that 24% were strongly opposed, 10% opposed, 27% neutral, 13% support, and 22% strongly support, so a plurality were actually in favor, with a large neutral group.[55] Only 34% of Republicans opposed or strongly opposed.

Since James Madison stressed over and over again that he desired legislators to be judicious, it's inconceivable that he would support America's current campaign financing system, which permits lawmakers to maintain themselves in office by taking campaign money from the same interests they regulate. Madison would understand the political campaign contribution for what it usually is: a currency used to facilitate a transaction that closely resembles a bribe or an extortion. He would likely argue that it makes as much sense to allow legislators to collect campaign money from special interests as to permit jurors in court cases to solicit cash from prosecutors or criminal defendants. Undoubtedly, Madison would have us ban nearly all private political campaign donations.

Unfortunately, it's not that simple. Banning or radically limiting campaign contributions would lock in huge incumbent re-election rates because incumbents have significant institutional advantages other than fundraising. Large staffs, ongoing media attention, the ability to bring federal money back to their districts and perform constituent "services" all tilt the playing field in favor of the incumbent. Just the first step in mounting a successful challenge against an incumbent, establishing name ID, requires significant money; voters will not vote for someone they don't know. Without resources in the hands of challengers, competitive elections are impossible.

Though some conservatives may choke on the words "public campaign finance," campaigns must either be financed privately, which almost invariably bases the system on institutionalized bribery and extortion, or all funding – other than small dollar donations – must be somehow publicly financed. Those are the two choices. Small dollar donations are not enough to adequately fund competitive campaigns.

For too long, conservatives have listened to the Republican establishment's cheap rhetoric about "welfare for politicians." But when the state pays for criminal defense, conservatives don't call it "welfare for murderers, child molesters and rapists." We understand that for the justice system to operate fairly, the state must insure an adequate defense for everybody. It is the only way to serve the cause of justice. Our political system is not much different. Madison teaches us that it, too, should be based on "justice."

If we don't end self-interested political campaign donations, legislation will continue to be profoundly corrupted by interests. If we don't make sure that sufficient resources get into the hands of those citizens who would run against incumbent politicians, then incumbents will continue to be re-elected at rates of 85% or more, no matter how poor their record of performance.

Conservatives are not anarchists. They believe that government is there to do for society what society cannot do for itself. The question, then, is this: Can the private and narrow interests found in modern free society fund political campaigns without corrupting the political system and destroying our republic? Madison would recognize that the answer is clearly, no, and so should we.

◊◊◊

There are several approaches to a clean elections system. A detailed discussion of each is beyond the scope of the book. Moreover, I found the tendency of reformers to become bogged down in the intricacies of a specific clean elections system to be unhelpful.

The first step is for us to decide together to reject the current system, which of course permits elected officials to perpetuate themselves in office by taking campaign contributions from the same interests they regulate, thus corrupting both legislation and elections.

The second step is to recognize the number of clean election concepts that by themselves, or in combination, would be superior to the status quo.

The simplest clean elections concept is that embodied in the *Fair Elections Now Act*. Under this system, citizens are permitted to make small uncorrupting political contributions of, say, up to $100. These contributions are then immediately matched and multiplied by public money. The key here is for the multiplier to be sufficiently high so that challengers can have a realistic chance to defeat incumbents. To defeat a House incumbent, it must be possible for the matching system to put $1.5 to $2 million in the hands of a challenger. The system must also be weighted to take into consideration more expensive media markets, along with the relative sizes of each state when it comes to US Senate elections.

This system is similar to public campaign finance systems currently working at the state level in Arizona, Connecticut and Maine. Each of these state clean elections systems is voluntary, as required under current law; politicians cannot be compelled to participate. And each state clean election system is under regular attack by incumbent politicians because public campaign financing has been shown to make elections more fair by leveling the playing field between incumbents and credible challengers.[56]

Another approach, designed by Yale University professors Bruce Ackerman and Ian Ayers, has two components.[57] The first is a blind trust, through which all private contributions must pass. Under Ayers and Ackerman's system, there would still be private campaign donation limits, but with a properly operating blind trust these limits could actually be raised. The idea is that bribes and extortions don't work if the candidate can't be sure who is donating to the campaign.

Ayers and Ackerman also assume that the system would be underfunded if all the self-interested money were removed, so they add another mechanism, "patriot dollars," which is a voucher system for voters. The idea here is that every voter would get his or her first $50 in taxes back (everyone pays at least $50 in federal taxes of some kind), in the form of a campaign contribution voucher, which the voter could then donate to candidates of their choice. The advantage of this system is that it is highly voter-centric, and since voters are actually keeping their own money, it doesn't feel like "public campaign finance."

The beauty of Ayers and Ackerman's system is that citizens would retain more liberty to support candidates financially and at the same time it would democratize the campaign funding process with the vouchers. But the plan raises some questions that may expose flaws. First, could the blind trust be trusted? Ackerman and Ayers create a complicated system to protect the integrity of the trust. It might work, but it's untested. Also, the plan would continue to permit the wealthy to give more, and might in fact raise the allowable donation limits. Asking whether or not the wealthy should have any more influence than the rest of us over the election process is a reasonable question. Is this just?

Though little discussed, another clean elections approach is for the media to pay much or all of their taxes and broadband fees in the form of free air time and content space for candidates. Using this method, there's a great opportunity to improve the tone and quality of political debate. Rather than give away air time and content space for political attack advertising, debate time could be frequently required. Making sure that challengers get to share the debate stage with incumbents would undermine an incumbent's favorite tactic: to ignore the challenger. On screen together, their statures become equalized. In person, whether together or in a first-person statement, politics is usually less vicious (the 2016 presidential race not withstanding). In fact, as long as taxpayers are going to pay for campaigns, we can reasonably insist that all ads be delivered in the candidate's own voice. This would go a long way toward reducing the nastiness in political advertising; candidates know that in most cases, when they sound vicious, they undermine their own likability. Free media time for candidates, like the other approaches, has its challenges. Determining which media must contribute in air time and content space, and how much, is complicated. Then there is the question of which candidates should qualify and by what criteria. These are difficult questions, but surely not unsolvable ones.

A final option is to publicly fund political parties. There would need to be some reasonable threshold for smaller parties to obtain funding, along with the Democrats and Republicans. Given the large number of registered Independents, they too would have to be accommodated in some way. An independent candidate could qualify for funding through petition a drive, for example.

Creating a workable clean elections system necessarily means bumping up against the First Amendment and freedom of speech, an issue the Supreme Court wrestled with in its controversial *Citizens United* decision, which gave private interests the unlimited ability to pay for "independent" political advertising. As long as interests can "independently" urge the election or defeat of candidates in paid advertising, clean and fair elections are impossible. The *Citizens United* decision, as well as other related Supreme Court rulings, would need to be modified as part of a comprehensive clean elections solution.[58] Reversing these decisions is a top priority for progressives, so the task of staunching the flow of big-dollar private money is as important politically as it is in terms of policy.

A very careful line should be drawn here. In *Federalist #10* Madison warned of the danger of losing liberty in the pursuit of discouraging special interests. He wrote, "liberty is to faction what air is to fire, an aliment without which it instantly expires."[59] Money may or may not be speech, but government control of speech is censorship. Madison would likely agree that the right to speak and broadcast about any policy issue through any and all media, including the purchase of advertising, must remain politically sacred or the liberty that characterizes free society becomes compromised.

There is, however, no constitutional right to bribe or extort; these are crimes. A broader definition of bribery and extortion when it comes to politics suggests the appropriate demarcation. The logical place to draw the line between free speech and bribery, or extortion, is where campaigns paid for by special interests support, name or clearly indicate candidates for public office or political parties in advertising. In such cases, the risk to the public is too great that the nature of relationship between interests and candidates is transactional. In other words, advertising in support of, or against, ethanol subsidies, fracking, saving the whales, higher teacher salaries, genetically modified foods, or any other interest, should never be curtailed. But once the name or image of a candidate or political party is mentioned in one of these ads, or any privately funded ad, then it becomes all too likely that something resembling bribery or extortion is taking place. At that point, interest buying and selling, as well as the disproportionate influence of the very wealthy over the election process, tips the scales of justice.

Some progressives will worry that interests could still run issue-advocacy ads that parallel candidates' political campaigns. For example, the natural gas industry would still be permitted to run ads trumpeting the benefits of fracking generally (without mentioning a candidate or a political party), at the same time a candidate is running ads featuring her support of fracking. Teachers' unions would still be able to run ads against the cutting of school budgets (without mentioning candidates or a political party) while candidates, at the same time, run ads in support of the same message. Interests may, therefore, still have some impact on political campaigns for elected office. But in these cases the connections will be indirect, the ads not obviously targeted *for* or *against* any particular candidate, and the interests behind the advertising, rather than being hidden, will be clear. The alternative is to forbid interests from promoting or defending themselves through advertising. This would give the state, along with the political interests that control it, the power to silence whole industries, labor unions, professional associations or other groups of citizens. It would cross the line into the dangerous territory about which James Madison warns us, where liberty becomes suffocated.

For some conservatives, any proposed modification in our understanding of free speech under the First Amendment with regard to political campaigns will draw criticism as a corruption of a fundamental constitutional right, but this concern must be weighed against the failing political system as a whole, in which incumbent re-elections are almost always assured, and legislation is pervasively and self-evidently corrupted by special interests. Our Constitution was built on compromises. Restricting what big and potentially self-interested money can say about candidates and political parties, but not issues, strikes a reasonable balance. This balance, between the need to reform our political system and uphold the First Amendment, probably represents the *minimum requirements* for progressives, when it comes to money and speech issues, and the *maximum restrictions* acceptable to conservatives. It is one of the biggest political and policy obstacles we must address.

◊◊◊

With all of the time waiting for the meeting between Coburn and Lessig, I worked to form the first state chapter of our organization in my home state of New Hampshire. Just before Christmas, 2010 I attended a small meeting in Concord hosted by a local erstwhile centrist activist who was always focused on Left-Right accommodation and consensus building. This activist had tried to start a local Coffee Party chapter, before that movement for civility in politics proved incompatible with its initial anti-Tea Party orientation. It was an unlikely time to be looking for middle ground; the Tea Party-fueled Republican capture of the US House had just taken place in the wake of highly partisan pieces of legislation passed in the Democratic Congress. My expectations for the meeting weren't very high and indeed it was poorly attended.

But when in walked Arnie Arnesen – one of New Hampshire's leading progressives, the state's first female candidate for governor, and radio personality – I took notice. Arnie was no centrist and she didn't bite on any of the centrist solutions. She later indicated that she came to the meeting because the intense polarization suggested to her that something profoundly unhealthy was happening to our politics.

The topic of conversation turned to No Labels, a new bipartisan organization richly funded by Washington insiders. Arnie said, "If they are not for public campaign financing, then be afraid. Be very afraid." Indeed, I had experience with the No Labels people. Though No Labels' stated mission is commendable, and there are some fine leaders involved, its money-driven, top-down organizational structure was troubling to me also.

After I got around to explaining my fledging organization's three-reform solution − a clean elections system, term limits and an end to gerrymandering − Arnie looked at me intently and said, "Yes, doing those three things could change everything." They would reform "the architecture of our democracy" in a healthy and necessary way, she said. Arnie had recently come around on term limits. She believes in government by citizens and not professional politicians. Arnie had been a Democratic leader in the New Hampshire House, "But do you know what?" she asked. "I was not indispensable. No one is indispensable."

At least one story Arnie shared about her experience running for governor has really stuck with me. It was just a few weeks before Election Day in 1992. Arnie's campaign was low on money, so she worked the telephone, desperately dialing for dollars. Finally, after God knows how many calls, Arnie the idealist couldn't take it anymore. To wash away the filth built up after all that cajoling for campaign cash, she put down the phone and headed off to the shower, where she collapsed in tears. "I felt like a whore," Arnie said.

Is it any wonder that good people, who might have a problem begging for money or taking it from special interests, don't want to get involved in politics? And are people who thrive on this kind of activity really the ones who should be leading us?

Arnie would soon become my best progressive ally in New Hampshire. I began looking for conservatives to partner with her at the state level.

I had lunch, at a Manchester restaurant fittingly called "The Republic," with Andrew Hemmingway, a top Tea Party leader in the state. The youthful Hemmingway would later run for governor. (Throughout the project I would keep tripping over candidates and former candidates for governor of New Hampshire. To the reader, it will seem like one in five citizens of our small state has run for this office!). Andrew was intrigued by the prospect of an alliance with the Left against the political class. I told him how supportive Larry Lessig was, and what we were trying to accomplish. Andrew was certainly for term limits and an end to gerrymandering; he appeared to be open-minded on clean elections. His priorities at the time, however, struck me as personal. He knew that he wanted to work in politics. Public policy is his passion. I get it. I am the same way. He explained that the guy I needed to get on board was Tea Party leader Jerry Delemus.

While Andrew Hemmingway struck me as a calculating political operative and policy wonk, Jerry Delemus, who I met with over beer in his town of Rochester, had the aura of a sturdy working man, with hands that looked like they were accustomed to real labor. Indeed, he is a small-time building contractor and a former marine. "Intense" is certainly a word that applies to Jerry Delemus. Highly focused on conservative politics, he had started the Rochester 912 group (the "912 Project" was inspired by media personality Glenn Beck) and the NH Liberty PAC. Jerry, like so many citizens of all political persuasions, believes the government has been captured by interests hostile to the well-being of the American people. He listened as we sat almost alone in a bar late one afternoon while I sketched out the deal. My fellow conservatives can be reflexively against anything that smacks of "public campaign finance." I was feeling pessimistic as I spoke, but Jerry didn't flinch. Finally, he said, "Maybe this is it. Maybe this is what we need to do."

A few months later Arnie offered to host a dinner at her house in Concord. Jerry and his wife, State Representative Susan Delemus, agreed to attend. Kevin Smith, the former executive director of New Hampshire's social conservative foundation, Cornerstone, was also coming. Kevin would soon launch his own campaign for governor. Needless to say, such a trans-ideological social event is not the sort of thing that happens very often. Arnie told me later that she didn't sleep the night before, worrying about the dinner. She invited some progressive activists, including the head of the local America Votes chapter.

At first it was all very awkward. The small talk was forced. When we sat down, Arnie urged each of us to tell a personal story about ourselves. It was a brilliant move because it humanized everyone. Jerry Delemus explained his background as a marine, an evangelical Christian and his grave concern that the United States was straying from the wise principles set down by its founders. He characterized himself as "to the right of Attila the Hun." Indeed, in time I would discover that Jerry occupies about the farthest position on the Right in American politics. None of this, of course, would have made the progressives at the table enamored of Jerry, except maybe his honesty. Then he spoke about his first marriage, and how his first wife was diagnosed with schizophrenia. And how hard it was for him. But Jerry would never leave his wife. She was ill, he was a Christian and had made a vow. Eventually his schizophrenic wife divorced him. They had been living in California. Jerry climbed up on his motorcycle and drove cross country to New Hampshire, where he started a new life and met his new wife, Susan, whom Jerry considered a great blessing.

Obviously the progressives in the room could disagree with Jerry, but only a real jerk could hate him. And at least one of them, the young woman who ran America Votes, almost reached out and hugged Jerry when he said that he opposed the trade agreements NAFTA and GATT. It was clear to me that she really wanted to agree with him on something. This is what happens when good people personally like each other; they look for places of agreement. On the way out the door Jerry declared that he could collaborate with Arnie. "I can work with you Arnie, because you have integrity." Then Jerry Delemus hugged Arnie Arnesen. If only there had been a photographer present from the *Union Leader* to capture the moment!

During this time, America's self-described "most noto-rious lobbyist," Jack Abramoff, had been released from jail and had a book out, *Capitol Punishment.*[60] He had a change of heart in prison and emerged as an advocate for clean government political reform. I met him at Harvard, where Lessig had invited him to speak.

A couple of big points need to be made about the Abramoff case. First, the legal things Abramoff did (and most lobbyists do) were far more damaging to the country than the illegal ones. He was convicted of mail fraud, tax evasion and conspiracy to bribe public officials. Though such crimes may sound quite serious – and indeed they can be – there is little to be found when drilling down into these convictions in the Abramoff case. For example, "the conspiracy to bribe public officials" – while it sounds omi-nous – was about violating the gift ban and handing out a stream of tickets for DC-area sporting events to members of Congress and their staffs. The "conspiracy" was not about contributing thousands and thousands of dollars for congressional re-election campaigns, which is what most lobbyists do and is, of course, perfectly legal. Consider which buys more influence, a ticket to a Redskins or Capi-tols game (each team makes it to the playoffs about as of-ten as a challenger beats an incumbent politician), or thou-sands of dollars every year toward re-elections?

Second, Abramoff went to jail because he was an ex-tremely effective lobbyist who charged exceptionally big fees, because he had the protection of neither of the politi-cal parties, and because he left himself vulnerable to con-viction on some relatively minor charges. His dealings in-cluded charging Native American tribes very high sums, which sounds sinister, except when you consider that these were casino interests and Abramoff was successful in de-fending some highly lucrative Native American casino in-terests against other highly lucrative Native American casi-no interests. It wasn't exactly another "Trail of Tears" for Abramoff's Indian clients, who benefitted from his ruthless advocacy. There is nothing exceptionally corrupt about Jack Abramoff compared to hundreds of other players in the Washington establishment who either legally thrive on the institutional rot that infests our political system, or get away with law-breaking because they are protected by the connected and powerful. In the case of the 2008 financial scandal alone, untold numbers of elites got away with grotesque corruption far worse than anything Abramoff did.

When I met Jack Abramoff for lunch he was a shrunken larger-than-life figure. Years before he had been jetting around the world with the rich and powerful, winning epic battles for various interests, and changing laws and would-be laws; he had even advised Imelda Marcos, wife of Philippine dictator Ferdinand Marcos. Now, all he had was his story.

Jack Abramoff was not like that gangster-looking character who appeared in a famous photo in which he is wearing a hat and trench coat. He was now my humble and thoughtful lunch companion at a kosher restaurant in DC. Strange as it may sound, I found in Jack Abramoff a kindred spirit of sorts. We were both in the College Republicans at the same time during the 1980s and had both come of age during the Reagan years. We had an acquaintance in common, Tony Rudy, who had worked for Abramoff and pled guilty to one charge of conspiracy. (Tony had also been in the Republican Club with me at the University of Massachusetts at Amherst, where I received my BA.) I have no doubt that Abramoff's conversion to an advocate for clean government reform is sincere. I was also sure that he was very worried about making a living and supporting his family. He had a whopping $44 million restitution bill to pay off. This is itself a kind of life sentence.

Though Abramoff approved of the plan to create a united Left-Right alliance for political reform, he thought that the partisan hatred was probably too intense for such a thing to happen. He believed that a conservative reform organization was necessary, but that would take money. I replied that I could see how in theory a conservative reform organization might be helpful to the extent it could bring reform-minded conservatives together to engage with the many progressive reform groups. But ultimately, I argued, we'd have to work together. I maintained that the American people were craving something idealistic and inspiring. Partisan reform groups, to raise money, naturally become more partisan, which is a fatal flaw in all of the existing progressive reform organizations. My whole experience working on political reform has taught me that partisanship is a tool of the status quo.

Jack was planning a trip to Raleigh, North Carolina, as part of his book tour. Michael Schwarz had referred me to John Skvarla, who ran a term limits group there. Skvarla was trying to encourage politicians to keep their term limits pledges (they are notorious for breaking them) with his group, the Alliance for Bonded Term Limits, by offering to assist with a bonded pledge: candidates would legally bind themselves ahead of time, so that if they broke a term limit pledge they would lose a big pile of cash. I set up a meeting between Abramoff and Skvarla, also a conservative, and brokered another meeting between Skvarla and the head of a progressive North Carolina voter organization in the hope if seeding a chapter of our embryonic organization in that state.

Back in New Hampshire, Arnie Arnesen and Jerry Delemus hosted a Left-Right breakfast for the project. We had some impressive people in attendance. Of course there were current and former candidates for governor, including Jim Rubins, an iconoclastic Republican very concerned about climate change who would later recast himself as a Tea Party Republican. The man who would be the upcoming Republican candidate for governor, Ovide Lamontagne, showed up (he would defeat Kevin Smith in the primary). The former head of the New Hampshire Charitable Trust, Lew Feldstein, was there. He had co-authored a book, *Better Together: Restoring the American Community,* with *Bowling Alone* author Robert Putnam. There were a few business people in the room, long-time activists from every side, and some current and former legislators.

They were all curious and generally supportive, but no one was writing checks or offering to serve on my board. The North Carolina effort was stillborn when the progressive leader took another job. It was clear to me that some big names would have to lead this movement or it was going nowhere. I needed a credible conservative partner for Lessig — either Coburn or somebody else.

5: Citizens Disunited – Reform to the Left, Reform to the Right

America has had so many organizations working on political reform for so long that you'd think we would be getting somewhere by now. The biggest and best known is probably Common Cause, founded in 1970, with millions of dollars to spend and offices all over the country. But there is also Public Campaign, Democracy 21, and the Public Interest Research Group (PIRG), along with Larry Lessig's Rootstrikers. Other reform organizations come and go. United Republic appeared around 2011 and Americans for Campaign Reform disappeared in 2014, subsumed under the new reforming financing hub group, Issue One, formerly Fund for the Republic, which had briefly been associated with United Republic. While some of these groups have their own niches, and others have broader missions beyond campaign finance reform, they look much alike. All of them have the important mission of getting the corrupting influence of money out of politics. And all of them have something else important in common: they are all controlled and run by progressives.

I have suggested that the biggest policy challenge to fixing our political system comes from the Right, with its knee-jerk reaction to anything that looks like "campaign finance reform" or "public campaign financing." But I was finding that conservatives at every level understood the corrupting nature of money in politics. I believed when I began my project what I now know: most conservative resistance to cleaning up the campaign finance system will give way if conservatives are treated as partners by reformers on the Left, because conservatives increasingly understand that any system that permits lawmakers to accept money from the same interests they regulate is inherently corrupt.

The first big obstacle to fixing our corrupted political system is partisanship, and though conservatives play the partisan game too, the first problem we must solve is the partisanship on the Left that dominates the so-called progressive reform "community."

During the course of my work I reached out to virtually all of the above progressive reform organizations and got a range of responses in return. In one case I was ignored. In other cases, cordial discussions followed with staff that went nowhere. There were also high-level meetings, including ones in which I brought prominent conservatives to the table. But Larry Lessig was almost the only nationally-recognized progressive reform leader who seemed to want a genuine partnership with leaders on the Right.

My sense is that when members of the "reform community," which is largely based in Washington, go looking for allies, they begin with their "friends" on Capitol Hill, who are almost all Democrats. They ask their allies in Congress what sort of reform might have a chance of getting signed into law. In the wake of the *Citizens United,* the reform community, with the support of most Democratic politicians, decided that overturning this decision with a constitutional amendment would be their priority. It is a deeply flawed strategy in terms of both policy and politics.

First, as Lessig frequently points out, reversing *Citizens United,* while necessary, does not solve the problem. Yes, the specter of unlimited "dark money" from undisclosed sources flowing into American elections, which became completely legal after *Citizens United,* is ominous sounding. Corporate and foreign interests can impact American elections at will. And yes, the removal of limits makes institutionalized bribery much easier. But influence buying and selling long predated the Supreme Court decision. The entire financial collapse of 2008, and all of the unseemly greasing of wheels connected to that debacle, predated *Citizens United.* Even if there had been no *Citizens United,* the campaign finance system itself would remain largely based on behavior that closely resembles bribery and extortion through campaign contributions.

One of my closer relationships in the reform community was with Rob Werner, a staffer at Americans for Campaign Reform. Rob invited me to speak before a gathering of Occupy DC, an offshoot of the Occupy Wall Street movement. For me, it was an intriguing opportunity. Would an Occupy group be open to me, a conservative reformer, and what I had to say?

From the moment I walked through the door, the Occupy activists treated me very courteously. When it came time for me to speak, I explained that while I am conservative, I came there to advocate something radical, and by that I meant change "from the root," which is a literal definition of "radical." I argued that we needed a system-wide fix that would address all of the mal-incentives and dysfunctions in our government, and not merely those associated with *Citizens United.* The Occupy folks cheered my three-reform proposal for clean elections, term limits and an end to gerrymandering. It was nice, but the most gratifying moment was yet to come.

After I spoke, a representative from Public Campaign stood up to address the audience and explain his organization's strategy of reversing *Citizens United* with a constitutional amendment that would do just that and nothing more. He, too, was received warmly. I stood in line to ask him what were, for me, the essential questions: Given that a constitutional amendment is by far the most difficult thing to achieve in American politics, why was Public Campaign calling for a solution that only fixed part of the problem? Given the enormous cost in money and effort required to have even a chance of passing a constitutional amendment, why not instead go for an amendment that would clean up the whole system and completely eliminate the institutionalized bribery and extortion that fund political campaigns? After I got this question out, the Occupy crowd cheered me, the conservative, while the Public Campaign staffer glared back in anger.

The true answer to the question illustrates an aspect of the fundamental political problem in the American reform movement. The "reform community" has been allied with the interests of Democratic politicians, who have an insider's agenda that is not necessarily in keeping with fundamentally cleaning up the system.

It's important to understand why the Democratic establishment favors overturning *Citizens United*. First, an incumbent's fundraising advantage, built up over years of leveraging the power of their offices, can disappear in a second if some interest decides to back the incumbent's challenger. Before *Citizens United,* such a threat could only come from a wealthy self-funding challenger willing to drop millions of dollars of his or her own money into a self-funded campaign. Now the threat can emerge from anywhere at any time and out of nowhere, and suddenly – horror of horrors – cause a competitive election.

Second, if the incumbent-protection system is based at least partly on the threatening of interests that might donate to a challenger, then the ability of interests to support challengers anonymously, as permitted under *Citizens United,* eliminates the threat of retribution against the financial backers of an unsuccessful challenger. Yes, I am arguing that *Citizens United* does something good: it makes incumbents less secure and has the potential to make the playing field more level between incumbents and citizens who are brave enough to attempt to dislodge them from their long-held offices.

Some Republican incumbents would probably be happy to see *Citizens United* overturned for the same reasons. Republican incumbents don't want fair elections any more than Democratic incumbents do.

Ideologically, however, pro-business Republicans are supportive of empowering industry against government regulation, or over-regulation. That's likely one reason Republicans may not be interested in overturning *Citizens United.* Democrats are probably more comfortable with the extortion and Republicans more comfortable with the bribery in our system. Make no mistake, however. Both sides engage in both activities; it's probably more a matter of degree and ideological comfort.

Constitutional First Amendment issues, addressed in the previous chapter, are also a concern to many conservative opponents of "reversing" *Citizens United.* And, as we will see, the IRS scandal, in which conservatives were allegedly targeted and harassed by that agency, plays into the debate. It stiffens conservative resistance to addressing *Citizens United,* since anonymous campaign donations are the only defense against a potentially politicized federal bureaucracy.

Super PACs and mega-donors, empowered by the *Citizens United* decision, also have encouraged competition in the presidential primaries. Whereas in the past, lower profile candidates would seldom get much beyond the New Hampshire primary for lack of funding, now many have the resources to continue on deep into the primary process. As a New Hampshire voter, I enjoy the privilege of my state's first-in-the-nation primary, but I think every voter in every state should play a role in the primaries. The ability of many presidential candidates to potentially go the distance all the way to the convention is another benefit of *Citizens United.*

That our next president might be financially beholden to his or her mega-donors, however, is another matter. We all want candidates responsive to the public and not the donors who have made their elections possible. The point isn't that the progressives are wrong about the harmful effects of *Citizens United*; it's that the issues are more complex than the simplistic rhetoric suggests.

The campaign to reverse *Citizens United* got down to specifics in the Udall Amendment, which spelled out exactly what the reform groups and their allies in Congress intended. The language in the amendment would have permitted Congress at the federal level, and state legislatures at the state level, "to regulate the raising and spending of money and in-kind equivalents" with respect to elections. In other words, the amendment proposed to give members of Congress, with their bottom-dwelling 20% public approval rate alongside their 85%-95% re-election rate, the power to regulate money and political speech in the form of advertising, as it relates to their own re-elections. For anyone concerned about fair elections and the current incumbent re-election rate, the implications are beyond shocking. The professional reformers seem content to give the foxes the key to the hen house by permitting the professional political class to regulate political speech. Public support for reversing *Citizens United* would surely plummet once the American people understood this reality and the implications. It should be self-evident that permitting the political class to regulate paid speech is an invitation to still higher incumbent re-election rates and less democracy.

In conjunction with the above approach, reformers are promoting the passage of a public campaign finance system through Congress. On the eve of the 2014 election, they happily announced that the Democratic Party was then on board with clean elections. The Democrats are always vocal about cleaning up the system when they are out of power the same way the Republicans are for term limits until they capture a majority in Congress. When the Democrats controlled both houses of Congress in 2009-2010, the Fair Elections Now Act never made it out of committee. It's wishful thinking to expect those with power and political advantage to willingly give up their advantages. Only broad-based popular political pressure can force the issue.

"Disclosure" is another related principle that's not all it's cracked up to be. Indeed, it's hard to find anyone opposed to "disclosure." It sounds like a no-brainer. "Sunlight is the best disinfectant," they say. But disclosure has its limits. For example, we can clearly go online, to a terrific web site, OpenSecrets.org, and see the trail of Wall Street money flowing to incumbent office holders from both parties. Yet, though we see the corrupting money trail, our banks are still too big to fail and white-collar criminals get away with terrible financial crimes. All of this disclosure is doing us little good in an information age in which the average citizen is overwhelmed with almost infinite arguments and data, both true and deliberately misleading, some trumpeted and some whispered. Sunlight is useless and even blinding when the public is expected to keep its eye on each detail swirling in the chaos of modern, or post-modern, society. Citizens have lives to lead, and if they follow politics at all they follow the lead of the Democratic and Republican-oriented political interests that keep public attention focused on hatred for the other side.

Even in his own time, James Madison understood the earlier version of this information problem when it comes to popular government. Citizens of the early republic had too little information, while today we have more information at our fingertips than we can handle. The challenge, however, is essentially the same now as it was then. It's not necessary or possible to make a policy wonk out of every citizen. Rather, the objective should be to structure the system to encourage relatively trustworthy and judicious political leadership.

◊◊◊

Larry Lessig was very helpful connecting me with reform-minded citizens and groups on the Left. I was eager to speak with Common Cause, because of the size and prestige of that organization. Larry helped arrange a meeting with Common Cause President Bob Edgar, a former Congressman. I had heard that Edgar supported term limits, so I knew going in that a big obstacle among progressive elites would not be a factor in his case.

I met Edgar and two Common Cause staffers, attorneys I believe, at their headquarters in downtown DC, not far from K Street, known for its lobbyists. It was a marvelous opportunity. Common Cause's potential support would definitively engage the American Left in the project. With Lessig, we'd have more than enough credibility to show conservatives that some leading progressives were serious about a collaboration and alliance. With Common Cause offices all over the country, they could call Left /Right meetings together from coast to coast, and jumpstart truly bipartisan state movements as well. In fact, they did this sort of thing regularly at the state level, up to a point.

Edgar was congenial and laid back, maybe too laid back, as he seemed to utter whatever came into his head regardless of how it sounded. He referred to Larry Lessig as "arrogant" and said that he had "given up Lessig for Lent." That was awkward, since I was working with Lessig and he had facilitated the meeting. I mentioned Jack Abramoff when Edgar chimed in that he had "given up Abramoff for Hanukkah. "

I tried not to let Bob's eccentricities get us off track. He confirmed that he backed term limits, which was good. I explained that our plan was to bring leading progressives and conservatives to the table and negotiate around a framework that included term limits and a clean elections system.

"What sort of term limits do you have in mind?" Bob asked.

I explained that I did not have any set limits in mind. The idea was to get the parties to the table and negotiate the specifics of both the term limits and the new clean elections system.

"I can't take anything to my board without specifics," Bob said.

"You can't?" I didn't understand.

"No," he replied.

"But it's a negotiation. The process needs to be deliberative. It needs to reflect a Left-Right consensus."

"I need a specific proposal," he insisted.

"You can't propose a negotiation or a process built around a conceptual framework of clean elections and term limits?"

"No."

"But we can't decide for everyone. This won't work unless it's a negotiation, unless it's a collaboration. If it's all pre-arranged most won't bother to come to the table," I pleaded.

"Can't be done," Bob said, finally.

I left the big Common Cause office shaking my head. "What a waste," was all I could think.

Lessig set me up with another reform leader I was excited about, Dylan Ratigan. I had watched Ratigan for several years on CNBC. A brilliant, passionate, and articulate financial news celebrity and television producer, Ratigan became especially disillusioned with the political /financial system in the wake of the 2008 financial crisis, and like Rick Santelli, made a memorable rant on live television after he went over to MSNBC. While Santelli became the founding inspiration of the Tea Party, Ratigan became closely associated with the Occupy Wall Street movement. Even as a conservative, I think Ratigan had the better rant. (It can be viewed on YouTube by searching under "Ratigan" and "Extraction." I call it "the Extraction Rant.") As always, I was considering how I might unite influential progressive-conservative pairs to stand up together for political reform. Ratigan and Santelli, the righteous ranters of the Left and Right, would make a perfect pair — and surely they knew each other, having both been on CNBC for many years.

I was honored to have two long telephone conversations with Ratigan. I kept trying to sell him on the essential idea of getting leaders on the Left and Right into a room together to fix the political system. But Dylan kept diving down into the nitty gritty of campaign finance reform with a specific proposal. I knew that our first problem was political. We needed to get both sides to the table to come up with answers together. The problem was not entirely different from the one I had with Bob Edgar. No specific plan was going to move the nation to reform the system. Philosophically diverse leaders had to develop it and move it *together*. I wanted Dylan to reach out to Santelli and help lead the project jointly. Politically it would be wonderful, and those two commentators, connected as they are to the world of finance, would surely be able to bring in some cash to help fund the project.

But Ratigan seemed emotionally exhausted. In our first conversation, he ranted to me on the phone. I guess I should have been thrilled to get my own private rant from Dylan, but there is a time for drama and a time for calm. I didn't disagree with Dylan at all, but I worried about him. I remembered watching him on MSNBC once kick the living daylights out of a Tea Party activist strawman, and I remembered thinking that this really wasn't the true Dylan Ratigan. He was playing to the market. He was not an obnoxious partisan and he was not being true to himself. Now, on the phone with me, he seemed overly volatile. He

kept talking about working with some veterans on hydro-
ponic agriculture. He couldn't help me. He needed to, as
he said, read on the beach, and help some veterans for a
while. It was too bad, because I believe that Ratigan is
someone who could truly bridge the gap between the
Right and Left when it comes to cleaning up the system.

◊◊◊

Based on my own experience I found that progressive
reformers associated with the various reform organizations
fell into one or more of four tendencies.

First, for a few progressive leaders, getting the money
out of politics is hopelessly entangled with Democratic
Party and progressive political interests. They do more
harm than good when it comes to cleaning up our political
system. They divide us and permit the insiders to win every
time.

Second, there are the reformers who draw salaries.
They're dependent upon the progressive funders of their
organizations, who would revolt if the organizations they
backed actually partnered with conservatives. While some
might be sympathetic to Left-Right collaboration, their
hands are tied by their funders and by professional consid-
erations.

Third, a plurality of progressives I met were prisoners
of groupthink. This group included highly partisan reformers and partisan progressive funders mentioned above, but
also more open-minded people who simply were not getting any perspective from the Right. Conservatives were
almost never permitted into the group and certainly not as
partners.

My favorite illustration of a reformer victimized by
groupthink is journalist Elizabeth Drew, author of a good
and fair-minded book focused on political corruption in
the 1990s, *The Corruption of American Politics: What Went
Wrong and Why.* In 2015, she engaged in a debate with Lar-

ry Lessig in the *New York Review of Books* over the wisdom of calling a Constitutional Convention of the sort permitted under Article V of the Constitution. Lessig trusted that it could not be a "runaway convention" while Drew feared otherwise. Lessig had the better argument, in that as a general principle we should trust the people, and furthermore, with states divided between Republicans and Democrats, no crazy or extreme constitutional amendment is going to make it through three-quarters of our state legislatures, as required for the passage of an amendment.[61]

As an alternative to a convention, Elizabeth Drew arrives at a catastrophically wrong conclusion. "The situation," she says, "calls for partisan action: the election of a Democratic president who will appoint justices open to campaign finance reform." Putting aside just how far-fetched this notion is of fixing our broken political system by judicial fiat, Drew seems to have no idea just how open grassroots conservatives are to reforming the system, nor how the consequences of her approach would alienate her essential would-be allies on the anti-establishment Right. A Washington, DC insider, Drew assumes that grassroots conservatives hold the same views on reform as Republican politicians. The "partisan action" she calls for on the Left will encourage solidarity on the Right between grassroots conservatives and the Republican establishment, and continue to keep Americans divided on the cause of reform. It's exactly the wrong approach. It's what's been happening for decades and is why we are not getting anywhere.[62]

Fourth and last, the smallest group of reform-minded progressive leaders I would meet were the ones with pure hearts and open minds. They were capable of reading the good intentions of their conservative counterparts, and were excited or intrigued by the possibility of a common alliance against the current interest-based system. The right progressive leader, with sufficient credibility, could potentially burst the groupthink bubble of the progressive reform community, help raise some resources, and lead progressives into a balanced alliance with conservatives at the popular grassroots level.

◇◇◇

On a list serve for one of the big reform organizations, I get links to the news stories and opinion pieces important to the reform community every day. Scanning the headlines over the course of weeks and months, one could easily get the impression that the most corrupt and dangerous funding source in the country was the Koch brothers, Charles and David, who are among the richest people in the country and own one of the nation's largest privately-held businesses, Koch Industries. Oil and gas holdings are a major part of their business, which helps make them perfect villains for an American Left focused on climate change. I never bought into the notion that the Kochs were singularly or especially corrupt.

Generally, two types of political contributions exist. First, there is the corrupt kind, in which interests hope to get something tangible in return for what they give; they donate to advance or protect their profits, market position, future financial or employment prospects, tax status or stream of government funding.

But there are also many political contributions that are given out of belief, principles and ideology. There is nothing wrong with this kind of giving. Indeed, it is sign of civic-mindedness when citizens willingly donate their own resources to further some cause that they believe will benefit their community, the nation or the world. One kind of political contribution is corrupt and harmful to the public good, and the other is noble and perhaps beneficial, depending on whether or not you agree with the donor's ideology and principles.

A sure way to spot a corrupt self-interested donor is when that donor gives to both sides, to Democrats and

Republicans. The financial, healthcare, tech and defense industries, for example, give generously to both Republicans and Democrats. They play the political game for their own self-interests. Many of these interests feel compelled to give to both sides, depending on who has the power at the moment, but there's nothing principled or noble in this sort of transactional campaign donation.

Often it's hard to discern the motivation of the interest, or sometimes maybe the motivations are mixed. Does a liberal trial lawyer give to the Democrats because he believes the same things they do ideologically, or because he wants to make sure that the Democrats in Congress continue to oppose any tort reform that might limit the damages in medical malpractice lawsuits? Maybe it's both.

In 2011 Senator Patty Murray, (D-WA) who was Chair of the Democratic Senate Campaign Committee (DSCC), in what appears to be a robo-call, tried to shake some campaign cash out of Koch Industries with the offer of a nice retreat at a resort on Kiawah Island in South Carolina. "We'd love to have you join us," Senator Murray purred. The Washington Democrat soon deeply regretted her office's mistake. The tape of the call went viral.

Since the rise of the Tea Party, the Kochs had been characterized by Democratic political interests as the worst of all possible corrupt political villains, corporate plutocrats who cared only about their big business interests, but the truth was something different entirely. Murray's robo-calls to special interests to sip mint juleps with Democrats on the veranda of some South Carolina resort was going out to every possible corporate interest imaginable, all of which might have a desire to buy some influence.

Some foolish low-level DSCC staffer had evidently neglected to take the Kochs off the list. The Koch brothers are libertarian free-market activists who are not only violently opposed to the crony capitalism that Murray and the DSCC proposed to practice, but with the enormous amounts of money they were pouring into free-market/

small-government causes, the Koch brothers had put themselves and their businesses in the crosshairs of the Democratic-controlled White House and progressive activism.

Going in, the Kochs knew there'd be blowback, but they were nevertheless caught off guard by the volcanic reaction. By 2011 they were being singled out by the White House as public enemies. There had been death threats so that David Koch felt compelled now to ride around in a bullet-proof car. Undoubtedly Koch Industries risked finding itself under the microscope of regulators sympathetic to the Democrats. Only a privately held company could afford such activism. Shareholders, fearing for the bottom line, would want no part of it.

Unlike Wall Street and the many other interests at the trough of power, the Kochs don't want any special government favors for their company. Rather, they support a free market system and wish to take a sledgehammer to government power and what conservatives call "crony capitalism." They aim to change the rules of the game entirely. Their motivations are ideological.

Hate the Koch's activism if it is inconsistent with your own political beliefs, but understand that they are propelled by their principles and not their interests. If it was all about their business interests, the Kochs would have shut up, kept their heads down, and considered attending Senator Patty Murray's South Carolina retreat.

Consistent with their ideological motivations, Charlie Koch published an article in the *Wall Street Journal,* "Why Koch Industries Is Speaking Out."[63] He no doubt wanted to explain himself to a nation in which he and his business were increasingly being characterized as monstrous bad guys. The first part of his article explained that the Kochs were most concerned about the nation's public debt and our "looming bankruptcy," for which Charles blamed both Democrats and Republicans. I agreed with Koch, but then, further along, he hit on a subject that really grabbed my attention as a political reformer.

Koch wrote, "Too many businesses have successfully lobbied for special favors and treatment by seeking mandates for their products, subsidies (in the form of cash payments from the government), and regulations or tariffs to keep more efficient competitors at bay." He lamented that this crony capitalism "erodes our overall standard of living and stifles entrepreneurs by rewarding the politically favored."

Charlie Koch's article got me thinking. Here was exactly the sort of thing that progressive reformers were complaining about all the time: "the rewarding of the politically favored." Surely he understood the role that campaign contributions play in the crony capitalist game. The progressive reformers treated the Kochs as a public menace, but was that because the Kochs truly supported the current system of institutionalized bribery and extortion, or was it because the Kochs were the nation's most aggressive funders of libertarian-oriented conservatives? If the Kochs were funding progressives instead of conservatives, would the big reform organizations even care about them? And the big take-away question from the article: Was it possible that the Kochs could support a new clean campaign financing system for the United States?

I wanted to find the answer to this question, and if the answer was yes, then what? I was always thinking about Left-Right partnerships. Without something close to a counterweight to the Kochs on the progressive side, to balance their infamy on the Left, I could never associate with them. It would be the kiss of death for my project; the progressives would head for the hills.

Only one name came to mind to potentially partner with the Kochs: George Soros. Like the Koch Brothers, Soros is ideologically motivated. He, too, only gives to one side, the progressives. And he's given millions if not billions. Finally, conservatives hate Soros as much as progressives hate the Koch brothers. (I had one conservative threaten to have nothing to do with my project if Soros got involved.) Obviously the Kochs and Soros are a match made in heaven. Or maybe in hell. But uniting them and their financial muscle would be the political/financial game changer the country needed. Either that or both progressive and conservative activists would be simultaneously so disgusted that nobody at all would ever go near this "alliance of the hated." But I reckoned that more likely the two negatives coming together could create a massive positive charge. Heads in Washington would explode.

Obviously it was a long shot, but so was everything else I was trying. I wrote Charlie Koch a long letter, making an argument similar to the one in this book about Madison, and how he intended that American government should be judicious rather than motivated by selfish and narrow interests. More controversially – some would say absurdly – I suggested that Charlie Koch partner with George Soros. I was writing a lot of unlikely letters at the time, but this one was the biggest Hail Mary of them all. I put it in the mail to Koch corporate headquarters in Wichita and practically forgot about it.

I was surprised two weeks later to find a voicemail waiting for me from an official at the Koch Foundation in Arlington, Virginia. My letter had obviously reached its target. It seems that Charlie Koch had read it, and it had escaped the destiny of the circular file. The call I would make to the Koch Foundation goes down as one of the strangest conversations I would have during my political reform brokering business. The executive I phoned there was no mere clerk. He was a player at the Koch Foundation, which I had confirmed, and he let me know this fact right away.

When I identified myself, he said "Yes," he hesitated, "I will take *this* call." The opening greeting was an odd message to me that the foundation considered the subject matter of some importance. But he was also saying, implicitly, that he didn't talk to just anyone, which suggested an arrogance of the sort that I always find off-putting.

I pressed for answers to two questions. Would Charlie and David Koch consider supporting a clean elections system along with congressional term limits? Would they consider an alliance with George Soros?

On the clean elections piece, the Koch Foundation executive said, "We find the ideas expressed in Ayers and Ackerman's book interesting." (Ayers and Ackerman developed the blind trust and campaign contribution voucher concept). However, then he offered that it would also be "interesting to give every child in America a puppy," but that didn't mean that they were necessarily for giving every child a puppy, only that it was an interesting idea. Then he repeated this fascinating illustration in case I missed what he meant the first time.

I was dumbfounded. What on earth does fixing our corrupted political system have to do with puppies? God, I wished he would just say what he meant, which I assume is that "interesting" should not be necessarily construed as "support." The conversation annoyed me, so I was probably more combative than I should have been. I kept pressing.

"So Charlie Koch wouldn't be interested in a partnership with George Soros?" I asked.

"I didn't say that," he replied.

Reflecting on the conversation later, I realized that Charlie Koch had a three-part message for me. First, there would not be any money for my organization "this year." I hadn't asked for money. Taking money from one partisan source, especially the Kochs, without taking money from a counterbalancing partisan source, was out of the question. But it was eye-opening that they'd consider funding a balanced Left-Right anti-corruption alliance.

Second, they'd be watching our web site. Our web site never went anywhere, unfortunately. Social media was not my thing and I never found someone willing to devote time and effort to it.

Third, the Kochs find the clean election reform ideas of Ayers and Ackerman "interesting."

It was astounding. Now it was more than ever necessary that I get some leaders on the American Left to listen.

A good friend's dad, a prominent doctor connected to Harvard, had recently passed away. There was a service at the University for him. Afterwards I headed over to Lessig's office to share the news about the Kochs.

Larry Lessig is not very good at concealing his feelings, and when I arrived at his door I knew I was imposing. He was behind schedule writing his next book. He stared at me, blankly at first, as I explained about my contact with Charlie Koch.

His expression eventually changed. "Good move," he finally said. I asked him if he had a channel to Soros. He did, and he agreed to float the idea of a potential alliance. I handed him a copy of the letter I sent to Charlie Koch.

I asked if he'd like some feedback on his manuscript, which would become the book, *Republic Lost*. "Love it," Larry responded, and handed me a draft. I got right back to him with some comments as soon as I finished reading it. He would thank me in the introduction, which was nice.

At the end of 2015, it was announced that the Kochs and George Soros were both pursuing similar visions for criminal justice reform, though it's unclear just how much they were collaborating. These political financiers each believe in insuring that the accused are provided with an adequate legal defense, and each believes that the American system of justice should be reformed to ensure that the punishment always fits the crime. It's a very interesting area for collaboration, since I frequently make the point that public campaign financing is analogous to the funding of public defendants. Public money is necessary to protect the integrity of the political system as well as the judicial system, the absence of which leads to unjust outcomes based on the ability of one side to overpower the other with self-interested money.[64]

Larry never got back to me about the trial balloon we sent up to Soros; I only found out it went nowhere many months later when I asked him about it. I have informed many progressive leaders about the Kochs' apparent willingness to explore political reform in cooperation with the American Left, but it's clear that no one believes me. No progressive ever expressed the least bit of enthusiasm or interest, except Lessig. I thought that one of the creators of the most imaginative clean election system, Yale professor Bruce Ackerman, might be intrigued that Charlie Koch considered his plan "interesting," but after I told Professor Ackerman on the phone about this message from Koch's people, there was nothing on the other end of the line but a dead silence. How could my story about Charlie Koch carry any weight when pitted against the richly funded and relentlessly broadcast villain narrative shaped by some of the nation's most powerful political interests? Looking back, all I succeeded in doing by talking about the Kochs with progressive reformers was to damage my own credibility.

◊◊◊

There should be little doubt that progressives who are focused on getting the money out of politics will never succeed without help from conservatives. Gallup has been tracking the self-identified political orientations of Americans for decades. Although "liberals" have been closing the gap, conservatives still outnumber them 36% to 25%, with 34% of respondents calling themselves "moderate."[65]

Most pollsters will say that there are very few true political moderates. Drilling down into the 34% of Americans who identify as moderate, we'd probably find that most break right or left in equal numbers. Others would prove to be fairly apathetic. But for the sake of argument, let's suppose that in the case of political reform, that the Right can be marginalized and that all of the moderates break left and join the liberals for a reversal of *Citizens United* and some kind of public campaign financing system to be passed legislatively, which seems to be the current strategy of the so-called "political reform community."

If progressives controlled both houses of Congress and the presidency, with a veto-proof majority in the Senate, then they could pass a public campaign financing measure. Recall, however, that the last time Democrats controlled Congress and the presidency, they failed to bring such a bill up for a vote. Currently, the Republicans have a firm grip on the House, and given the institutional advantages of incumbency, seem unlikely to lose that chamber anytime soon. As of 2016, Republicans controlled 237 House seats, compared to 193 for the Democrats.

Securing a constitutional amendment to overturn *Citizens United* without conservative support is even less likely. All paths to a constitutional amendment require thirty-eight states (three-fourths of all states) to approve the amendment either in the legislatures or in state conventions. Although there has been much talk in the media and progressive blogosphere about how demographics will doom conservatives and Republicans, the trend certainly is not moving that way yet. After the 2016 election, the Republican Party controlled thirty-two state legislatures, compared to twelve for the Democrats. The rest were split.

Some progressives may point to some evidence of success in winning over Republicans for a reversal of *Citizens United* at the state and local level. These victories reflect the desire of grassroots Republicans to fix the system but, were a real debate underway, most grassroots conservatives would never accept any reform that permits Congress itself to control political speech through the regulation of campaign advertising. Republican establishment money and resources will crush this effort should it ever become a serious threat.

Even if progressive reformers could be sure that the

Democratic Party is committed to fixing the system, including making certain that elections are fair – and that's a big "if" – it is next to impossible for them to reform the system without cooperation from conservatives.

In one way, it's easy to see why progressives assume that conservatives are not interested in reform. While numerous progressive organizations employing hundreds of people are at work trying to get the corrupting influence of money out of politics, there is no comparable movement on the Right, not even for term limits or any clean government reform. Rather, there is only Peter Schweizer and his small Government Accountability Institute, which is dedicated to research and not political action. Seen from this perspective, conservatives appear to care little about political corruption, and shame on them for not organizing themselves to fight it.

Up until the rise of Donald Trump, however, I would have argued that so-called "civil war" inside the Republican Party is really an anti-corruption movement. True, conservatives perceive "corruption" differently than do progressives. For conservatives, the growth of the federal government, the weakening of the 10th Amendment (which leaves unremunerated powers to the states), the increasing power of the bureaucracy, judicial activism, the actions of the Federal Reserve, etc., all constitute a corruption of the enlightened system laid down by Madison and his fellow founding fathers. But part of the conservative perception about corruption converges with progressive concerns about the money and politics.

Conservatives may have no formal political reform movement per se, but they are attacking the Republican political establishment as well as the Democratic one, and part of that attack is motivated by a disgust with the selfish interests associated with political careerism, crony capitalism and the K Street lobbying industry. Conservatives may not have any organization that looks anything like Common Cause or Public Campaign, but they are putting up

primary challenges against Republican establishment candidates and sometimes winning, as in the case of former
House Majority Leader Eric Cantor, who was defeated in
his Republican primary in 2014 by economist and insur-
gent politician David Brat. The case against Cantor very
much included issues relating to institutionalized corruption and the influence of money.[66]

The political success of Donald Trump signals a whole
new and powerful front in the GOP's civil war, this one
stoked by the anger of alienated working-class voters.
While entirely different and often at odds with the more
intellectually-driven faction mentioned above, supporters
of Donald Trump cheered their candidate's financial independence and his freedom from binding ties to special
interests. Trump's campaign was also an assault on the
status quo system.

In contrast to the Republicans, there has been no "civil
war" in the Democratic Party, but maybe there should be.
When is the last time a powerful establishment Democratic
incumbent was primaried by a clean government populist
on the Left? Why not challenge Nancy Pelosi, who declined to have the Fair Elections Now Act brought to a
vote when the Democrats controlled the House? This is
the same Nancy Pelosi whose husband seems to have
scored a special deal on the IPO of Visa stock while Visa
had business before the US House when she was Speaker.
Herein lies the biggest initial obstacle to fixing the system:
the unwillingness of the progressive reformers and media
to challenge the Democratic Party and the most corrupt
Democratic politicians. Time will tell if the presidential
campaign of Bernie Sanders, his reform agenda, and his
unfair treatment at the hands of the Democratic National
Committee, will finally lead to a more rebellious posture
among grassroots Democrats against their party's elites
and the corrupt system they defend, alongside their Republican insider counterparts.

6: Scenery on the Road to Nowhere

Back in March of 2011, I first met the would-be president of the United States. I am referring to that vote-amassing juggernaut, Buddy Roemer, the former Republican governor of Louisiana. Well, he received a few votes anyway. In the New Hampshire primary, where he devoted significant time and energy, Roemer garnered 945 votes, or 0.4% of the total cast in 2012.

It's hard to imagine now, but at one time a Roemer campaign for president seemed like a really promising idea. Not only had he been a governor, but also a member of Congress. After he left politics, Roemer had started a community bank in Louisiana and from that point of view he watched in disgust as Wall Street looted the American taxpayer and helped crater the economy. Roemer is articulate, intelligent and passionate about fighting the corruption in our political system, so I was pretty enthusiastic when Lessig invited me to have dinner with him.

Joining us was Arthur Hiatt, the former CEO of Stride-Rite shoes and the former number two donor to the Democratic Party, who in 1996 was publicly scolded by President Bill Clinton when Hiatt, raising his voice from the audience at a fundraiser, argued for ending the nation's corrupt system of private campaign finance.[67] Americans for Campaign Reform's Rob Werner was also there, down from New Hampshire with me, as was Josh Silver, a veteran leader of the reform movement.

I grabbed the seat next to Buddy Roemer. I was eager to discover what he thought of our plan to combine a clean elections system with term limits. I figured that as a Republican, he would love it. While he was for term limits, he explained to me to me that he "did not want to muddy the message," which was going to be all about the corrupting influence of money in politics. I thought to myself at the time, "You are running as a Republican and don't want to 'muddy the message' with the single reform that is wildly popular with conservatives? Instead you are going to run on campaign finance reform, something many Republicans are dubious about because it always tangled up in Democratic political interests? Really?"

Roemer went on to hire a McCain operative as his campaign manager, which was the kiss of death. The first rule of a Republican political campaign should be never hire someone who has worked for John McCain. As outgoing President George W. Bush noted in amazement, McCain's "organization" couldn't even fill a room in his home state of Arizona with supporters on the eve of the 2008 election.

My first encounter with Josh Silver, who actually knew how to make things happen in Arizona, was more promising. Josh had impressively led and won the battle for clean elections in Arizona with a clean elections law passed in a citizens' initiative referendum. When I explained about our plan to wed clean campaign finance and term limits, the favorite reform of the Left with the favorite reform of the Right, and throw in a prohibition against gerrymandering, Josh looked me in the eye from across the table and asked enthusiastically where he could sign up.

My relationship with Josh would be up and down. At one point he flirted with hiring me at United Republic, a new reform organization he would head. During that time, he described what he said would become the most powerful force in American reform politics. Deep-pocketed funders were already lined up. The new organization would have two missions. First, it would itself be an extremely well-financed giant that could get the job done. It would be edgy, no-nonsense, bipartisan and huge. Josh wanted to kick corrupt politicians out of office. Now it was my turn to cheer. The secondary mission was to seed smaller reform efforts all around the country. Josh revealed that, in fact, the funding of other groups would not amount to much. The real action would be at United Republic.

In the end, Josh couldn't hire me, and it's easy to see why not in hindsight. I was committed to a balanced Left-Right organization, an integrated progressive-conservative collaboration at every level, and Josh was not. His "bipartisanship" did not go much farther than his desire to win over some token Republicans to join his effort. I would never let go of the idea of a full and balanced Left-Right partnership. Our differences became clear the more Josh and I talked. Josh would later criticize me for always trying to change the nature of other people's organizations. When those other reform organizations are partisan, as they all are, Josh is right; I do try to change them.

At one point Josh asked me hopefully if I was an "Eisenhower Republican." But a moderate Republican on his staff would be useless to him, and he didn't seem to understand that. In the age of polarized politics, any united reform movement must be anchored firmly on each end. Moderate Republicans in league with the true believers on the other end will be considered traitors by their own side. The same would hold true with moderate Democrats in league with orthodox conservatives. True centrists in American politics are going the way of the dodo bird. A united reform movement must be led by real progressives and real conservatives. Hard-core idealists from each side should be welcome. If you pick up both ends of a net, you capture everything in between, including the remaining moderates.

A telling moment came with Josh when I tried to get United Republic to support term limits. Josh agreed that it was a good idea and something he wanted to do. The problem, he explained, was that he had board members opposed to term limits. The irony here was inescapable. The would-be biggest and baddest get-the-money-out-of-politics organization would itself, like all the other groups, be controlled by money.

It would also be partisan. At one point his group foolishly decided to go after Coburn for his opposition to the *Stock Act,* which was a result of Peter Schweizer's research and was intended to prevent members of Congress from trading stocks on inside information. I didn't agree with Coburn's position on the Stock Act either, but his was simply a wrong-headed idiosyncratic policy position; Coburn wasn't corrupt. More importantly, Coburn was the big pro-term limits conservative I hoped to win over to clean elections and partner with Lessig. With so many ripe targets, why go after Coburn? United Republic's rhetoric was hopelessly left-leaning. Conservatives would want nothing to do with it. I said as much in an unrestrained e-mail to Josh.

Despite our disagreements, I owe Josh Silver a debt of gratitude. Mine was one of the small organizations that United Republic funded. By "funded," I mean $10,000, which seems like a laughably small amount, but this money, with a few thousand dollars more from my board, was crucial to someone of modest means like me. It enabled me to keep the lights on and cover travel expenses.

Larry Lessig had been terrific. Not only had he introduced me to some key American figures interested in political reform, but early in 2012 he promoted my efforts to a Boston-area financier and philanthropist, Bill Burgess, who was a venture capitalist and old-school pillar of the community. The Dartmouth-educated Burgess reminded me of the Princeton-educated Charlie Kolb, the former head of the Committee for Economic Development, with whom I had become acquainted. Both Ivy Leaguers are highly successful, gracious, inquisitive, and committed to true public service. They are privileged citizens who implicitly recognize their positions in the world and gratefully give back accordingly.

Burgess had read Lessig's *Republic Lost* and became motivated to do something about money in politics. He met Larry for lunch and indicated an interest in getting behind political reform financially. Lessig recommended two organizations to Burgess: mine, then called Americans United to Rebuild Democracy (later renamed Clean Government Alliance) and United Republic. On the surface of it, to be considered alongside United Republic was crazy. We were a minnow next to a burgeoning whale.

◊◊◊

After Roemer went nowhere in the Republican primary, Lessig began toting him around as a presidential candidate under the "Americans Elect" ticket. This massive privately funded fiasco was supposed to help Americans find a consensus candidate for president outside of the major parties via the internet. It was a dubious idea even if executed flawlessly, but the online voting protocols were so stringent that very few people ever participated. It was just more reform-related money down a rat hole.

Still, there was Larry at the DC Occupy event I attended, with Roemer in tow. Here Larry made the case to a far-left leaning audience that they should nominate, online through Americans Elect, the pro-life, pro-fossil fuels, pro-free market capitalist Republican, Buddy Roemer, because he was also foursquare for getting the money out of politics, never mind that Justice Party member and former Salt

Lake City Mayor Rocky Anderson was also running. Rocky was for public campaign financing too, but without all the conservative baggage that Roemer carried. Larry never mentioned Rocky Anderson. I could tell that the Occupy crowd wasn't much interested in supporting a conservative "good old boy" like Roemer.

I could appreciate Larry's desire to get a Republican clean elections advocate into the spotlight. For all the flaws in the Roemer campaign, the former Louisiana governor had charisma and could be an excellent spokesman for the cause. But when explaining the strategy to the Occupy audience, Larry revealed something very harmful to any potential Left-Right reform alliance. He said that because Roemer was prioritizing the issue of money in politics, Roemer was his "first choice" for President. This was fair enough on the face of it, but no one seriously believed that Roemer had a snowball's chance of getting elected president of the United States. Lessig then declared that his "second choice" for president was Barack Obama. Since Roemer was really a Republican, he would drain more votes from the Republican nominee Mitt Romney than he would from Lessig's "second choice," President Obama. Lessig was gaming the system to promote both clean elections reform *and* re-elect Obama (despite the president's poor record on clean elections issues, a record Lessig acknowledges). Here in a nutshell was everything that is wrong with America's progressive reformers and their organizations. They are trying to advance the cause of clean election reform while at the same time protect Democratic partisan interests. For them, it's about reform *and* electing Democrats/defeating Republicans. Obviously no conservative would want any part of this.

I wrote Larry to warn him how his tactic would be perceived by any conservatives who might consider partnering with him. If other conservatives had heard what I heard, they would run the other way.

Distressingly, Lessig denied what he had said. While

Larry's tactics and disingenuous sounding response were a warning sign, I had to write the whole episode off. We are all subject to partisanship sometimes. Larry was helping me in some very big ways that made the Roemer maneuver look minor by comparison. If he had a real and credible conservative partner, I had faith that he would not be making the same mistake.

By the spring of 2012, as I waited for an opening in Larry's calendar to coincide with Senator Coburn's schedule so we could hold that dinner meeting, things were looking up in every respect.

Financially, we badly needed to make something happen. I went down to Massachusetts to meet Bill Burgess. Eric MacLeish, one of my board members, who is also a very impressive Boston-area attorney, joined me. Eric had served as lead counsel in the horrific child pedophile case against the Boston Catholic Archdiocese (his character is in the movie *Spotlight*) and more recently he has won another high-profile court battle against a state mental hospital that had been abusing its patients. Among other benefits, knowing Eric has served as a reminder to me of the good work that trial lawyers can do. He also raised $5 million for the families of Massachusetts' 9/11 victims. A Democrat, Eric supports term limits and was committed to our bipartisan approach. He could obviously become a serious fundraiser for us, but I always got the feeling that we needed to gain more traction first. As it was, he made modest contributions that helped keep me going. Our first meeting with Bill Burgess went well enough, but as a venture capitalist, Bill would take the time to do his due diligence on us.

Another board member had a very promising connection, a professional relationship with an heir to one of America's great family fortunes. While it's not wise for me to name names, the family name is a universally recognized brand. The heir was committed to political reform and was saddened by the extreme partisan acrimony that has infested our politics. If we kept moving forward, we'd have a chance to get in front of this great potential funder.

I became a little frustrated waiting for Larry's schedule to free up so we could schedule the dinner with Senator Coburn. During the summer of 2012 I reached out to Peter Schweizer via e-mail. I didn't know much about Schweizer at the time, only that he had discovered the inside trading in Congress that had led to the Stock Act, a story that had been featured on *60 Minutes*. I also knew that he had penned a book about corruption on Capitol Hill entitled *Throw Them All Out*. My e-mail to Schweizer outlined what I was trying to accomplish. He shot back a response instantaneously: "Great project!"

Soon I was on the phone with Schweizer and realized that in terms of pairing, he was the best possible conservative partner for Larry Lessig. Schweizer is an author, Hoover Fellow, and as I would increasingly appreciate, the nation's most respected anti-corruption voice on the conservative side. One thing extremely refreshing about Peter is that he skewers powerful Republicans, such as Speakers of the House Hastert and Boehner, just as much as Democrats.

I thought Larry might help me reach out to former Democratic Senator Russ Feingold, who Michael Schwarz said might work well with Coburn. I still had hope for a Ratigan-Santelli partnership. I learned through Larry that Soros wasn't interested in talking to the Kochs, which was no real surprise; the Soros-Koch alliance was always an extreme long shot. At least Charlie Koch was still out there, and apparently interested.

Peter Schweizer, who was based in Tallahassee, was ready to fly up to Boston and meet Larry just before Labor Day. Meanwhile, Bill Burgess offered to host a cocktail party at his house in the suburbs, with Larry and Peter as the honored guests. The invitees were almost all high-ranking corporate executives, a variety of CEOs and CFOs. I was overjoyed. The pieces were really coming together. America's first truly balanced and bipartisan political reform organization looked about to be born.

◇◇◇

Peter Schweizer caught me gazing at a photo of my 5-month-old son, Thomas, as he approached the table at the Rialto, a restaurant in Cambridge where Larry Lessig liked to have lunch.

Thomas is my third child, all sons. It seemed like the appropriate moment to be thinking about my boys, because what we were doing was for them, and their generation, and generations of Americans to follow. Also, like most fathers, I suppose, I want my children to be proud of their dad. Prior to working on political reform, my resume had become spotty and unfocused. Now well into middle age I felt like I had found my calling. I was happy and excited by the work I was doing. I needed to draw a salary, but I was sure that my first paycheck was right around the corner. This day would be a turning point; in retrospect, at least that much I got right.

Soon Larry joined Peter and me at the table and the two of them seemed to get on cordially. Larry remarked how he had enjoyed Peter's book. After a while, I tried to steer the conversation to the business at hand, launching a Left-Right alliance for political reform.

Larry delivered some news about his relationship with Josh Silver's United Republic. It seemed that he and other influential reform activists never intended United Republic to be *the* giant political reform group, with only token support for other groups. Rather, it was supposed to be the reverse. Seeding smaller reform efforts all around the country should have been its principal mission, according to Larry, so he had broken with the group, but not before an ally of his had donated $250,000. I didn't see how this story related to what I was doing, except maybe mine was one of the smaller organizations that might now benefit.

That thesis turned out to be incredibly wrong.

At the table, Larry spurned my efforts to make any concrete plans. Perhaps I was again being overly aggressive, but this was the only time scheduled for these two leaders to be alone together. Larry's posture was nothing like when we met with Senator Coburn. He was neither warm nor supportive. Then he dropped what was, for me, a bombshell. He suggested maybe not pursuing a clean government constitutional amendment at all, and instead working toward ordinary legislation. Peter quickly agreed, but of course we couldn't do term limits or address *Citizens United* without a constitutional amendment. In a flash, all my work for the past two years was undone. I immediately realized that this was not so much a change in strategy. Rather, it was Larry Lessig backing away as fast as he could from me and my project. Lessig made it clear that everything was but a preliminary exploration, at best.

I couldn't believe it. After all that work, Lessig was bailing on me. Did he realize that I was on the verge of recruiting the nation's three best possible conservative partners for him, Peter Schweizer, Tom Coburn and Charlie Koch? You could not ask for a more influential or powerful team of conservatives.

I departed lunch highly dejected. Peter and I decided to grab a beer. I suppose he wondered if I was always this morose. He didn't fully know all I had done or appreciate what had just transpired.

At a dimly lit bar I explained that it sure looked like Lessig was abandoning the project; more would become clear at the cocktail party scheduled for that evening. I had no clue how I was going to handle that event, because with Larry's retreat it meant that I now had no plan at all. I had two leaders who had agreed to absolutely nothing. Whatever would I say to all those well-heeled would-be funders that evening? It was all out of my hands now. I glumly tried to stay in the moment.

At least I had the opportunity to begin to know the

remarkable Peter Schweizer. He is the William J. Casey Fellow at the Hoover Institution, Stanford University, as well as president and founder of the Government Accountability Institute, and a partner at Oval Office Speech Writers in Washington, DC. He is the author of numerous books, including *New York Times* bestsellers. In 2015 Schweizer would famously publish *Clinton Cash*, a blockbuster that suggested serious corruption issues relating to Bill and Hillary Clinton, Hillary's role as secretary of state, and the Clinton Foundation. Primarily an investigative journalist, Peter focuses his efforts on uncovering unknown corruption stories and, although he is a conservative, he strives to be strictly non-partisan; as already noted, he does not hesitate to expose corrupt Republicans as well as Democrats. Indeed, I think he enjoys going after corrupt Republicans, because it bolsters his credibility.

As we talked at the bar, I realized that it was Peter who had broken the Solyndra/green-energy corruption story. Here was an issue that progressives concerned about climate change should be just as concerned about. Peter and his organization had found that around 80% of the billions of dollars that went to green-energy ventures as part of the 2009 stimulus package were funneled into enterprises run or owned by campaign donors to Obama and/or other prominent Democrats. If one cares about green energy, then it is essential that projects get funded based on their merits rather than the influence of campaign contributors. Failed green energy projects, like the solar panel manufacturer Solyndra, are politically costly to those who desperately want government to do more to curb carbon emissions. If you want green energy to succeed, then the best projects must receive the funding rather than those that have the best political connections. Progressives should have been up in arms, but insiders were more interested in protecting the reputation of the Obama administration. Pointing the finger at Democratic corruption once in a while would enhance the credibility of progressive reformers and like-minded journalists and, in this case, help protect the reputation of viable green energy projects.

I told the soft-spoken Schweizer that I thought he deserved more credit for his accomplishments, but he explained that he found it better to simply try to do good work and not to worry about publicity or who gets the headlines. This wasn't just talk on Peter's part.

I brought up how little progressives understood conservatives and the irony of how the conservatives they hated the most were the ones most likely to believe as they did about the need for clean government reform. Peter agreed that the Koch brothers were indeed potential reformers.

The jockeying for position in the 2012 primary was underway and I asked Peter if he had heard a fine speech by another hated conservative, Sarah Palin. She had recently spoken in Iowa, warning against the influence of campaign donors and implicitly criticizing the crony capitalism of Texas Governor Rick Perry.

"Yes," Peter said. He had apparently heard the speech.

A few seconds passed in silence as Schweizer stared into his beer. Then it dawned on me.

"Peter, did you write that speech?"

"Yeah," he said.

I just had to laugh despite my gloom. And, having been dealing with so many oversized egos, I was truly amazed. Ninety-nine out of a hundred people would have taken ownership and credit for the speech immediately after I praised it, but not Peter Schweizer. He is about the highest-achieving humble person that I have ever met.

Peter's personality also makes him a natural diplomat. He is careful, he listens, he's tactful, and his lack of oversized ego makes him discreet. He's the perfect conservative to negotiate in the overheated partisan climate. As time went on I would increasingly realize how pivotal Schweizer was when it comes creating a Left-Right alliance for anti-corruption reform. First, Peter is by far the most respected authority on issues relating to corruption among conservatives. He's also respected even by the so-called "mainstream" media. In the rollout of *Clinton Cash*, the *New York Times* and the *Washington Post* actually partnered with him to build on his work about the most recent dubious dealings of the Clintons.

Second, I would learn that Peter is connected to major conservative power centers. He has relationships with high-ranking people at the Koch Foundation, Fox, and Breitbart media. Possibly as much as anyone in the country, Peter Schweizer has the ability to lead the anti-Washington-establishment Right into an alliance with the anti-Washington-establishment Left. But at the moment, Larry Lessig, the only leader on the Left I had met who was open to such an alliance, was running the other way.

We drove out to the cocktail party that evening. My disappointment weighed heavily on me as we pulled up into Bill Burgess' driveway in my family van. Bill arranged for Larry and Peter to each say a few words on the terrace, but he introduced me first. What could I say? I summarized the problem of partisanship when it comes to political reform, and described myself as a "political reform matchmaker." I characterized that evening as "a first date." Larry and Peter each made a few remarks, but said nothing memorable or anything that would suggest what was happening was at all exciting or groundbreaking, because it wasn't.

Then we broke up into two groups so that the guests could interact with Larry and Peter more intimately. I was in a separate room, which was fine, except that I felt like an idiot because thanks to Larry I had no plan going forward. Eric MacLeish tried to be helpful by asking the group in our room what they thought we should do. I groaned inwardly. How pathetic we must have looked coming into this with apparently no idea what we were doing or what came next.

An older blond gentleman, who originally hailed from

Iceland, asked the obvious. "Well, you have two capable leaders, one from each side, right here. They can lead the movement, no?'

I couldn't very well explain what was happening – or was not happening – so there was this awkward silence.

At one point someone who sat on Mitt Romney's finance committee approached me. "Are you a conservative?" he asked.

"Yes," I replied.

"I thought so," he said. "Do you know who you have in this room? Do you?"

Apparently there was so much money in the house that evening that even a member of Romney's finance committee was impressed. And herein lies at least part of the reason Larry Lessig ditched me and my balanced bipartisan approach to political reform: he regretted recommending that his wealthy contacts help bankroll my effort as well as that of United Republic.

At the end of the party Larry overheard me say to Bill that I'd be in touch. Lessig glared at me with some combination of distaste and panic before turning to Burgess. "Bill, we need to talk . . ." said Lessig as he hurried to Burgess's side.

Bill would go on to join the board of the Fund for the Republic (later renamed" Issue One"), run by Larry's friend Nick Penniman, a Bill Moyers and Arianna Huffington protégé. Their work would be indistinguishable from all the other progressive partisan reform campaigns going on around the country, except better funded than most. Any conservative involvement in their efforts would be bought and paid-for tokenism, including the seeding of a new "conservative" money-in-politics organization controlled with progressive money.

I later called Bill to confirm the obvious. Larry Lessig would not be working with me anymore. Bill said that I shouldn't rule out Larry partnering with me again sometime in the future, however. It was cold comfort given my time, my precious financial resources, and my credibility, all of which I had sacrificed to find Larry conservative partners. I was angry, to say the least.

Later I realized that money and group-think are so overwhelmingly powerful that Lessig walking away should not have come as a surprise. It's easy to imagine some progressive political operative telling Larry that he was insane to give away so much money – potentially millions of dollars – by urging his wealthy contacts to put significant resources and connections behind my embryonic organization. Why wouldn't Lessig want to control those resources himself? Or direct that money to his progressive friends?

Perhaps what's more surprising is how far I had come with Lessig's help. For a couple of years, Larry Lessig had been extraordinary. He had been the one and only big-name progressive who had supported a true alliance of progressives and conservatives, and he had done so in every way possible. Using Larry's name I had attracted the highly respected conservative statesman-Senator, Tom Coburn, and the nation's leading conservative reformer, Peter Schweizer, who, in my opinion, are the two most appropriate conservatives to help lead us out of the corrupt and partisan mess we are in. And again, Charlie Koch was interested. Now Larry's commitment was broken but, in terms of judging Lessig's conduct overall, it does not erase all that he had done to help. Larry Lessig had been extraordinary. Now he was acting in merely the ordinary and expected way, coveting money for his own use, and declining to truly partner with people too often considered "the enemy."

When it came down to it, Larry Lessig, like other progressive reformers, obviously did not want a full partnership with conservatives. The question is, why not? Here are some possible reasons:

#1 Progressive reformers may believe that conservatives are ideologically incapable of partnering with progressives on political reform.

All my experience shows that this assumption is wrong. It's completely wrong at the grassroots level, and reform has sufficient support at the conservative leadership level. If progressives will make a determined effort to be non-partisan when it comes to issues relating to political corruption and reform, conservatives can work with them.

#2 Partnerships with conservatives are impossible because of the controlling influence of partisan money. Progressive political messaging has portrayed conservatives as stupid, evil monsters in the eyes of their funding and activist base (it's all Saul Alinsky, all the time[iii]). How could any principled progressive partner with such awful people? Some would likely quit boards of directors rather than do so. I saw, not unexpectedly, how the moneyed boards of organizations like Common Cause and United Republic, who fund reform, control the activities of these organizations. Larry Lessig freaked out when he thought he might be giving away an enormous funding base when he should have been celebrating the launch of a united Left-Right political front to save our lost republic. Bob Edgar might have endangered his own job if the Common Cause board thought he was proposing an alliance that might include the Koch brothers and Sarah Palin.

#3 Perhaps the main purpose of political reform for some progressives is to further progressive ideological interests; conservatives get no place at the table because they are the enemy. No doubt that for many on the Left, a clean elections system is all about minimizing the influence of big business on government. For them, reform is primarily a tool to weaken capitalism, a system conservatives want to maintain or even strengthen. You can't be a progressive and work with defenders of the status quo. They believe that the only way to win is to elect Democrats.

[iii] In the influential *Rules for Radicals* (Vintage, 1989, originally published 1971), Alinsky wrote, "Pick a target, freeze it, and polarize it." Alinsky preached going after people rather than institutions, because people hurt faster than institutions.

#4 Some progressive reform organizations believe that token conservatives can be found to peel off enough support on the Right to form majority support for reform. Tokenism seldom works because people tend to see right through it. Tokenism is especially ineffective in our age of polarized politics, when any conservative out on his or her own, and probably without sufficient credibility, will be branded a RINO (Republican in Name Only) and ignored or ridiculed on the Right. In at least one case, I know of a progressive reform organization that actually paid a high-profile conservative to stand with them for reform.

My experience suggests that all of the above assumptions are in play when it comes to reform leaders in the United States today. The lesson that would be reinforced again and again over the course of the years that I worked to "save America" is that the reform movement, including its leaders and organizations, is plagued by the very same diseases that need to be expunged from the political system itself: self-interested partisanship, groupthink, and the controlling influence of money. It's more than just a little ironic.

7: Double Standards and Dead Ends

In September 2014, a Virginia jury found Republican Governor Bob McDonnell guilty on eleven counts of corruption, involving conspiracy, bribery and extortion. McDonnell's wife, Maureen, was convicted on eight counts of corruption, as well as another for obstruction of justice. Bob McDonnell would be sentenced to two years in prison, and his wife to one year. The jury was convinced that the McDonnells lent out the prestige of the Virginia governor's office in exchange for lavish gifts – a Rolex, Armani clothing, fancy vacation, etc. – and $120,000 in sweetheart loans from Johnnie R. Williams Sr., CEO of Star Scientific, the maker of a dietary supplement.

Though no quid pro quo was ever discovered, prosecutors showed a pattern of behavior in which gifts from Williams were followed by favors from the governor's office. For example, records show that Governor McDonnell e-mailed an assistant about dietary supplement issues six minutes after accepting a $50,000 loan from Williams. Virginia's loose ethics laws permitted McDonnell to legally accept gifts as long as they were not the fruit of bribery or extortion. Ultimately a parade of circumstantial evidence incriminated McDonnell. Notably, Williams never got what he really wanted: state-funded studies of his dietary product. Bob McDonnell would appeal and take his case all the way to the Supreme Court.[68]

To any average citizen, the guilty verdict delivered by the Virginia jury against their governor is completely understandable. While there was no explicit proof that bribery or related crimes took place, the accumulation of circumstantial evidence is sufficiently convincing to indicate that the McDonnells were using the office of the governor for personal gain. There's simply no other way to interpret the evidence. The Bob McDonnell standard is a reasonable standard that could, and perhaps should, be applied throughout the American political system, but is it?

In 2005, former President Bill Clinton stood alongside Nursultan Nazarbayev, the despotic president of Kazakhstan, who had governed since 1990 by abusing the human and political rights of his people. Clinton nevertheless praised Nazarbayev for "opening up the social and political life of your country," a characterization that contradicted the view of the US State Department at the time. Ostensibly Bill Clinton was there to promote his foundation's campaign against AIDS, though Kazakhstan doesn't really have an AIDS problem. He had flown to Kazakhstan on the private jet of Canadian mining tycoon Frank Giustra, who was keenly interested in acquiring the rights to mine some Kazakh real estate rich in uranium.

Meanwhile, Senator Hillary Clinton sat on a Congressional committee that controlled the generous spigot of foreign aid that had flowed to Kazakhstan since the end of the Cold War. Forty-eight hours after Bill Clinton's visit to Kazakhstan, the sales process for the mining concession began between Kazakhstan and Giustra's company, UrAsia. And soon after that, millions of dollars between people and entities connected to UrAsia started flowing into the Clinton Foundation. Maybe it was all just a coincidence, but it certainly looks suspicious.

And there's more. UrAsia was gobbled by another Canadian company, Uranium One, which was chaired by Ian Telfer, who, along with various associates and connected entities, also donated millions to the Clinton Foundation. Meanwhile, the Russian government, through a state-controlled corporation, had designs on acquiring Uranium One as part of that government's ongoing effort to control the global uranium market. Salida Capital, a Cypress-based company populated by former KGB agents, decided to donate a couple of million dollars to the Clinton Foundation and pay Bill Clinton $500,000 to make a speech in Moscow.

Because Uranium One held US uranium assets, an Executive Branch committee that included Hillary Clinton, who was by now secretary of state, would have to approve the acquisition of Uranium One by the Russians. Hillary Clinton had a reputation as a hawk in the committee when it came to preventing foreign state-controlled corporations from acquiring strategically important American assets, but in the case of Uranium One, not so much. The deal sailed through.[69]

The story of how Russia came to acquire US uranium assets and the connections to the Clintons is one of many involving circumstantial evidence uncovered by Peter Schweizer in his book, *Clinton Cash*. Here are some of the others:

Both Hillary and Bill Clinton had been firm opponents of nuclear proliferation and both were on record as resistant to supporting India's nuclear ambitions, but all of that too changed after millions of dollars from India flowed to the Clinton Foundation.

In 2009 Secretary of State Clinton traveled to Russia to urge officials there to sign a multi-billion-dollar airplane deal with Boeing. The Russians agreed, and two months later Boeing pledged $900,000 to the Clinton Foundation.

TD Bank, the biggest shareholder in TransCanada's

Keystone pipeline project, which proposed to bring oil from Canada to the US Gulf Coast, paid Bill Clinton $1.8 million to give ten speeches over the course of roughly two-and-a-half years. Hillary Clinton's State Department hired Environmental Resources Management to conduct an impact study of the pipeline project, even though the company had financial ties to TransCanada. The State Department would erase the biographies of individuals with potential conflicts of interest. Hillary seemed to support the project until she finally came out against it as her bid to become the Democratic nominee for president began to look shaky in 2015.

Between 2001 and 2013, Bill Clinton made $40 million giving speeches in foreign countries. The biggest speaking fees came when Hillary Clinton was serving as secretary of state.

Swedish telephone giant Ericsson, which was coming under criticism for providing surveillance equipment to oppressive regimes around the world, paid Bill Clinton a whopping $750,000 for a single speech. Less than six months later, President Obama signed an executive order imposing sanctions on telecom sales to Syria and Iran, but Ericsson's work in Iran was not included in the prohibition.

In 2011, the United Arab Emirates (UAE) was having its interests squeezed over issues relating to trade with Iran. A member of the nation's royal family complained in a State Department cable that his country was being left out of negotiations involving economic sanctions against Iran. The UAE paid Bill Clinton to give a speech for $500,000, and at the very same moment, the foreign minister of the UAE was flying to Washington to meet with Secretary of State Hillary Clinton.

While she was still in the Senate, Hillary Clinton had taken the lead in promoting peace and democracy in the Congo. She was one of the first to sign on to the Democratic Republic of the Congo Relief, Security and Democracy Promotion Act of 2006, legislation authored by then-Senator Barack Obama. The legislation gave the US secretary of state tools to help address the country's deeply ingrained corruption, violence and human rights violations. As secretary of state, however, Hillary Clinton would repeatedly intervene in the Congo, or abstain from intervening, in a pattern that seemed to parallel the flow of millions of dollars in contributions to the Clinton Foundation from shady sources connected to Congolese warlords more than it did to serve the noble aims of the legislation she had supported as a senator.

The list goes on. Hillary Clinton reversed her position on the Colombia free trade deal as close associates of Bill Clinton's stood to make millions exploiting that country's natural resources.

After the Haiti earthquake, the Clintons looked like the gatekeepers for foreign investment to rebuild that country. Among the highlights, an Irish telecom firm, Digicel, landed a telecom monopoly in Haiti while paying Bill Clinton to give three speeches at $200,000 apiece. Also, VCS Mining, a company with almost no track record of actual mining, was granted an open-pit gold-mining permit in Haiti; Hillary Clinton's younger brother, Tony Rodham, would be added to the company's board of directors shortly thereafter.

The Associated Press, following on Schweizer's work, found that more than half of all the people Secretary of State Clinton met with while in that office had donated to the Clinton Foundation.[70]

In the case of Virginia Governor Bob McDonnell, circumstantial evidence was enough to convict him and sentence him to prison for two years. In the case of the Clintons, it seems that no amount of circumstantial evidence can prompt a Justice Department investigation relating to possible corruption. Bob McDonnell's corruption consisted of acts paid for with tens and hundreds of thousands of dollars in loans. Straight cold hard cash flowed to the Clintons and their foundation on a much larger scale: hundreds of millions of dollars to their foundation and millions more to Bill Clinton personally. Diet pill entrepreneur Johnny Williams Sr. never got what he wanted most from Governor McDonnell. Other than the promoters of the Keystone pipeline, all the players who gave money to Clintons referenced above got what they ultimately wanted. Governor McDonnell's corruption wasted small amounts of tax dollars and compromised the integrity of his office. By contrast, the possibly corrupt dealings of the Clintons potentially wasted significant amounts of money in US foreign assistance, undermined US strategic interests, and weakened American attempts to promote human rights around the world. Yet one Clinton, the former president, remains one of the nation's most honored citizens, and the other Clinton came close to being elected president in 2016. Comparisons between the way the law enforcement authorities have treated Bob McDonnell on the one hand, and the Clintons on the other, seem strikingly unequal and potentially unjust.

Progressive journalist and author Matt Taibbi, in his book, *The Divide: American Injustice in the Age of the Wealth Gap* makes a strong case that in America today wealthy white-collar criminals get away with crimes involving huge amounts of money while poor people on the street, who may or not be criminals, are unfairly or disproportionately punished by our judicial system. According to Taibbi, to be rich and powerful in America in the 21st century is to have a keep-out-of-jail card for most white-collar crime.

But maybe the platinum version of this card goes to powerful individuals associated with the Democratic Party. House Speaker Nancy Pelosi's husband got special IPO stock shares of Visa while credit card legislation was before the US House, among others of Pelosi's questionable dealings.[71] Former Democratic New Jersey Governor John Corzine illegally gambled his client's money on European sovereign debt and somehow escaped prosecution at the same time he bundled $500,000 for President Obama's re-election in 2012 while under investigation.[72] Before Jack Lew was appointed treasury secretary, it appears that he had benefitted in a kickback scheme between CitiBank and New York University, where he was comptroller general, after which he moved on to Citibank itself, where he headed one of the divisions most caught up in the shady dealings associated with the 2008 financial crisis.[73]

Meanwhile, the conservative intellectual and political activist Dinesh D'Souza was convicted and sentenced to eight months in a halfway house. His crime? He had admittedly laundered $20,000 to a close friend running a hopeless campaign for Congress. If he had been better informed, D'Souza would have realized that he could have contributed the same money indirectly by forming a Super PAC. His probable real "crime" was producing a film, *Obama's America: The Unmaking of the American Dream*. D'Souza would end up threatened with a seven-year jail sentence and was forced to seek psychological counseling (this is something political dissidents some-times endured in the old Soviet Union), punishments unprecedented for a campaign finance crime as utterly meaningless as the one he committed. His friend, the candidate, was challenging an entrenched incumbent and she was, of course, crushed on Election Day. D'Souza's sentencing to a halfway house with hardened criminals on their way *out* of incarceration is otherwise unheard of.

The famous liberal attorney, Obama voter, and Harvard law professor Alan Dershowitz suggested the common nature of what D'Souza had done when he said that he was himself occasionally approached by other attorneys asking him to give money to various candidates and promising to "make it right," indicating that Dershowitz would be paid back for his "contribution," thus skirting the law exactly the way D'Souza had done. Dershowitz said that what happened to D'Souza looked like a "selective prosecution." Conservatives call it political persecution.[74]

The above examples suggest a double standard when it comes to prosecuting corruption based on partisanship. The 2015 indictment of New Jersey Senator Bob Menendez, a Democrat, however, might indicate a slightly different reason for the selective enforcement of anti-corruption laws. Like Bob McDonnell, Senator Menendez had received lavish gifts from a political supporter, in addition to $750,000 in campaign contributions. Menendez helped his generous political supporter obtain a port security contract in the Dominican Republic, and he assisted in a matter involving Medicare regulators. The New Jersey senator would insist that he was merely performing constituent services, something all senators do routinely. Was Menendez being singled out, and if so, why?

Speaking before the Seton Hall University School of Diplomacy and International Relations, Menendez, the ranking Democrat on the Senate Foreign Relations Committee, announced that he could not support President Obama's agreement with Iran on nuclear weapons. "If Iran is to acquire a nuclear bomb, it will not have my name on it," Menendez declared. "While I have many specific concerns about this agreement, my overarching concern is that it requires no dismantling of Iran's nuclear infrastructure and only mothballs that infrastructure for 10 years," he said.[75] It is one thing for a member of Congress to dissent from his or her own party for political reasons, as a couple of other Democratic senators did on the Iran nuclear deal issue, but Menendez was a leader of the opposition attacking what President Obama probably considers one of his greatest achievements. From a White House point of view, Menendez had been giving aid and comfort to the enemy (the Republicans, that is — not Iran). Was the prosecution of Menendez payback for his disloyalty? And if so, are selective corruption prosecutions really an exercise of raw Executive power designed to keep members of Congress in line? This too would be a form of corruption, and an especially dangerous one, because it tends toward the solidification of power in the hands of the presidency.

In 2016 Governor Bob McDonnell's prosecution was overturned by a unanimous decision of the United States Supreme Court. Writing for the Court, Chief Justice John Roberts pointed out that quid pro quo corruption, the exchange of something of value for an "official act," is illegal. But, he argued, using the standard applied against McDonnell means that "nearly anything a public official accepts—from a campaign contribution to lunch—counts as a quid; and nearly anything a public official does—from arranging a meeting to inviting a guest to an event—counts as a quo." In the case of McDonnell, the Supreme Court concluded that the definition of what constitutes an "official act" was far too broad. Roberts noted that conscientious public officials routinely arrange meetings for constituents, contact other officials on their behalf, and include them in events. The Court declared that these are not "official acts," which must involve the actual wielding of government power.[76]

So what is the average citizen to make of all this? Average citizens sat in judgement of Governor McConnell and Senator Menendez and they probably had no difficulty believing these officials were corrupt. Persons and entities with clear financial interests don't give away thousands or hundreds of thousands of dollars in campaign contributions, expensive favors and/or personal gifts for no reason. It's clear that the supporters of both officials wanted something. They gained access to and assistance from these elected officials that would have been nearly impossible for an ordinary constituent who had given nothing. The broad definition of "official acts" pressed by the prosecutors seems perfectly reasonable. It's clear that the donors and gift-givers were actually buying something.

Yet big problems would arise if the Supreme Court had ruled for the government and if the McConnell and Menendez standards were applied broadly. The fact is that nearly every elected official is doing favors for donors all the time. Sometimes an elected official acts in the interest of the donor, but is it the case that the donor is "bribing" the official, or is it that the official is "extorting" the donor, or is it simply that the elected official believes that he or she is acting in the best interests of the nation, regardless of the campaign contribution? Any attempt to untangle the motivations of thousands of elected officials all across the country would require a police state and the employment of mind readers.

Under the current system, a broad definition of bribery or extortion would invite still more partisan mischief and tempt the Executive Branch to go after political opponents, who would become easy targets, while leaving their own side alone. Indeed, as the above examples suggest, it may already be happening. Selective prosecutions, made lawful under a broader definition of corruption, could further political corruption by letting partisan allies off the hook, inflaming partisanship still more, and promoting an imperial presidency. Justice Roberts, writing for the Court in the McDonnell case, touches on this danger when he uses the case history to warn of "arbitrary and discriminatory enforcement" of anti-corruption laws.

When it comes to corruption in government, we are left with three paths from which to choose. First, we can stay on our current course, which permits interactions between wealthy donors and elected officials that very often seem indistinguishable from bribery and extortion, except in the strictly legal sense. Second, we can broaden the legal definition of corruption to a more commonsense standard, but in so doing we would create an enormous law enforcement challenge and make the system even more vulnerable to politically motivated prosecutions than it already is, all while prosecutorial discretion would still allow attorneys general to issue "keep-out-of-jail-free" cards to political allies. Or, third, we could simply ban all large gifts and campaign contributions altogether, and choose some other means to fund political campaigns. For most citizens watching from outside the system, it's not a hard choice.

Conservatives will recognize the partisan double standard I have described in this chapter as the absolute truth when it comes to the enforcement of anti-corruption laws. Most progressives, on the other hand, will lament that I have engaged in right-wing paranoia. In Chapter 9, we'll see why such responses are unsurprising and even normal. The good news is that even our profound differences of opinion about which side is actually more corrupt need not keep ordinary citizens on the Right and Left from working together. Yes, it would be helpful, politically, if grassroots progressives worked harder to hold their own side to higher ethical standards. But people of good will of all political stripes, including progressives, believe in equal justice under the law. If conservatives demand a new system that will be resistant to selective partisan anti-corruption prosecution, progressives will have no problem agreeing in principle. Typical citizens on the Left do not favor partisan witch hunts or corrupt political protection rackets any more than conservatives do; indeed, members of the American Left have been the victims of some of these practices themselves, historically. Progressives and conservatives will be able to agree on the clean government future we want to build together, even if we don't necessarily agree on the past.

◊◊◊

For almost the first two years of my project to unite leaders of the American Left I had the support of Larry Lessig, perhaps the single most influential progressive reformer in the country. But I struggled to find equally credible conservative partners for him. When I finally found Lessig's conservative counterpart in Peter Schweizer, Lessig bailed out on me. Now, in 2012, I had the nation's leading conservative reformer on board, but no progressive leadership. It was all very frustrating, but Peter's commitment sustained my efforts. Support from any one of the many progressive reformers and organizations in the country could get us off the ground, but on the conservative side, there was only one Peter Schweitzer. I saw him as the key to unlocking the American Right.

Two months after everything fell apart up in Massachusetts, Peter Schweizer and I were in Washington sitting at Ralph Nader's office, an unpretentious fluorescent-lit space with a 1970s feel, crowded with file cabinets and metal bookshelves. I recall my sense of delight when a spry-looking Ralph Nader entered the room. For all the frustration that went with trying to broker an alliance between the American Left and Right, it was always fun to meet famous and interesting people, and there was Nader, whose face was so familiar, large as life and eager to talk to us about our plan.

He was visibly enthused about our visit. "Gentleman, this just doesn't happen in Washington," Nader remarked. "I'll be at some meeting or testifying alongside someone from Cato who completely agrees with me on an issue, but the other side always finds some reason not to work together." Nader liked the plan I had drafted for a Left-Right alliance and had been circulating it among some of his colleagues.

As he spoke, I looked for signs of age in the then seventy-eight-year-old consumer advocate and citizen reformer. Nader liked to ramble and get diverted. The first time it happened I thought to myself, "this man is either brilliant or becoming senile." An old person may frequently lose track of a conversation, and someone academically inclined, with great intellectual curiosity, will also wander off topic as he or she makes interesting and often irresistible connections. The difference is that the senile person never finds his way back, and is led from one diversion to another until he's lost in a mental forest somewhere without a compass. The intellectual always finds his way back to the point, which Nader did again and again. Ralph Nader seemed as sharp as ever.

Frequently the subjects that rose to the fore in the conversation related to books that Nader happened to have lying around his office. He'd tell us that we must read this one, and this other one by so and so. Sometimes he pointed to a book that he himself had written, such as his fictional *Only the Super Rich Can Save Us,* about Warren Buffet and a bunch of other billionaires getting together to make a plan to save the world with their money. As with all his books, he typed this one, all 500-plus pages of it, on an old-fashioned manual typewriter (Ralph does not use a word processor or the Internet). Peter and I would end up leaving Ralph's office with books piled high in our arms.

Peter Schweizer's posture was different than it was in the meeting with Larry Lessig, where he had followed Larry's lead. Now Peter kept deferring to me. I appreciated the kind sentiment behind his new tack, but I was a facilitator; the really important thing for me was that at least one prominent or connected reform-minded conservative bond intellectually and personally with one reform-minded progressive. They would be the leaders, not me, and they are the ones who needed to establish a trusting and collaborative relationship.

Ralph Nader was so positive about the Left-Right approach that the nuances of the meeting were unimportant. He envisioned a "convergence movement" between the populist Left and Right in several important areas where there is agreement and where an elite self-interested establishment stands in opposition. The convergence areas include crony capitalism/corporatism, banking reform, electoral/political reform, civil liberties, foreign policy and trade. Nader is surely correct that substantial numbers of progressives and conservatives could form powerful alliances in all of these functional areas. Unbeknownst to Peter and me at the time, Nader was in the process of writing a book on this very subject, *Unstoppable: The Emerging Left-Right Alliance to Dismantle the Corporate State.* [77]

Given his passion for the subject, Nader would have been the perfect progressive to lead a Left-Right alliance from the progressive side, but for his perceived spoiler role in the 2000 presidential election that put George W. Bush in the White House. Since then, the progressive establishment has exiled Nader. He was now living alone on his own little political cul-de-sac. As a conservative, I did not at first fully appreciate Nader's political isolation on the Left today. To me, he was and is a progressive of historic proportions. But I had noticed that there was no connection between him and the progressive reform organizations to which I had been talking, even though Nader had actually founded a couple of them.

At the meeting with Schweizer, I defined the goal, which was of course a comprehensive anti–corruption /clean-government amendment to the Constitution. "Good," Nader said, "so there is a final objective."

I think I know what was behind this simple statement. All the reform organizations become institutions, and institutions exist to survive and grow. Nader wasn't interested in creating another organization that would end up existing for its own sake. He wanted the focus to be on solving the nation's problems, not institution building. He liked the fact that there was an end-game to what we proposed.

Unfortunately, Nader's political liabilities as a result of the 2000 election go well beyond his lack of sway with the big reform organizations. The Democratic establishment has done an excellent job convincing the rank and file that Nader is the reason that Al Gore lost that election. The Democratic establishment has done to Nader what it has done so well to conservatives: it turned us all into politically and socially unacceptable enemies.

I was pretty shocked by the response I got from some Democrats when I told them I was working with Nader. One board member e-mailed me on the eve of my meeting with Ralph and asked me to punch him in the nose.

Our best funding prospect, the heir to one of America's great fortunes mentioned earlier, wanted nothing to do with Nader.

A former New Hampshire state senator proclaimed that Nader had "blood on his hands," suggesting he was responsible for the Iraq war (yet Hillary Clinton and John Kerry, both of whom voted for the war resolution, are not?).

I understand about the infuriating nature of the spoiler campaign. Many Republicans believe that Ross Perot lost the 1992 election for George H.W. Bush. Every election at least one of my Libertarian friends votes for that ticket and I get annoyed that they are helping Bill Clinton or Barack Obama. But who is really to blame for the spoiler phenomenon? Is it the spoiler candidate or the people who vote for him/her? The spoiler candidates are always categorized by their opponents as "selfish," but isn't denying voters the widest possible choice of candidates the truly selfish act? Ralph Nader didn't throw the election to the Republicans in 2000; his supporters did. And the answer to frustrated Democrats is what? Would you deny voters the choice?

Another person to blame for Al Gore's loss is Al Gore, who failed to carry his home state of Tennessee.

Speaking at the libertarian Cato Institute, of all places, Ralph Nader observed in 2015, "It was quite clear to me, many years ago, that power structures believe in dividing and ruling" by distracting "attention from the areas where different groups agree to where they disagree." On this, and quite a number of other things, Ralph Nader's wisdom is spot on.

I can personally attest that Ralph Nader is decent, fair, principled, open-minded, intellectual and yet down-to-earth. He has devoted his entire life to public service in a selfless way that is in complete contrast to the self-serving and demonizing nature of American politics today. I don't think Nader is constitutionally capable of betraying any of his core principles – he would be a miserable wretch if he did – which is exactly why he's the sort of leader the American Left so desperately needs. His record as a consumer advocate and anti-corporate power crusader speaks for itself. As if it mattered what one conservative thinks to the mass of citizens on the Left, I believe that progressives should forgive Nader for his role in the 2000 election. He's a progressive tragic hero, not a villain.

Since we are interested in reforms that would improve the functioning of our republic, there is one reform that, had it been in place for the 2000 election, could possibly have put Al Gore in the White House and kept Nader from being tossed into the Democratic Party's political dungeon. It's called an *approval voting* system. Under such a system, it would say at the top of every ballot: "Vote for one *or more* of the following candidates. The candidate with the most votes wins." Thus, in an approval voting system, a voter is permitted to vote for multiple candidates running for the same office, allowing citizens casting ballots to choose all the candidates they find acceptable, which weakens the tendency of like-minded voters to divide their support between the most similar candidates, helps marginalize candidates whom the majority of voters find unacceptable, and nearly eliminates the possibility of a spoiler. (We can assume that citizens taking up ballots in an approval voting system, who would have supported only Nader in 2000 without also voting for Gore, would have stayed home without Nader in the race and therefore would have taken no votes from Gore.) An approval voting system would also have been helpful in 1992, when Ross Perot is said to have played the role of spoiler to George H.W. Bush's reelection.

In the Republican Primary of 2016, Donald Trump would have had a harder time capturing the nomination had an approval voting system been in place, since the more conventional Republican vote was divided among the many other candidates. No winner-take-all primaries would also help cancel the effect of dividing like-minded voters and allowing a relatively unacceptable candidate to gain the party's nomination.

◊◊◊

Peter Schweizer and I connected over the phone on New Year's Eve, 2012, when he had some time to talk. Back when Peter had agreed over lunch with Lessig that our Left-Right reform alliance should pursue something legislatively rather than constitutionally, he wasn't merely being deferential to Lessig. He didn't believe that we should go straight for a constitutional amendment. "You have to date before you can get married," Peter said.

I was wedded to an approach that would fundamentally reform and transform our political system to make it more judicious and therefore also more consistent with the founding vision of James Madison. There could be no term limits and no truly clean elections system without amending the Constitution. Anything less, in my opinion, was just nibbling around the edges, and without constitutional change, I feared that anything achieved legislatively would be inevitably undermined over time by the same selfish interests we sought to control. I had thought legislative solutions a waste of time and resources. In terms of messaging, I wanted to do something big and consequential that would capture the imagination of the American people. Ordinary citizens, who don't necessarily appreciate the many facets of the systemic failure, have a profound sense of its overall corruption and dysfunction, and they want it fixed. I still believe that news of high-level conservative and progressive leaders coming together to fundamentally and finally fix the system would generate the popular wave of enthusiasm necessary to drive an amendment process forward. Anything less would not generate sufficient popular energy. As someone far outside the system, I was thinking more like an ordinary citizen, and ordinary citizens want nothing short of solutions that will change the awful trajectory of American politics and government. So I was a little stubborn on this point.

Peter was thinking more along the lines of an insiders' game, and by that I mean working with established centers of political influence on both sides. "We are going to need people with some real power to drive this forward," he said.

The more Schweizer talked, the more he convinced me. The two approaches – legislative and constitutional – were not mutually exclusive; they were complementary. Progressives and conservatives could build trust and momentum with smaller legislative achievements on the way to a constitutional amendment, which is a necessarily long process. Working with members of Congress for commonsense reform legislation would help identify reform-minded congressional allies in the run-up to the big battle for the amendment.

We could start with reforms so commonsensical that only the most corrupt politician could oppose them. Schweizer has listed a number of these in his excellent book, *Extortion*. The key, to get us off the ground politically, is to first pursue nothing that would be the least bit controversial among grassroots conservatives and progressives. I call them "the no-brainer reforms." I'll begin with the ones that I think are most obvious. The first five are from Peter's book:[78]

Ban contributions from government contractors. Accepting campaign donation checks from private entities that do business with the government is "in your face" corruption. While ending this obnoxious practice through a change in the law is preferred, the president probably has the authority to stop it through executive action.

Ban political contributions from lobbyists. We could call this one "The Help Lobbyists Sleep Well at Night Act." Lobbying could be a noble profession if money wasn't changing hands between interests and politicians. This reform, as well as the ban on donations from would-be government contractors, should be immune to judicial reversal, since Connecticut has them on its books at the state level.

Ban leadership PACs. In the words of Schweizer, "Leadership PACs have essentially become money-laundering operations" and are often used as slush funds, with very few restrictions placed on how these monies are spent. They exist to enhance the power, and often the lifestyle, of leading members of Congress and serve no public purpose.

Prohibit fundraising while Congress is in session. Most fundamentally, when members of Congress are on the clock working for the taxpayers, they should not be out raising money for themselves. This reform should limit members' ability to extort money from interests using implicit threats and the tactical timing of votes on various bills. It would also eliminate some of the most grotesque forms of fundraising, which normally consists of members driving off Capitol Hill to money-raising luncheons hosted by lobbyists at fancy DC venues. It would, however, be difficult to police a member's political operatives from fundraising. Checks can be post-dated and the prospect of partisan enforcement is also an issue.

Ban immediate family members of representatives and senators from becoming lobbyists. The current practice can turn the buying and selling of influence into a lucrative family business.

Prohibit campaign donors from becoming US ambassadors. Ambassadorships are regularly for sale to generous campaign donors, a corrupt practice that undermines US foreign policy by putting deep-pocketed political hacks in places where talented diplomats are needed.

Several of the above reforms would limit an incumbent's ability to fundraise, which is essential to enhancing a challenger's ability to defeat an incumbent. Since one of the paths for a constitutional amendment goes through Congress, anything we can do to make it easier for clean government candidates to defeat incumbent status quo politicians is important.

I was wrong to dismiss all legislative reforms as "nibbling around the edges." If written into law, the reforms suggested by Peter Schweizer would improve the system. If we could agree on nothing else, these commonsense ideas would be enough to justify a popular-based Left-Right alliance. These reforms should be enough to rally even the cynics, who believe that wholesome and fundamental structural changes in our system are politically impossible.

Progressive reform organizations are hungry for a public campaign financing system, a goal they would always prioritize with me in conversation. Undoubtedly, entrenched incumbency is a massive obstacle to any kind of wholesome change in American politics. A public campaign financing system, one that could put adequate amounts of resources in the hands of challengers, would serve as a giant backhoe to dislodge the career politicians. It is a necessary tool that would help clear the road to a constitutional amendment, but it's going to take Republican support to make it happen. (Also, expect many Democratic members of Congress to back away if it looks like it might become a reality.) An established Left-Right partnership that builds trust, along with the successful passage of some of the "no brainer reforms" above, will help conservative reformers go to their base and explain the necessity of a public campaign finance system as part of an overall plan to restore James Madison's vision for government relatively free of manipulation by narrow interests. Imagining these steps ahead of us shows the wisdom in Peter Schweizer's approach.

In early 2013, the National Press Club offered us space to announce our Left-Right reform alliance, featuring Peter Schweizer and Ralph Nader as leaders. In hindsight, it may have been a mistake, but I hesitated. If we raised our standard with Nader as our sole leader on the Left, would progressives rally to our cause in sufficient numbers?

Ralph seemed a little surprised that the National Press Club had offered us space. "I used to speak there all the time," he said ruefully, "before I became involved in politics." I concluded that before we announced our presence, we needed the participation of more leading citizens, balanced on the Right and Left.

I called or wrote every American leader that I could imagine possibly supporting a Left-Right reform alliance. There are too many to mention them all and there's no point in bringing up most of those who never got back to me.

At least some who declined to help wrote me kind responses. Former Supreme Court Justice Sandra Day O'Connor couldn't be of assistance because she was still a practicing judge. Bill Moyers was focused exclusively on media production, but said that he appreciated my efforts. Former Senator David Boren, who in his little book *Letter to America*[9] had advocated doing something very close to what I proposed, said thanks, but he was too busy running the University of Oklahoma.

I had a series of promising telephone conversations with former Democratic congressman and presidential candidate Dennis Kucinich, who has in abundance the combination of qualities we need in our leaders. He's a politician of strong convictions, unlikely to sacrifice his principles or ethics, but he's not partisan; he genuinely welcomes an opportunity to work with the other side. Kucinich and I got sufficiently far in the discussion process that he offered to host an open-ended progressive-conservative conclave at his house in Washington for interested leading players on both sides. Peter Schweizer informed me of the impressive guests on the Right he could invite. Shortly thereafter, Dennis said that he was thinking about running for office again and needed to focus on that possibility. The would-be gathering at his house was off.

In the end, a short list of some outstanding people

were supportive of the project. First there was former Comptroller General of the United States David Walker, whose centrist proclivities had involved him in No Labels. He thought Nader's participation was fine, but he wanted other prominent voices on the Left side of the political divide to participate.

I was still in touch with former Council for Economic Development President Charlie Kolb, whose interest in election reform was undiminished and who surely has some ability to help with fundraising, a critical need.

Finally, Joan Blades, a founder of MoveOn.org, and I became friendly. Joan's work to bring progressives and conservatives together into conversation and community, the goal of her "Living Room Conversations" project, is – in the current political context – nothing short of heroic. Joan was eager to see more women involved.

As a group, Ralph Nader, Joan Blades, David Walker, Charlie Kolb and Peter Schweizer span the entire political spectrum, with maybe only a "center-left" position missing. (David Boren would have fit that bill nicely.) Each is principled, brilliant and accomplished, and each appreciates the value of a principled compromise. If only the United States were being led by such admirable citizens.

And if only I could have gotten them all on the same conference call. Herding cats would be easy by comparison. Here is where my own lack of political influence and status was an acute liability. Who was I to try something this big? I'm sure that in many instances my efforts were written off as the work of a crank, unworthy of a busy and relatively influential person's time. I'm certain that my own lack of a track record limited the commitment of even those who supported me. I kept suggesting things were about to happen that did not, after one big player or another backed out. By now, with Peter Schweizer, my credibility must have been flagging, or at least the credibility of the reformist American Left through me was flagging. Why should Schweizer keep wasting his valuable time with me? Nader kindly wrote of me that I "exuded energy." And my favorite compliment was from Jerry Delemus, who referred to me as "like a battering ram." As 2013 drew to a close, my head was hurting and once again things were stalling out. All my energy and hard-headed effort could not budge the partisan mountain I aspired to move.

◊◊◊

Finally, at the beginning of 2014, we had one of our biggest breaks yet. A friend of Arnie Arnesen's, Miles Rapoport, was named president of Common Cause. Rapoport was replacing Bob Edgar, whom I had met previously, and who had passed away the previous year. We arranged a dinner meeting between Miles and Peter Schweizer. Common Cause was and still is the granddaddy of all reform organizations. Its size, credibility and reach are second to none.

Common Cause is chaired by former labor secretary and scholar, Robert Reich. He was someone I had written to on two different occasions because he seemed the perfect person to lead an alliance from the Left. Reich understands the value of bipartisanship; he had authored op-eds on the subject and had penned a supportive blurb for Nader's book. Joan Blades, who lives in Reich's part of the country, also knows him. Now here was another way to approach Reich, through Miles Rapoport, if Miles would prove amenable.

Arnie Arnesen offered to help make the case for an alliance with willing conservatives to her old friend, so we flew down to DC together. During all the time that I worked to bring conservatives and progressives together for reform, I had no better friend than progressive Arnie Arnesen. She had me on her radio program on several occasions and was always on the lookout for opportunities to advance the cause and bipartisan approach that we both understand is essential. She maintained her commitment even as her husband, Marty, fought and ultimately lost a long battle with cancer. Arnie told me that she sometimes felt guilty for not doing more to help me, but truthfully, along with Peter Schweizer and Ralph Nader, there was no one I appreciated more than her and no one I'd rather have at the table with me making the arguments that needed to be made to Common Cause.

Arnie and I sat down at a pricey Washington steakhouse with Rapoport and three Common Cause staff members, including Vice Presidents Karen Hobart Flynn and Arn Pierson. Peter Schweizer hurried in straight from the airport as his flight had been delayed. With both Arnie and Peter there to make the case to the entire staff leadership of Common Cause over a long meal, the situation could not have been more ideal.

To get us started, I laid out the proposition for a Left/Right partnership that would fundamentally reform our political system with a negotiated clean government amendment to the Constitution, which would include a clean elections system in federal elections and term limits for members of Congress. Along the way we'd work on and pass at least some of the "no brainer" reforms mentioned above. I noted how delighted I was to be talking with Common Cause. With its nationwide presence, Left-Right clean government alliances could be launched everywhere.

As I recall, Miles Rapoport spoke next. I am sure he expressed some words of welcome, but what I remember distinctly is Miles describing the dual nature of Common Cause's mission. The organization was dedicated equally to democracy and ethics in government on the one hand, and progressive policy solutions on the other. He made it clear that Common Cause was a progressive organization with a progressive mission, and those facts were not going to change.

My heart sank. These did not sound like the words of

someone looking to discover common ground or make any principled compromises. I felt like Rapoport had just torpedoed the whole proposal, and we had not even gotten to the appetizer. As others talked, I kept thinking about what he had said. Maybe because I am an optimist by nature, I looked for a silver lining. All the other reform organizations disingenuously claim to be non-partisan. At least Common Cause was being honest.

When the opportunity arose, I turned to Miles to address that fatal-sounding statement. "Look," I said, "no one is asking Common Cause to change its mission. The point is simply that we must work together. The system is just too entrenched for either progressives or conservatives to do it alone." I went on to point out that we needed to fill seats on both sides of the table. If Common Cause could help fill the chairs in the Left side, I knew that Peter could help fill the ones on the Right. Karen Hobart Flynn would later add helpfully that Common Cause sometimes worked with conservative groups at the state level in pursuit of shared goals to good effect.

We didn't have a Left-Right debate at that restaurant's table. That's not how the teams were aligned. Rather, the very progressive Arnie Arnesen and the very conservative Peter Schweizer and I moved the ball down the field together.

The usual objections came up. There were some of the typical arguments against term limits, which didn't seem especially heartfelt. Common Cause was keenly interested in resisting voter ID laws, a subject Miles spoke about with passion, but we weren't proposing to touch that controversial issue.

Overall, resistance to our argument was tepid. What could anyone say? That maintaining rigid partisan positions was more important than finding solutions to the grave and mutually understood failings of our political system? That it was better to maintain a politically hopeless posture than work with willing members of the other side? I could sense the mood turning our way.

Toward the end of the evening, Common Cause Vice President Arn Pierson, who had been listening thoughtfully at one end of the table, offered up something intriguing. He wondered aloud if the model could be tested at the state level. Many states have a citizens' initiative process for state constitutional amendments. What this means in practice is that conservatives and progressives could unite in one of these states and pass a constitutional amendment for term limits and a clean elections system without the need for approval from even one sitting politician. In theory it could be done through petition drives and statewide referendums. We'd need to find a state that had neither term limits nor a clean elections system in order to test the theory that packaging the two reforms together could unite the whole political spectrum at the grassroots level. And, as Arn warned, the packaging might be a problem. At least some states, he said, restricted constitutional amendments to single subjects. Still, it was a wonderful idea worth exploring and demonstrated some real interest in our proposal among Common Cause senior staff.

As the dinner broke up, I had no idea where we stood. I watched Karen Hobart Flynn linger over my business card, with our Clean Government Alliance logo on it, which features a handshake between a blue hand and a red hand. Maybe it was the optimist in me again, but I thought I spotted an approving little smile on her face.

The weeks went by and I heard nothing from Common Cause. Arnie Arnesen pointed out repeatedly that Miles was new on the job, and he'd need time to settle in. She urged me to be patient, which I wasn't. Since Arn Pierson lives in my part of the country, just up the road near Portland, Maine, I suggested that he and I get together again. I wanted to make sure he understood the backstory prior to our meeting, and give him some idea of the lay of the land on the conservative side. I figured such a briefing could only build trust.

Many times I would meet progressive reformers who I sensed thought of me as an enemy. Other times it was more of a wariness. But with Arn Pierson there was none of that. It felt like we were completely on the same side, the side of the people trying to take back their government from selfish interests. So I provided him with more background as we munched down pizza on the Portland waterfront, where this book opened. I thought we were about done when he said, "OK, let's make a plan."

Arn proposed a leadership conference populated by equal numbers of progressives and conservatives, with ten to fifteen per side. We'd recruit influential people, including media types, leading activists, scholars, financiers closely associated with progressive or conservative constituencies. He proposed that our goal would be to emerge with three politically balanced working groups, one to work on the "no brainer" reforms to get us started as Schweizer suggested, another focused on the idea of a clean government amendment to the Constitution along the lines I had advocated, and a third group that would explore the possibility of testing a Left-Right alliance at the state level, which is the idea Arn had raised at our first meeting over dinner.

I was thrilled. I drove home flying high on the plan. When I told Peter Schweizer about it, he described the proposal as "terrific." But I never heard from Arn Pierson or Common Cause again.

8: Lost with Darkness Descending

On May 10, 2013, speaking before the American Bar Association, Lois Lerner, the Director of the Exempt Organizations Division at the IRS, took a question from the audience that she used as an opportunity to make a startling revelation. Lerner explained that the IRS field office in Cincinnati had been singling out applications for nonprofit tax status from Tea Party organizations for "further review." Although she insisted that this was done not for political reasons, but for the sake of "consistency and efficiency," the special scrutiny reserved for these conservative groups was "absolutely incorrect, insensitive, and inappropriate."[80]

And there was more. She acknowledged that, in some instances, these cases "sat around for a while." She added, "They also sent some letters out that were far too broad, asking questions of these organizations that weren't really necessary for the type of application." In some cases, Lerner admitted, they wrongly asked for the lists of the group's financial contributors.

The question in the audience was apparently planted by

Lois Lerner herself to give her a chance to head off an inspector general's report due out in a few days, which would find that the IRS had improperly targeted Tea Party groups. When Lerner stated that applications were held up "for a while," what she really meant was *years*, in many cases.[81] Also, one social conservative group proved in court that IRS employees leaked confidential contributor information to their political opponents, who had the names published.[82]

The IRS "scandal" is typically dismissed by progressives, but it is of very serious concern to conservatives. Government actions against conservatives at the IRS, perhaps also in other federal agencies, and as we will see, in Wisconsin, are intimately tied to issues of money and politics, and the partisan enforcement of campaign and election laws. For progressives, it should be a matter of applying the empathy test. As we go over the particulars, imagine if the tables were turned, and all the progressive players were conservatives and all of the conservative players were progressives. How would progressives feel and what would they demand?

◊◊◊

The groups mentioned by Lois Lerner at the American Bar Association meeting were seeking to be recognized by the IRS as either legal 501c3 or 501c4 non-profit tax-exempt organizations. Traditional charities typically apply as 501c3s, which cannot engage in any political activity. Organizations that are recognized under chapter 501c3 of the tax code have a major advantage because financial donations to these groups are tax deductible. What is less well known is that financial contributions to organizations recognized under chapter 501c4 are not tax deductible, but these groups can legally engage in political activity. Essentially, as compared to 501c3s, 501c4 non-profits give up the major tax advantage in order to be involved in politics.

The vast majority of conservative non-profits targeted by the IRS were applying for 501c4 status, so none of their financial backers would be able to write off their contributions.

It can all get pretty murky. It's quite common in Washington to see 501c3, 501c4 and Political Action Committees (groups that can give money directly to candidates) that look legally separate on paper but work essentially as one organization and in some cases share resources, like office space or staff. The opportunities for abuse of the law are high in these cases because it's not especially hard to shift tax-deductible contributions into political activity. Staff can easily declare they are spending their time working on something charitable or educational when in fact they are engaged in politics. The IRS might reasonably dig deep into these organizations, but stand-alone 501c4s have no similar opportunity to violate the tax code. The major objection to 501c4s is that their financial backers can donate unlimited amounts of money for a broad range of political advocacy and that these backers can remain anonymous.

In the months that followed, Democrats in Congress and their allies in the media and blogosphere would throw up smoke screens claiming that progressive groups had been denied non-profit status also. This was true to the extent that the IRS went about its normal business using customary evaluation standards and denying applications from aspiring non-profit groups, including a few progressive-sounding ones, when they failed to meet those customary standards. No one has argued that progressive groups were systematically given a pass from routine scrutiny, so naturally a few applications for progressive organizations would be questioned.

But progressive groups do not appear to have been *targeted* like conservative-sounding ones. Two-hundred and ninety conservative groups received extra scrutiny as opposed to six progressive ones, and those six did not get the same treatment as the conservative groups. No progressive group had their application sit around for years, and they simply were not asked the same kind of intrusive questions. No evidence exists in the inspector general's report that Occupy Wall Street organizations, groups on the Left that most parallel Tea Party groups, got any unusual scrutiny at all from the IRS. IRS agents testified that among the six progressive organizations that received extra scrutiny were five ACORN groups that appeared to be old organizations applying as new ones, and another left-leaning group because of a possible "improper private benefit" for someone. [83]

In 2014, it would be discovered that not only were IRS applications for conservative groups targeted, but so were existing 501c4 conservative organizations. Dozens of 501c4 organizations were subject to "surveillance." Of these, 83% were right-leaning. Of those that got audited, 100% were right-leaning.[84]

In 2016, under court order, the IRS finally released its own list of 426 targeted organizations, adding progressive organizations to the inspector general's initial list and making the IRS political dragnet look less ideologically prejudiced. Conservative leaders immediately cried foul, claiming that the Left-leaning organizations were only added later as a smokescreen.[85]

We know for certain that Lois Lerner did not tell the truth when she claimed the targeting of Tea Party groups was an action instigated by rogue agents at a field office in Cincinnati, and that the targeting came as news to her. We know she spoke falsely because field officers testified that they had been following instructions from higher-ups in Washington, including Lerner herself. An acting IRS commissioner uttered the same untruth when he blamed the inappropriate treatment of conservative non-profit applications on frontline "rogue" agents in Cincinnati and that these agents had been disciplined. Thrown under the bus is more like it.[86]

IRS attorney Carter Hull revealed that the criteria for scrutinizing the targeted organizations were developed at least in part by IRS Chief Counsel William Wilkins, a political appointee of President Obama's located in Washington, DC. It was Lerner's assistant who instructed Hull to send applications on to Wilkins' office. At one meeting, in July 2011, Lerner instructed those present that the applications should be referred to as "advocacy" applications, rather than "Tea Party" applications. It appears she was trying to hide the targeting.

But what did all this actually mean to a conservative activist trying to organize politically at the grassroots level? The most famous example is that of Catherine Engelbrecht, a woman as heroic to conservatives as Lois Lerner is infamous.

Engelbrecht testified before the House Committee on Oversight and Government Reform on February 6, 2014, but her story goes back to 2009, when working the polls at her local precinct, she perceived "fundamental procedural problems" in the voting process. As a result, she and other citizens founded a civic organization, "True the Vote," dedicated to making sure that "every American voter has an opportunity to participate in elections that are free and fair." Or, to put it another way, True the Vote is an anti-voter fraud group (Yes, Engelbrecht's group uncovered significant voter fraud in Houston).[87]

There is no more heated subject between activists on the Left and Right than the battle over voter IDs. Conservatives demand laws that require voters to present picture identification when voting, like almost every other democratic country in the world. Not to do so is an invitation to voter fraud, conservatives argue. Progressives say such laws are anti-democratic and promote the suppression of the African-American vote, since poor people and impoverished African-Americans who might depend on public transportation might have no photo ID driver's licenses to present for voting purposes. The racial element in the difference of opinion makes this debate particularly incendiary. And maybe it made Catherine Engelbrecht a lightning rod.

Shortly after founding True the Vote, Engelbrecht also helped found a Tea Party group, King Street Patriots. Prior to filing these applications for 501C3 and 501c4 non-profit status with the IRS, Engelbrecht never had any trouble with the government. She and her husband ran a small manufacturing company. "In nearly two decades of running our small business, my husband and I never dealt with any government agency," Englebrecht testified. They filed their taxes every year and were never audited or investigated.

Now, after filing the applications with the IRS, everything changed. Since 2010, Englebrecht, her organizations, and her business were subject to more than fifteen instances of audit or inquiry by federal agencies. In 2011, her personal and business tax returns were audited. In 2012 OSHA inspected her place of business and found some minor infractions (like the wrong type of safety belt on a piece of machinery) that somehow resulted in fines of more than $20,000. In 2012 and 2013, the Bureau of Alcohol, Tobacco and Firearms conducted audits of her business (Englebrecht Manufacturing makes a part for a gun). Beginning in 2010 the FBI contacted Englebrecht's non-profits, demanding membership lists in connection with a domestic terrorism case. Meanwhile, as she was waiting and waiting to get her non-profit applications approved, Engelbrecht says the "IRS was subjecting me to multiple rounds of abusive inquiries with requests to provide every Facebook and Twitter I'd ever posted, questions about my political aspirations and demands to know the names of every group I'd ever made presentations to, the content of what I'd said, and where I intended to speak for the coming year." This sort of questioning is certainly reminiscent of the darkest days of McCarthyism.

Catherine Engelbrecht has either been the subject of a

remarkable set of coincidences and/or rogue behavior on the part of individual government agents or she has been unjustly, systematically and unlawfully targeted by the government for her political views and activities. The IRS now acknowledges that the line of questioning was inappropriate.

The inspector general's findings of wrongdoing at the IRS and scope of his investigation were limited to unjustified scrutiny and delay relating to 501c3 and 501c4 applications for non-profit status recognition. But Catherine Engelbrecht and her business were also audited during the same period. As any taxpayer knows, the prospect of an IRS audit is terrifying. The possibility of ongoing politicaly-motivated IRS wielding tax audits as a partisan weapon raises the potential abuse to a whole other level. Still more serious is the implicit inter-agency coordination in the Engelbrecht case, which has grave implications for political liberty.

During the 2012 presidential campaign, wealthy Romney Super-PAC donor Frank VanderSloot was described on an Obama campaign web site as one of eight "wealthy individuals with less-than-reputable records." Shortly thereafter he was subject to three IRS audits, personally and for his businesses. VanderSloot reported that other donors to the Super-PAC were similarly audited but that they had no interest in coming forward to discuss the matter. "They took their own beatings," VanderSloot said, "and they don't want any more and they don't want to even talk about this."[88]

Conservative media personality Wayne Allyn Root, a relentless opponent of President Obama and a fellow classmate of his at Columbia, was audited by the IRS in 2011 in a process that he says began, most unusually, with a voicemail left by an IRS agent. (The IRS insists that the subjects of audits are never first informed this way.) The agent also called Root's accountant, who told him not to call Root, but to address all tax matters through him. The

IRS turned around and called Root again anyway. Root was shocked when he discovered that the agent on the line knew all about his political views. "I felt like I was being stalked," writes Root.

After spending thousands of dollars in tax court, Mr. Root won his case. The next day, he says, he was audited again.

Now Root went to the conservative advocacy organization Judicial Watch, which took his case. Judicial Watch filed to obtain a copy of Root's IRS file under the Freedom of Information Act, a process that is supposed to take thirty days, but the documents were not produced for fourteen months. The IRS stated that the reason it took so long to turn over the file was because a United States senator from Oregon was involved (both are Democrats). Why was a US senator concerned about Mr. Root's tax filings?

When the file finally arrived it was marked "sensitive case," but what made it "sensitive?" The file included notes about Root's political perspective and activities. Judicial watch claims to hold a copy of the file, which they say has also been shared with an investigative committee in the US Senate.

Root's case was formally closed on May 23, 2013, the same day that Lois Lerner was suspended from the IRS. The previous day, she had pleaded the Fifth, asserting her constitutional right to remain silent rather than potentially incriminate herself. In September 2013, Lerner was reprimanded by an internal IRS panel for "neglect of duties" and retired from the IRS that month.[89]

At the same time that the IRS was allegedly violating the civil rights of citizens connected to conservative organizations, Lois Lerner had been having dinners and phone calls with a man named Kevin Kennedy, who ran the benign-sounding Wisconsin Government Accountability Board.

In Wisconsin, Republican Governor Scott Walker had made himself hated by Democratic political interests by effectively striking at one of their most important power centers: the public unions. In 2011, amid raucous demonstrations by progressive protesters, Walker successfully passed reforms to limit the collective bargaining power of public unions in his state and end automatic union dues collection, a portion of which flows into Democratic campaign coffers whether the individual member likes it or not. The next year, progressives attempted a recall election to remove Walker from office. It was a high-stakes contest, because if public unions could be similarly undermined throughout the country, it would represent a significant blow to Democratic political interests nationally. Money poured into the campaign from everywhere to both sides.

Lois Lerner's friend, Kevin Kennedy, worked alongside Milwaukee prosecutor John Chisholm, who launched a "John Doe" investigation against the politically conservative citizens in Wisconsin who funded an issue advocacy campaign that paralleled Scott Walker's political bid to survive the recall election. A "John Doe" investigation is when the party suing is not sure if there are known persons or businesses being sued. In effect, the investigation begins with fictitious defendants, named John Doe #1, John Doe #2, etc., who are either replaced by real people as evidence is uncovered, or the case is dropped if no criminality or no criminal defendant is found. As this process suggests, a John Doe investigation is well-suited for a witch hunt. So, what did this investigation mean in practice?

In the dark of night, teams of police arrived with battering rams at the doors of conservative financial backers of the law to reform the public unions. They yelled in the faces of the shocked home owners, terrified children, seized computers and files, gave no explanation for the raids, and placed gag orders on the targets of the investigation, denying them even the right to call an attorney.

Chisholm, the Milwaukee district attorney, had managed to get a court order to search for evidence of coordination between the Walker campaign and advocacy groups, notably the Wisconsin Club for Growth, which advocated for reforms opposed by the state's public unions. It's also worth noting that District Attorney Chisholm's wife is a teacher and union shop steward at a Milwaukee high school.

Political campaigns and advocacy groups are not supposed to coordinate their activities. That would be illegal. But wherever in the United States political campaigns take place, it's likely that the candidates' campaigns, and the issues advocacy campaigns that run alongside them, involve overlapping circles of people. Law or no law, it is reasonable to think that members of the same political community working on the two different kinds of campaigns, with nearly identical goals, will interact and talk about what they are doing or not doing. It seems almost inevitable. Therefore, if you could get your hands on virtually all the communications between activists on one side or the other, chances are you could find them in violation of the law.

This is probably what Milwaukee prosecutor Chisholm had in mind when he embarked on this constitutionally dubious fishing expedition. A similar investigation into Wisconsin progressive advocacy organizations and political candidates was as likely to reveal coordination as the investigation of conservatives did. But again, progressives were not targeted.

In 2015, during her second bid to be the Democratic nominee for President, Hillary Clinton's campaign and a Hillary Clinton Super PAC tweeted out identical messages.[90] Here was a "smoking gun" of campaign coordination. But for some strange reason, in this case, there were no police raids at the Clinton compound in Chappaqua, or anywhere else. Nobody in any position of authority cared.

Should this "coordination" really be considered a serious crime? Does coordination between a political campaign and an issues advocacy group ever make the difference in an election? Not likely. The issues advocacy campaigns are usually run by slick professionals who know what sort of ads to run and when to run them. At some level some coordination probably always occurs and it probably doesn't matter very much in the end.

In the case of what went down in Wisconsin, there is simply no justification for spending millions of taxpayer dollars and potentially violating the civil liberties of ordinary citizens through paramilitary-style raids to prosecute a crime as meaningless as "campaign coordination." The Wisconsin prosecutor's investigation and aggressive police actions were obviously not really about campaign coordination; they were acts of partisan retribution and intimidation designed to silence opposition.

In May of 2014 a Wisconsin judge ordered a halt to the investigation and ordered the state to return everything it seized to the lawful owners and destroy any copies made. From there the case went to the Wisconsin Supreme Court, which ruled that the prosecutor's actions were "unsupported in either reason or law" and constituted a "fishing expedition into the lives, work, and thoughts of countless citizens."

Far more serious than the potential coordination between advocacy organizations and political campaigns is the potential coordination between partisan political interests and the police power of the state. But there have been no police raids at the IRS or Lois Lerner's house.

What might an investigation of Lois Lerner's files uncover? Former Illinois State Representative Al Salvi has a notion of what sort of behavior she might be hiding. Back in 1996 Republican Salvi was in the late stages of an election against the future senator from Illinois, Democrat Dick Durbin, when some Illinois Democrats and the Democratic Senatorial Committee leveled charges against him with the Federal Elections Commission (FEC). The charges themselves became a major distraction and focus of media attention as Election Day approached. Salvi later complained that as a result he couldn't get his message out to the voters. The news was all about his alleged violations.

Even after losing the election, Salvi refused to settle with the FEC, even though attorney Lois Lerner, head of the FEC's Enforcement Division at the time, made him an offer. "Promise me you will never run for office again, and we'll drop this case," she is reported to have said.

But Salvi didn't back down because he believed he had done nothing wrong. FBI agents came to his house. Another set of agents interviewed his elderly mother, asking where she came upon $2000 to give to her son. Almost $100,000 in legal fees later, Salvi won when a judge dismissed the case.[91]

Meanwhile, Dick Durbin, Salvi's opponent back then, is enjoying a nice career in the US Senate. In 2010, he wrote to the IRS urging the agency to "quickly investigate" Karl Rove's group Crossroads GPS and other 501c4 organizations.[92] The letter was part of a wave of pressure being put on the IRS by mostly Democratic politicians and members of the progressive reform community. The result may have been the abuse of ordinary citizen-activists like Catherine Engelbrecht and others by partisan interests unjustly wielding government power.

All the above examples – and more could be added – are troubling, but the Engelbrecht case, if she was subject to political retribution, is the darkest and most threatening of them all, because if it happened, it involved inter-agency coordination between multiple departments of government: the IRS, FBI, OSHA and ATF. This kind of coordination can only be orchestrated at the highest levels. It would constitute a new kind of McCarthyism and, if tied to the White House, a scandal of proportions not smaller than Watergate.

Progressives may be skeptical, and perhaps they should be. Maybe all these stories are exaggerations, fabrications, and/or hallucinations. In these partisan times, we are disinclined to believe extreme charges when made by the other side and embrace the flimsiest accusation made by our own side because it's psychologically comforting and because it fits a pre-existing narrative developed by media-savvy partisan interests. But, again, how would progressives feel if the ideological identities were reversed? What if progressives were the ones who felt targeted by government agencies allegedly captured by conservative partisan interests? In that case, it's obvious that progressives would demand a fair and thorough investigation. That's all conservatives ever wanted, but they did not get it.

By any stretch of the imagination, it's hard to deny that there has been an obstruction of justice in the case of Lois Lerner. IRS attorney Thomas Kane, in sworn testimony, declared that Lois Lerner's Blackberry was illegally "removed or wiped clean of any sensitive or proprietary information and removed as scrap for disposal in June 2012."

By August 2013, a congressional committee subpoenaed the IRS for all of Lois Lerner's e-mails. Seven months later, in March 2014, John Koskinen, a new IRS commissioner and a major Democratic campaign donor who has shelled out $100,000 to Democrats and left-leaning groups over the years, admitted that the IRS had yet to find Lois Lerner's e-mails. In fact, it doesn't seem that the IRS had even bothered to look. Under questioning, the commissioner pointed out that all e-mails are backed up on servers and, "We can find, and we are in fact searching, we can find Lois Lerner's emails."[93]

In June 2014, the IRS claimed that many of Lerner's e-mails could not be recovered because of a computer crash at the IRS back on February 4, 2013, though Commissioner Koskinen had made no mention of this lost data in his March testimony. On the contrary, he said everything was backed up. On June 17, the IRS reported that it also could not produce the e-mails of six additional key employees, all related to alleged IRS targeting of conservatives, because of computer crashes. The next day, after technical experts said they could recover the data from the hard drives, the IRS revealed that the hard drives had been destroyed. In September, more IRS hard drive crashes were reported, including those of key employees in the Cincinnati office, bringing the total to twenty IRS employees who have lost e-mails related to the IRS' alleged targeting of conservatives. Republicans in Congress would later begin impeachment proceedings against Koskinen for lying to Congress, failing to protect subpoenaed documents, and obstruction of justice. [94]

Finally, in November 2014, the inspector general for tax administration, made it known that 30,000 of Lois Lerner's e-mails were indeed backed up at a storage site in West Virginia. It's alleged that Justice Department officials blocked some lower-level IRS officials from accessing the site. [95]

In June 2015, the IRS was still refusing to release Lerner's e-mails, despite a court order.[96]

Another Democratic campaign donor, attorney Barbara Bosserman, was put in charge of the investigation at the Obama Justice Department.[97] Eight months after the investigation purportedly began, the FBI had only begun to interview the alleged victims of abuse at the hands of the IRS. In the middle of the investigation President Obama famously prejudged the outcome, when in an interview on FOX, he claimed there was "not even a smidgeon of corruption" at the IRS regarding the targeting of conservatives.[98]

During the summer of 2015 it was revealed that Richard Pilger, director of the Elections Crimes Branch at the Justice Department, had contacted Lois Lerner to know who at the IRS the DOJ people should contact about potential fishing expeditions against 501c3 groups, presumably conservative ones, an idea being promoted by Senator Sheldon Whitehouse (D-RI). The goal, Lerner said, was to "piece together false statement cases about applicants who 'lied' [Lerner's quotations] — saying they weren't doing political activity, then turning around making large visible political expenditures," all in the hope of bringing criminal charges against these groups. Here was a proposition for targeting that began not in the Cincinnati field office of the IRS, but in the Obama Justice Department itself at the suggestion of a Democratic senator. [99]

As the facts emerge, it is increasingly clear that the Obama Justice Department had numerous conflicts of interest when it came to investigating the IRS targeting of conservative groups. Not only was the investigation placed under the authority of an Obama donor, but it appears that the department itself might have been complicit in actions to deprive citizens of their civil rights. Nevertheless, the investigation was formally, and some would say predictably, closed without any charges filed, in the fall of 2015. The public has little reason to believe that justice was served or that steps have been taken to prevent the future persecution of American citizens based on their political views.

Progressives will remain skeptical. Such is the nature of politics and human psychology. But progressives understand well the right of every citizen to a fair hearing. It's obvious that in the case of the IRS "scandal," the IRS obstructed justice and the Justice Department was completely unconcerned about this fact. Progressives would not tolerate a Republican campaign donor put in charge of investigating campaign-related violations in which the potential victims were Democrats. So that justice is served, fair-minded progressives should see the need for a non-partisan and independent investigation.

Progressives who prioritize cleaning up our corrupt campaign finance system would also do well to consider the political implications of the IRS scandal and the lack of a thorough inquiry. While many conservatives may agree with progressives about the corrupting influence of money in politics, they are never going to join with progressive reformers in a common effort to clean up the system so long as they believe that campaign finance rules are designed only to punish conservatives. Much less will they be willing to work with progressive reformers who have aided and abetted the potential violation of the civil liberties of conservative citizens. As long as conservative political interests can potentially be targeted by the federal bureaucracy, conservatives will defend *Citizens United* at all costs, because the anonymity for political activity protected under that ruling will continue to be their only defense.

◊◊◊

Among the people I had invited to the Lessig-Schweizer cocktail party back in 2012 was Jerry Delemus, Recall that it was Delumus, the NH Tea Party leader self-described as "to the right of Attila the Hun," who was more than willing to partner with New Hampshire's most progressive leaders to fight political corruption and help create a clean elections system.

Jerry's hardcore brand of populist and Christian evangelical conservatism horrified Larry Lessig. In fact, my own differences with Jerry Delemus on some issues are quite substantial. But I wanted to demonstrate to potential backers of our project, at that party and elsewhere, that support for a new clean elections system is not a left-center proposition, and that we can unite the entire political spectrum at the populist level if, and only if, conservatives are treated as full partners and not as enemies. It's not that I wanted radical leaders to be in charge, but rather that I intended to illustrate that a full-spectrum popular political reform alliance is possible, and necessary. Though Larry seems to have missed the point, I was told that some of the corporate and philanthropic elites at the cocktail party were impressed that a radical conservative like Jerry was there, and ready to roll his sleeves up to work alongside progressives to clean up our political system. It is also true that at the time I did not fully appreciate the extent of Jerry's radicalism.

In 2014, Jerry headed back out west, this time in his truck with his son, a couple of friends, and a .50 caliber sniper rifle. With his wife's blessing, he motored almost forty-one hours straight to the Bundy Ranch in Nevada where right-wing militia groups were gathering in a stand-off with the federal government. Hundreds of men showed up with all manner of military firearms, ready to use them against agents and officers of the Federal Bureau of Land Management. When Jerry arrived, they had already forced the Bureau of Land Management to return Bundy's cattle at gunpoint.

Jerry apparently soon found himself in the role of a mid-level leader at the Bundy Ranch. He "recruited, organized, trained, and provided logistical support" and "led armed patrols and security checkpoints." Jerry declared that he and his compatriots were ready to "give our lives" in the cause. Fortunately it never came to that and Jerry returned home claiming victory.

In the case of the standoff at the Bundy Ranch, most conservative media concluded that while the government might be overbearing toward Western ranchers, the threat of violence was a gross overreaction in a bad cause.[100] Bundy's neighbors were paying their grazing fees — why shouldn't he? Bundy's overt racism, revealed during the standoff, repelled most conservatives just as it did people on the Left.

After the Bundy Ranch episode, Jerry reappeared in the headlines again when he challenged Muslim extremists by promoting a New Hampshire version of the "Draw Mohammed" contest, an idea first promoted by Texas free speech activist Pam Geller, whose own contest was met by gunfire from Islamists. Jerry would end up calling off the New Hampshire event, claiming victory by drawing attention to the issue of free speech, even though no drawings were actually produced.[101]

After Islamist extremist attacks on US military recruiting centers, where soldiers are required to be unarmed, Jerry helped organize local fully-armed conservative militants to stand guard at a New Hampshire recruiting station. I recall Jerry posting on Facebook an exasperated photo of himself in military gear after long hours of standing watch.

Much to my surprise at the time, Jerry Delemus was soon promoting Donald Trump for president. It was surprising to me because Trump had previously held many political positions that I would have thought anathema to Delemus, the radical conservative. Trump's rhetoric on trade and immigration would naturally appeal to Jerry, but Trump is obviously not a small-government conservative; he supported Democrats for many years, and his commitment to the Constitution, a copy of which Jerry always carries in his pocket, is not clear. Jerry had frequently warned that if our country remained on the path it was on that God would remove His blessing from the United States. But now Jerry was backing a man whose casino business, divorces, buying of political favors, and love of money should have made him seem like a terrible choice to an evangelical Christian. Nevertheless, Jerry soon accepted a position as one of Trump's New Hampshire co-chairs.

I was astounded and told Jerry so. He and I went back and forth respectfully about Trump during the run-up to the New Hampshire Primary. At one point I messaged him, "All I can figure is that Trump is reaching out to you personally." Jerry did not respond.

I suspect that the personal connection between Trump and Jerry Delemus had been made by Corey Lewandowski, who, before he became Trump's campaign manager, had worked as a Koch-affiliated Americans for Prosperity operative in New Hampshire.[102] I was acquainted with Corey, who personally and publicly had supported the Fair Elections Now Act while working for the Kochs. I think the

Kochs' people would have fired Corey if he had personally and publicly supported climate change legislation or Obamacare, or the bombing of Iran, but speaking out for election reform was OK. Here was another way that Charlie Koch signaled his openness to issues relating to corruption and money in politics. Corey moving from the Koch brothers to Trump did not make any more ideological sense than Jerry's backing of Trump. For Corey, at least, it could be justified for the purposes of career advancement. The Kochs have made clear their dislike of Trump. Charlie Koch and Donald Trump are opposites in terms of commitment to small-government conservative philosophy and personal temperament. Yet all manner of rank and file conservatives flocked to Trump anyway, despite his lack of conservative bona fides.

The rise of Donald Trump represents something new and potentially ominous in American politics. For many on the Right, rage and the desire to fight have become more important than conservative principles. Donald Trump's campaign rhetoric suggested that he would not necessarily be faithful to the Constitution, which for conservative intellectuals now decapitated from the movement that had sought to lead, is unthinkable in a Republican nominee. Candidate Trump threatened to go around Congress, punish political enemies, and alter the First Amendment. He's perhaps going to do to his political enemies what conservatives perceive that Obama administration has been doing to them, and maybe much more.[103] And maybe that's part of his appeal.

The campaign on the Democratic side was not much more reassuring. Senator Bernie Sanders, an obviously decent man who ran a positive campaign, gave Hillary Clinton a run for her money — her Wall Street money that is — along with her other vast financial resources from self-interested people and entities. But Sanders fought Hillary with one arm tied behind his back. He did her a tremendous favor when he said in debate that people were sick of hearing about her "damn e-mails," as if the private server Secretary of State Clinton used for official business was not a big deal. Connecting the dots to Schweizer's work, Sanders could have instead painted the picture showing how a private communications system might have facilitated the co-mingling of official Department of State business with Clinton Foundation business. But Sanders would never go there. He would never draw on Schweizer's research because to do so might bloody Clinton too much, might help the Republicans in the general election, and might turn off Democratic voters trained to reject any argument made by conservatives, regardless of merit. On the Democratic side, partisanship trumps all, and as a result, corruption thrives, Democratic candidates are not fully vetted in their primaries, and Trump's moniker for the Democratic nominee for president, "crooked Hillary," stuck like glue.

The FBI investigation of Clinton's e-mails, which on the run-up to the election was focused narrowly on national security issues and not the potential pay-to-play corruption associated with the Clinton Foundation, resulted in nothing more than a verbal condemnation of Hillary's actions. Inexplicably to many, no charges were brought. Liberal professor and constitutional scholar Jonathan Turley called FBI Director Comey's decision to grant immunity to three top Clinton aides allegedly involved in concealing evidence, "baffling." One had cleaned Clinton's server with Bleachbit after its contents had been subpoenaed by Congress. Turley remarked, "The easiest way for prosecutors to scuttle a criminal case is to immunize those people who are at the greatest risk of criminal indictment," which is exactly what Comey did in the case of Hillary Clinton and her private e-mail server.[104] To restore faith in our political system, there is every reason to go tough on the most powerful public figures, not easy.

Although the president is sworn to uphold the law, the Obama Justice Department was within its rights not to fully investigate or prosecute Hillary Clinton or Lois Lerner. Any president has the authority to issues orders to the FBI or exercise "prosecutorial discretion" because the FBI director and the attorney general work for, and report to, the president. The fact of this constitutional power has become a major problem, causing Americans of all political stripes to lose faith in the notion of equal justice under the law.

◊◊◊

In January 2016, Jerry Delemus again tangled himself up in the quarrels some western ranchers have with the federal government, this time in Oregon, at a rancher-occupied wildlife refuge. Jerry wanted to make sure that Trump got the "whole story" and thought it would "arouse" the Donald and motivate him to join Jerry out west in support of the ranchers.[105] That didn't happen. Instead, this time the FBI ended up shooting one of the protesters, an action Jerry would characterize as "murder."

After the event, back home I recall Jerry posting on Facebook something about his "willingness" to talk with the FBI. A short while later, at the beginning of March, Jerry was taken away in handcuffs. [106]

Many will be tempted to immediately condemn and scorn Jerry Delemus for his armed revolt in a dubious cause. Remember, though, that Jerry is also the Tea Party activist who praised our state's arch-progressive, Arnie Arnesen, for her integrity, and spontaneously hugged her, and hoped to work with her to help clean up our political system. Jerry can obviously be misguided, but he is not a bad man. When citizens lose complete faith in their government, radical political movements flourish, and good people can get sucked in.

Extremist conservatives, especially those who are part of the gun culture, have developed a dangerous doctrine of armed resistance to federal authority they deem unlawful.

They take very seriously Thomas Jefferson's prescription that "the tree of liberty must be refreshed from time to time with the blood of patriots." The astoundingly successful and peaceful civil disobedience of the civil rights movement should render Jefferson's advice happily obsolete and shows the way forward for anyone wishing to see radical change in our time. The resort to violence, conversely, will only lead to tragedy and also serve to legitimize and enhance the police power of the state.

Unfortunately, this seems where we are headed. When Senator Coburn warned us in his office of the danger of extremism from both sides, scenes like that at the Bundy Ranch are clearly what he had in mind.

The unequal application of justice based on political power and partisanship, as suggested by the possible scandal at the IRS and in other instances, has the potential to promote more extreme reactions among those who perceive that their rights are being violated. And more extreme action by right-wing militia-type organizations may embolden partisan forces in the government to double down on their current alleged heavy-handed approach and apparent double standards, unless it's all stopped now.

Meanwhile, political dysfunction and partisan hatred produced the two most publicly disliked presidential nominees since polling began: Donald Trump and Hillary Clinton. They are symptoms, products and drivers of a corrupted political system that no longer serves the broad and long-term interests of the American people. They are also harbingers of America's political future unless we the people take action.

Our story opened in 1786 with an alarmed James Madison reviewing the tumultuous events in Massachusetts as rebels and representatives of the government waged war on each other. Blood was spilled at the federal arsenal in Springfield, Massachusetts. There, two soldiers of the Revolution, rebel Daniel Shays and loyal militia officer William Sheppard, led their followers who stood ready to kill each other, not because any of these men held any mutual animosity that was personal. Rather, they were fellow citizens set on a course of violence against each other by the actions of selfish interests in a distant capital. The situation is not so different today as radical political polarization, fueled by selfish political interests, has partisan political hatred at a fever pitch. No, most of us are not ready to kill each other yet, but the hostility is reaching dangerous levels. Can Americans still reform their political system, or will the system itself continue to successfully foment the hatred that makes solving pressing national problems impossible?

◇◇◇

There wasn't much more I could do once Common Cause decided against the Left-Right reform leadership conference idea. I feel pretty certain their vice president, Arn Pierson, had wandered off the Common Cause reservation when he began planning that event with me. I hope he was not taken to the woodshed for it. The reform movement needs many more Arn Piersons.

Meanwhile, in my state, Larry Lessig had launched an organization called "The New Hampshire Rebellion," which featured 1) long marches to raise awareness about the corrupting influence of money in politics, 2) a plan to encourage citizens to ask presidential candidates what they intended to do about such corruption, and 3) and, perhaps officially led by another related group, a series of town and city resolutions in support of a constitutional amendment that would reverse Citizens United (and give Congress the power to regulate political advertising).

The fundamental problem was the same as always: the plan was created by a small group of like-minded partisan insiders. We don't need long walks in the snows of New Hampshire to make people aware of the problem; the American people get it. The problem is that the American people don't see the way to fix it.

Citizens should not be "asking" candidates what those candidates will do about corruption. Candidates for each party will offer up predicable partisan sound bites that say nothing and go nowhere. Rather, the people must unite as conservatives and progressives behind a comprehensive solution and demand of candidates what they must do to repair our broken political system. We are in charge. We must *tell* them, not ask them.

Cities and towns should not pass pre-packaged resolutions assembled by partisan groups. They should do as our ancestors have always done: debate and put forth their own solutions based on the views of the local people they represent.

It was especially hard for me to watch all this bungling and waste of reform-related resources in my own backyard. Larry Lessig hired Jeff McLean, the former vice president of my Clean Government Alliance (that hurt a little), who, along with the new Vice President Eric MacLeish, both Democrats, pleaded with me to join Lessig's New Hampshire Rebellion. I said that I would be more than happy to, so long as control of the organization was shared equally by progressives and conservatives, which of course didn't happen. Conservatives are not going to join a progressive-controlled reform organization any more than progressives would join a conservative-controlled one. That much should be obvious.

Still, I tried to work with the NH-based progressive reform organization, Open Democracy, which eventually merged with the NH Rebellion. My idea was that we could hold a balanced bipartisan Clean Government Convention to be held in the spotlight of the NH Primary. We'd organize bipartisan alliances all over the state and come together to demand reform from the presidential candidates, who would be invited to the convention. Arnie Arnesen, helpful as always, encouraged the NH Rebellion to sign on to the concept. They agreed in principle but offered no support, financial or otherwise. It was all left up to me.

A final flicker of hope and light appeared from the City Council of Portsmouth, NH, where I live. In the run-up to the would-be New Hampshire Clean Government Convention, I started organizing city and town governments to pass bipartisan resolutions in favor of holding the convention and for measures that would reform our political system. In Portsmouth, we passed a bipartisan resolution generally supportive of the concepts outlined here, including term limits, a clean elections system, and an end to gerrymandering, all to be enforced by some neutral and independent policing authority.

The resolution was, as it should be, a product of deliberation both before it was presented to the City Council and at the City Council meeting itself. Although Portsmouth is one of the most heavily Democratic communities in New Hampshire, we had several Republican or generally conservative council members who were full partners in the process and who supported the final draft of the resolution.

It was a pleasure for me, a conservative, to work with the Democrats on the City Council. No one was more supportive or active than Councilor Jim Splaine, a lifelong progressive activist and former state legislator. Jim envisioned a "buddy system," in which progressives and conservatives would reach out to each other and arrive at the Clean Government Convention Noah's Ark style, two by two.

Our non-partisan City Council, like many local governments all across the United States, is not gripped by debilitating political polarization. Rather, Democrats and Republicans collaborate there all the time. Often one bipartisan coalition will face off against another bipartisan coalition over issues usually related to the city's downtown development. Working together and developing solutions is normal at the local level.

Councilor Stefany Shaheen, daughter of the state's

Democratic US senator, Jeanne Shaheen, also helped craft the resolution. While she couldn't speak for her mother, she promised that our plan for a bipartisan reform convention and movement would get a fair hearing with Senator Shaheen when the time came. The possible participation of our Democratic senator was an exciting idea, since our other US senator, Republican Kelly Ayotte, had indicated to me an interest in the project. Notably Senator Ayotte could support a clean elections system, so long as it did not "favor one side." I liked to imagine our two senators chairing our New Hampshire Clean Government Convention.

But there would be no Clean Government Convention. I simply couldn't pull it off all by myself without resources. The idea of passing grassroots bipartisan resolutions for a Clean Government Convention in cities and towns throughout the state conflicted with the professional reformers' top-down campaign to pass cookie-cutter resolutions to reverse *Citizens United*, a campaign that was already underway. That train had already left the station.

Over the course of four-and-half years I had contacted every American leader I could possibly think of on the Left and Right, practically begging each of them to put partisanship aside for the sake of reforming a corrupt political system that is doing terrible damage to the country we all love. With reluctance, I finally had to acknowledge that it wasn't working. I had no one left to ask.

But I had a story, which you have been reading. And I believe my experience suggests answers to some of the most difficult questions regarding the failure of our political system and our ongoing inability to do anything about it. I think I know what needs to happen, not because I am smarter or better educated than anyone else, but as a result of my obsession and my experience acting on that obsession.

Let's now look to the way forward.

9: Overcoming Intuitive Partisanship

I n a study, a test subject is undergoing an MRI brain scan when information is introduced that is contrary to the subject's political ideology. Immediately the part of the brain "associated with negative emotion and response to punishment" lights up. Synapses fire in this area, the brain's unhappy place. Meanwhile, the part of the brain associated with reasoning, the dorso-lateral prefrontal cortex, is fast asleep, unmoved by the new information that should be intellectually stimulating. Then, when the ideologically hostile information is somehow discredited, the brain's reward center starts humming. "Ah, that feels much better," says the brain. The study found that the subjects got a small pleasant hit of dopamine when their own previously held partisan notions and identity seemed to be confirmed and reinforced. Partisanship may be actually addictive, just like a drug.[107] Factor in that massive amounts of partisan money, media and messaging are heaping fuel on a partisan fire rooted in DNA, and is it any wonder that people seem close-minded and hopelessly divided?

James Madison believed that inevitable partisanship was driven by interests and passions, though he hoped that political structures and systems could be put in place to encourage political leaders to discourse calmly together, share diverse viewpoints, and find solutions that serve the common good. Unhappily, implementing Madison's vision is harder than even he imagined.

Modern-day moral psychologist Jonathan Haidt argues that partisanship is hardwired into our DNA through the process of evolution. We think we are acting on reason, Haidt concludes, but research shows that most of the time humans follow their intuition, then use reason as a justification for their beliefs or actions. Reason is mostly just a tool to defend our kneejerk positions and keep our minds closed.

Haidt's findings, the result of a persuasive argument laid out in his book, *The Righteous Mind: Why Good People Are Divided by Politics and Religion,* are hard to accept about ourselves. While we can easily acknowledge partisan irrationality in others, virtually everyone is sure that his or her own political views are based on reason (I *know* mine certainly are!). But Haidt proves otherwise. Our reason is like a presidential press secretary, an inflexible defender of positions established elsewhere, in our cases by our pre-programmed intuitions.

To make his argument, Haidt points out that in modern Western societies most people have concluded that every individual should be free to do what he or she wants so long as it does not hurt others (a relatively new and radical idea, historically). But when he asked these fully modern people if it was acceptable to engage in cannibalism or commit one-time incest, they resisted by looking for an argument to justify their opposition to these social taboos. It did not matter to the subjects that no one was getting hurt or having his or her rights violated. It seemed to the subjects that these activities just had to be wrong; the unconscious self-appointed mission for the subjects was to find a reason why. The people in the study "seemed to be flailing around," writes Haidt, "throwing out reason after reason," even after each reason was proved not relevant. Intuition came first; reason, second. It's the same with our political ideologies, argues Haidt. We adopt our group or team position, then seek to justify it.[108]

One would think education would help, but it does not. Haidt shows that education usually does not make us more open-minded; it only makes us better able to defend our own intuitive positions. (This is why Haidt has been taking the lead in calling for greater intellectual diversity on university campuses.) It makes us better presidential press secretaries, more capable of arguing the party line. Viewed this way, education can actually make people more close-minded as students and scholars pile up facts to support their own arguments while presumptively dismissing opposing viewpoints.

Haidt theorizes that our brains are hardwired for group identity and defense through the process of human evolution. Humans are "groupish" says Haidt. We love to root for sports teams, wave the flag, bond in fraternities and join religions. Yes, evolution moved forward in time through each individual's pursuit of self-interest, but a strategic self-interest expresses itself in group interest, or what we routinely call "enlightened self-interest." Haidt uses the examples of bees operating in their hives as an example of group interest in nature. He suggests that humans are 90% selfish ape, and 10% communal bee.

As primitive humans began to congregate, "groups composed of true team players" were the most successful and nature rewarded us accordingly. This is good news in terms of our desire to rescue the American political system from selfish interests. If we can learn again to identify first as Americans, and second as progressives or conservatives, then we can use our groupish DNA for constructive common interests.[109]

Haidt's work, which does so much to demonstrate the irrationality of partisanship, has taken any rough edges off his own politics; knowing the biological tendencies has made him less partisan and more open to differences of opinion. Still, Haidt remains a self-described "liberal" nonetheless. He tells a funny story juxtaposed against the horrific 9/11 terrorist attacks. The violence against his country and its citizens aroused nationalistic feelings in Haidt that he found awkward and perplexing. Most bizarrely from his point of view, he had an urge to put an American flag bumper sticker on his car. Now, liberals just don't do this, says Haidt. In the university lot where he parked his car, the only vehicles with flags belonged to custodial or maybe administrative staff, but not faculty, who were almost all on the Left. People on the Left "think globally;" they are most concerned about "the fate of the planet." Flag-waving is obviously nationalistic, and nationalism leads to all kinds of trouble, according to liberals like Haidt. Still, he really wanted that American flag bumper sticker. He resolved the dilemma of his competing groupish impulses by putting an American flag sticker on one side of his bumper and a UN flag on the other.

Conservatives hear a story like this and think, "how pathetic." Conservatives wave the flag every chance they get and with great satisfaction pledge allegiance to it, and "to the republic for which it stands, one nation, under God, indivisible, with liberty and justice for all."

I will go out on a limb and suggest that the chasm between how people on the Left and Right view the American flag suggests both a source of our division and an opportunity. Citizens on the American Left obviously have a weaker group identity as Americans than do citizens on the Right. They identify strongly with their progressive politics, by sub-groups such as gays, feminists, environmentalists, etc., and by their roles as global citizens. It's not that they don't love their country, but it's difficult for them to embrace a national heritage that in their minds is characterized by so much race, class and gender oppression, as well as regular aggressions against other peoples and the environment. The America portrayed by left-wing "historians," such as Howard Zinn, is eminently unlovable, and Zinn's *A People's History of the United States* has sold over two million copies.[110]

The good news for progressives who want to get the corrupting influence of money out of politics is that conservatives are not hopelessly partisan. As they say in the Pledge of Allegiance, they really do see us as "one nation, under God, *indivisible*." Some progressives might take issue with the "under God" part, but the message should be clear: conservatives genuinely feel that we should be united in sentiment as one people around our founding principles. The progressive depiction of a nation torn apart by race, class and gender is anathema to them. They want unity. To convince a conservative, appeal to our shared identity as Americans.

Dr. Ben Carson, one of the most socially conservative of Republican candidates running in the 2016 presidential campaign, stressed the point again and again. When asked what is the most important issue, he was likely to say, "the divisiveness that's going on in our nation, that's creating a war between everybody."[111] Appeal to conservatives as fellow Americans dedicated to restoring James Madison's vision, and the conservative brain centers that cherish their Americanism will start firing big time.

Please note, no one is claiming that the principled debate between conservatives and progressives on the appropriate size and role of government is by any means irrelevant or unimportant. Far from it. Principled progressives and conservatives cannot be expected to give up their most sacred values, nor should they. But where we can agree is that *principles* and not *selfish interests* should guide public policy. We have it in ourselves to work together for our common good, if we can overcome the partisan myopia rooted in our evolutionary psychology and inflamed by self-serving interests in politics and media. So how do we make it happen?

◇◇◇

Recall that my initial approach to political reform had two major elements. First I tried to recruit balanced teams on the Left and Right of credible leaders who could serve as unofficial representatives of progressive and conservative grassroots constituencies. Second, from polling data and endless personal anecdotal evidence, I surmised that the American people had arrived at a consensus about what needs to be accomplished, generally, to clean up our political system: Americans want term limits on members of Congress, in order to discourage political careerism, and they want to get the corrupting influence of money out of politics. I was trying to recruit leaders on the Left and Right who would acknowledge this consensus and work together toward fulfilling the wishes of the American people. Seven years later, I remain convinced that the approach is essentially a sound one.

Political reform requires a group of political leaders, balanced on the Left and Right, to do the work of crafting reforms, including ordinary legislation and almost certainly a comprehensive anti-corruption amendment to the US Constitution. This ideologically balanced wonky leadership team also needs to formulate and implement a political strategy for enacting these measures. This Left-Right leadership team would be constructed along the lines suggested by Jonathan Haidt and the advocates of deliberative democracy. As Haidt writes, "If you put individuals together in the right way, such that some individuals can use their reasoning powers to disconfirm the claims of the others, and all individuals feel some common bond or shared fate that allows them to interact civilly, you can create a group that ends up producing good reasoning as an emergent property of the social system."

One study showed that when groups of six, including two sets of three with strongly opposing views, were compelled to collaborate, views moderated and each side's command of information became more accurate. As James Surowiecki reports in his enlightening book, *The Wisdom of Crowds*, "non-polarized groups (by this he means groups with balanced viewpoints) consistently make better decisions and come up with better answers than most of their members, and surprisingly, often the group out-performs even its best members."[112] This is the objective to be aimed at by creating a balanced team of conservative and progressive leaders and policy wonks.

As Peter Schweizer rightly emphasized to me, a diplomatic temperament among the leaders is also important. Rigid partisan bomb throwers could potentially blow up the whole negotiation. But even an ideologically balanced and even-tempered leadership team is not enough.

Let's think back to the theoretical principles established by the ancient Greeks and admired by James Madison and the other founders. Public decision making works best through a division of labor between wisdom and virtue, or put another way, between brains and hearts. The reform of the American political system must be a collective act of the American people, and therefore the people themselves must play an essential role in the process.

This is exactly the course James Madison and his fellow founding fathers followed. After they drafted the would-be US Constitution, they didn't merely send it on to the state governments for ratification. Instead, they called for conventions of the people in every state to approve the Constitution. At the time, these conventions were the most democratic bodies ever assembled for any meaningful purpose, let alone tasked with approving the fundamental laws of a burgeoning nation. Utilizing large state conventions allowed citizens to be represented as directly as possible at the time and helped circumvent the politically ambitious class who would naturally be gathered in the state assemblies.

At the state ratifying conventions, approval of the Constitution was touch and go and was only narrowly accepted by the people. The citizens of America grudgingly approved the new Constitution, with caveats. Many delegates were alarmed that the proposed Constitution did not explicitly guarantee their liberties. While the framers understood any power not expressly given to the federal government to be unlawful, the people gathered in their state conventions nevertheless called for a series of amendments to insure the rights of citizens against a potentially oppressive government. Out of respect for the wishes of the people, the first US Congress, under the leadership of James Madison, drew up and passed the first ten amendments to the Constitution, which ultimately became known as our Bill of Rights.

So, in fact, the adoption of the Constitution involved a dialogue and a process between two classes of citizens that can be understood several different ways: as leaders and the people, brains and hearts, or 18th century policy wonks and ordinary folks. First, Madison and the other framers drafted the Constitution. Second, the people meeting in convention approved it with changes. Third, leaders in Congress made the changes requested by the people. It was a back-and-forth process between leaders and the people. Today we have the ability to recreate this successful process, and in the 21st century we are fortunate to have tools at our disposal to make it even more effective.

First, however, we probably need to rethink the relative strengths of the people and the leaders since the American founding. There's no doubt that the founders were elitists. Their society was very hierarchical; it was a system in which ordinary folks were expected to defer and tip their hats to their betters. Yes, the founders were theoretically committed to the ideas that all men were created equal and that the system must rest on the will of the people, but as we all know, women and slaves were denied rights, which strikes us, in our time, as extremely unjust. The founders also had little faith in the capacity of the average person to make judicious political decisions. They believed that the people needed to be led by the best and brightest among them, and that the rest should know their place and follow. So in the partnership between elites and ordinary people, the founders would put the elites in the driver's seat.

In their time, it was not an unreasonable choice. Information of any kind, let alone accurate information, was in short supply for ordinary people. Formal education beyond grammar school was rare, books were precious items, newspapers were partisan and hard to find outside of the major towns, and relatively few people had time to read even if they knew how. No doubt many people relied on a single perspective, uttered by a member of the clergy on Sunday morning from the church pulpit, for their view of the world. For people living in what was largely a rural society, the information sources simply weren't to be found even if one had the time, ability and desire to learn more about the world. Deferring to those who were worldlier was a perfectly rational choice for ordinary 18th century Americans.

But are elites really smarter than the mass of the people? And if they were in the 18th century, is it still true today? James Surowiecki, who has closely examined the body of research, argues emphatically, no. He concludes that the collective wisdom of large groups and whole societies is usually greater than that of any one person or small group of experts, and is always greater over time.

A large group, when estimating how many marbles are in a jar or how much something weighs, will usually outperform the expert. An expert may beat the crowd once, but he or she will not do so consistently. "If you put together a big enough and diverse enough group of people and ask them to make decisions on matters of general interest, that group's decisions will, over time, be intellectually superior to the isolated individual, no matter how smart or well-informed he is," concludes Suro-wiecki.[113] "The crowd" he says, "is holding a nearly complete picture of the world in its collective brain."[114] Surowiecki goes on to suggest that four conditions characterize wise crowds.

First, there must be a diversity of opinion, because diversity removes or weakens "the destructive characteristics of group decision making." Even if one is sure that one opposing side is poorly equipped to solve the problem, the mere presence of alternative points of view will cause the smartest participants to perform better than they would alone. Diversity of opinion is especially important for small groups in avoiding groupthink, where dissent is not so much suppressed but made to seem somehow impossible (this is exactly what is happening at virtually all of America's existing political reform organizations).

The second quality in successful group decision making is that there must be independent judgment among the members. This is a tough one in politics, because conservatives and progressives are already organized into tribes set up to maintain orthodoxies. A lack of independence can lead to what Surowiecki calls an "information cascade," a phenomenon that can bring out the worst in group decision making, like when speculators inflate a stock market bubble until it inevitably bursts. In these cases, group members do not follow their independent judgement but instead follow those around them, led by a few influential people. In politics, this is how demagogues rise to power.

Third, there must be decentralization, which brings in points of view from outlying perspectives. Decentralizing infuses specialized opinions into the mix, that might be relevant but are not typically consulted. It also encourages the application of "tacit knowledge," which is based on long and general experience not easily conveyed to others.

Fourth, and critically, the information must be aggregated. After some disaster we usually learn that the information that could have averted or mitigated the bad outcome was already in the system, but this information never got to the decision makers. Diversity, independence and decentralization are useless unless the valuable information produced by these healthy group characteristics can be aggregated and used.

Our job, as citizens who want our political system to work better, is to develop ideas that will promote diversity of opinion, independence, decentralization and aggregation in decision making, first to a political movement that will effectively reform the American system of government and elections, and ultimately, to the political system itself. In other words, our movement should model the very same qualities we want to see in the political system we wish to reform. Surowiecki's concepts seem like a good place to start.

As one citizen representing a very small, practically unfunded organization, I could only surmise from limited polling data and everyday conversation that a popular consensus exists for congressional term limits and a new clean elections system, and that it made political sense to assemble what appear to be the favorite reforms of the Right and Left, respectively, into a single package. Nothing in my experience has changed my view that these goals reflect the collective wisdom of the American people, and that the strategy is sound, but only a formal public opinion survey process can prove the point. And that requires money.

Ralph Nader admits that he has become a little obsessed with the idea of a billionaire or two, or more, saving America. He's got a chapter in his book, *Unstoppable,* entitled "Dear Billionaire." Nader is right to suggest the potential of just one or two members of the super-rich to come to our collective rescue. Five-hundred-thirty-six of the world's billionaires reside in the United States. Any one of these individuals could change everything.

The first step is the funding of a public opinion diagnostic test to establish whether a popular consensus exists about reforming our political system. No one, no matter how wealthy, is eager to throw money away. Millions and millions of dollars have already been flushed away on various political reform schemes. All that is required to test the feasibility of a national bipartisan reform movement is some relatively inexpensive public opinion research and a professional and ideologically balanced team to create the study. It should have at least two elements: first, a traditional public opinion telephone survey, and second, a series of focus groups balanced by progressives and conservatives.

The focus groups could take several different forms. Some could be made up of ordinary citizens on the Left and Right, but others should be populated with political activists. Some groups could employ professional mediators, others not, to get a sense of how much might happen spontaneously once a movement got rolling.

Winning over the activist class on both sides is essential. Currently, the political communications system begins at the top with the political parties and their allies in the media and the professional punditry. They, in turn, influence the citizen activists, who have influence over their concerned but less politically active neighbors. The professional political class has a self-interest in the status quo. They will always come up with a reason why progressives and conservatives must remain mutually hostile, or why any reasonable compromise is unacceptable. Therefore, the messaging of the political class must be interrupted at the citizen-activist level. It's up to us to block out the partisan noise generated by the self-interested professional political class and media, work together, and rally our fellow citizens in a united effort.

The sole purpose of this diagnostic first step is to lay the groundwork for a great common ground Left-to-Right alliance to fix our political system. There are no shortcuts. We must proceed methodically by crafting a well-designed campaign and laying a strong foundation for an enduring national movement. The initial public opinion diagnostic will reveal one of three things: 1) an existing bipartisan consensus for reform, 2) a potential bipartisan consensus for reform achievable through a campaign of education and deliberation, 3) an unbridgeable partisan divide when it comes to political reform. My guess is that the results will fall somewhere between #1 and #2. Such a result will demonstrate the credibility of a wholly bipartisan approach to reform and begin to make possible the aggressive fundraising necessary to do the hardest thing in American politics, which is to amend the Constitution, a task made still more arduous since it's the entrenched and self-serving powers of the status quo interests that we wish to overcome. But overcome them we must.

Enlisting the vigorous participation of the public will be essential. Such fundamental change to our political system must be an act of the people. The people as a whole, however, while potentially excellent at choosing between alternatives, are less adept at creating the alternatives themselves. Ordinary people will be able to express quite clearly the goals they wish to see accomplished with a new reformed political system. I predict the goals will include 1) congressional term limits to promote citizen government instead of government by career politicians, 2) clean elections system in which elected leaders can no longer accept money or otherwise benefit from the same interests they regulate, 3) fair elections, without advantages for incumbents, particular political parties, or the wealthy, and 4) some kind of independent enforcement mechanism for the new system to insure that our elected leaders no longer have the authority to police themselves in cases where their interests collide with those of the general public.

We should continue to adhere to the classical model that includes a balanced wonky leadership committee to help establish the mechanisms of reform, and the people to establish the goals and approve the final Clean Government Amendment, before deploying it as the people's weapon against the entrenched status quo system and its defenders.

Therefore, the second step, assuming that our public opinion diagnostic test is favorable, is to deploy significant resources to foster a national popular deliberation about political reform that will express the will of the people in as many ways as possible. The practice of bringing teams of conservatives and progressives together can be radically expanded into communities all around the country and will be a healthy activity for its own sake. There can be informal discussion groups, book groups that study multiple perspectives, or potentially formal alliances between local Republican and Democratic committees (the parties at the national level will hate this). These groups can lobby their local governments in town meetings, city councils and county boards, to develop their own resolutions through deliberation, to express the will of the citizens they most closely represent. Such a practice is deeply rooted in American history and was used extensively in times of crisis during the run-up to the American Revolution and the Civil War. Likewise, state legislatures can pass similar resolutions, with the strong encouragement of the people they are supposed to represent.

Some groups will want to get down into some detail in support of specific term limits or a particular type of clean elections system, which is fine, but also difficult and not necessary. Choosing the general *objectives* for a comprehensive clean government amendment to the Constitution will be sufficient for this phase. The story of the ongoing discussion and the parade of resolutions will help keep the campaign in the public eye − along with a robust advertising campaign.

Citizens would also be directed to a web site, where they could choose from a list of reform objectives or add their own, sign up as volunteers, or donate funds.

Another way to keep reform in the news, and to make progress along the way, is to do as Peter Schweizer urges, and immediately pursue some obvious reforms (the "no brainer" reforms) legislatively, such as banning campaign contributions from government contractors, prohibiting campaign contributions from lobbyists or forbidding incumbent fundraising while Congress is in session (see pages 162-164). Pursuing these or other reforms together as progressives and conservatives will build trust, and success will help maintain forward momentum.

After some predetermined period of time, at least one year and maybe two, all the information would be aggregated from the web site, the local government resolutions, polling data, and focus groups, which in total would clearly express the will of the American people, specify the problems with our political system that they want solved, and set forth the *objectives* for a comprehensive clean government amendment to the US Constitution (assuming that the public concludes that ordinary legislation is inadequate to the task).

With all the data in hand, our leadership committee of policy experts, scholars, and high-profile activists, balanced on the Right and Left, would craft the constitutional amendment, which we can call *The Clean Government Amendment.* The committee would construct a proposed mechanism capable of achieving the reform objectives laid down by the American people to be built into the amendment. The committee would also likely choose to back some of the "no brainer" reforms mentioned above, which can be pursued legislatively.

Populating the leadership committee is a tricky proposition. An election might produce a committee with the wrong temperament, and an election process would be cumbersome and time consuming. I was working on a "team captain" approach, in which one credible leader on each side would choose his or her own team. Each team should include members with 1) a diplomatic and collaborative temperament, 2) standing in his or her own ideological community, and 3) policy expertise.

Selecting the two team captains, or maybe pairs of captains, for the committee, might be accomplished by the board of directors. As we have seen, just as in political campaigns for office, funders of political reform groups are a source of corruption. They can prevent the organization from doing what is right and necessary. It won't come easy for those who write the checks, but they would need to understand from the outset that they are investing in a collaborative process between progressive and conservative leaders, activists and policy wonks, who are the ideological stakeholders, who would in turn engage in a dialogue with the American people and together with the people create the solutions. The funders must support the model rather than call the shots.

Once the committee has completed a draft of the Clean Government Amendment, it would be vetted and voted on by the people via the internet. Final approval of the amendment draft should require supermajority support of 67% from both progressive and conservative communities and should require the voluntary participation of 1% of the voting population, which is close to the round number of one million voters. Voters will self-identify ideologically or they might be asked a series of litmus test questions. My view is that there are too few centrists in the country to form their own group and that it's better to make everyone choose the Right or the Left, but if our public opinion data suggests a strong demand for centrists or moderates, then they can form their own third category. The essential point is that each grouping gets a veto over the final products, and that the so-called "moderates" are not allowed to outvote one end of the political spectrum by allying with the other. The ultimate product must be the result of a consensus.

Voting protocols need not be especially strict since fraud is only meaningful in close elections, while we are aiming for supermajorities. An e-mail address combined with a physical address should suffice for voting. Voters would obviously have the choice of approving or rejecting the proposed amendment. There should also be an opportunity for voters to propose specific changes, which could be aggregated on the site. It might be possible for everyone voting to review a list of the leading proposed changes and vote on these as well. It should be understood going in that the amendment will likely go through a vetting process that involves it moving back and forth from its drafting committee to the people via the Web.

Keep in mind that this admittedly elaborate process assumes that Americans will decide on the need for a comprehensive Clean Government Amendment to the Constitution and is designed to make the amendment as strong as possible. Currently, proposed constitutional amendments are drawn up in back rooms by political insiders. Creating the strongest possible constitutional amendment through a popular process is of critical importance and may require some patience. It's critical because we propose to reform the fundamental law of the United States for all time. Altering the structure of the system will change everything, perhaps forever and presumably for the better. We must get this right.

Getting the amendment right is also critical because we will be deploying it as a political weapon that we must use to dislodge our nation's entrenched political establishment. The final amendment must not only fix the broken system, but it must contain so much common sense that no politician would dare oppose it (though we know that many, with more ambition than common sense, will oppose it anyway). We will need to do the seemingly impossible: vote incumbent status quo politicians out of office.

There are essentially two ways to pass a constitutional amendment. First, the way it's always been done, is through Congress. Two-thirds of both houses of Congress are required to pass the amendment on to the states. Note here that Congress will want to monkey with our amendment. They'll want to change it to benefit themselves or to protect a partisan interest. Here is one of the political reasons that our Clean Government Amendment must be the product of a highly deliberative process involving large numbers of citizens, and why we want supermajority support from both sides. We must make it impossible for incumbent politicians to justify altering the amendment to serve their own ends.

After passage in Congress the amendment goes out to the states, where three-quarters of the legislatures, or state ratifying conventions called for that purpose, must approve it for ratification.

The second way to amend the Constitution is through an Article V Convention, in which two-thirds of the state legislatures call a convention to amend the Constitution. This approach has never been tried, though an Article V convention was threatened during the run-up to the 17th Amendment, which led to the direct election of senators. With the handwriting on the wall, Congress caved and passed the amendment before the convention was called.

An Article V Convention is not like the founding convention that took place in Philadelphia in 1787. We would be amending the Constitution, not recreating it. An Article V convention cannot be a "runaway convention," as is sometimes feared, because whatever that convention produces must be ratified by three-quarters of the states, either through their own conventions or through the state legislatures. The states are still evenly enough divided between Republicans and Democrats. Nothing new is going into the Constitution without a broad-based popular consensus.

Currently there are a number of efforts afoot to call a Constitutional Convention for various purposes: to reverse *Citizens United*, enact term limits, add a balanced budget amendment, and so on. I believe the real danger is that most proposals will run aground on partisan interests whether before or at the convention, or at the state level, or that we would end up with a partial or incomplete solution that will only serve to discourage and sour the public on the process. It makes a lot more sense to decide as a nation what it is that we want to do before we start doing it. A fully fleshed-out, popular, comprehensive Clean Government Amendment to the Constitution that is the product of a national deliberation can be the political engine that pulls us to a Constitutional Convention as permitted under Article V.

The founders left us a very conservative process for amending the Constitution. Changing our founding document is hard to do and undo. Unfortunately, the specifics are not spelled out about how the various conventions called for in the Constitution would work. How would delegates be selected, and how many of them would there be for both the federal and the possible state conventions? No one knows, so this process, when and if it approaches, requires thought and monitoring to ensure that the outcomes are produced by the people and not the interests. The convention or conventions, as the founders intended, must be strictly popular in nature.[115]

Once the constitutional amendment is written, the American people will have "weaponized" reform. That is, reform will have been turned into a political weapon that can be deployed against status quo politicians. Because of the critical role that states play in both constitutional amendment processes, the Left-Right teams will have to vet both state and federal office seekers to make certain that clean government candidates who support our amendment are elected at all levels of government. In other words, support for our Clean Government Amendment must become an issue in every state and federal election.

The tactical model is similar to what was used during the Progressive era, when there were "progressive" Republicans and "progressive" Democrats. The added word," progressive," suggested agreement on a set of issues that transcended the usual debate between the two parties. Similarly, we would have "clean government" Republicans and "clean government" Democrats that we can put up against status quo politicians of both parties in primary elections.

Now let's see if we can poke some holes in the soundness of the process I am suggesting. What might go wrong with it?

First, *the partisanship may be too powerful to overcome.* If so, this barrier will be revealed in our first step, the diagnostic test, which would limit the amount of time and money wasted. Even if partisans can't agree on a constitutional amendment, it seems impossible that there would be any significant resistance to at least some of our no-brainer reforms, like banning campaign contributions from government contractors. If progressives and conservatives, together, accomplished only that one reform, it would justify the initial investment in effort and resources.

Second, *the Clean Government Leadership Committee might produce a flawed amendment.* Since the process includes a vetting by the public with support from supermajorities of both progressives and conservatives, it's likely that the final product will be very strong. An initially weak leadership committee would slow the process down, but a back-and-forth dialogue between the committee and the people would eventually reflect the wisdom of society-at-large.

Third, *the entrenched interests might not yield and the power of incumbency would make the removal of enough status quo politicians too difficult to pass an amendment.* It seems unlikely that even entrenched incumbents could indefinitely resist upwards of 67% of the public mobilized to support a Clean Government Amendment. But in the event that we can't remove sufficient status quo politicians in Washington, we would have the option of working at the state level to call a Constitutional Convention. Incumbency is much less powerful at the state level in most states. Or both paths can be pursued simultaneously.

Fourth, *maybe the obstacles are all the above.* If fixing the system is impossible today, maybe it won't be impossible five, or ten or twenty years from now. Maybe some awful disaster must strike the United States first in order to mobilize our people into action. In that case, we must organize now and be ready with the solution when the time comes.

There's no question that the process outlined above is going to take some time and money – just how much time and money is impossible to say. The abolitionists and women's suffragists never bothered to ask such questions; they simply went to work to change the system because it was the right and necessary thing to do. So it must be with us. We do have some distinct advantages over these other great campaigns. First, and most significantly, whether we realize it or not, we are far more united as a people in our desire to see political reform than 19th century Americans were to free the slaves or give women the vote. We also have the internet and social media to help us organize public participation and aggregate feedback. On the negative side, the issues we must address are more complex than the questions of slavery and women's suffrage, and we must overcome political interests that have unjustly entrenched themselves in power through the very system we wish to reform. Whatever the strengths and weakness we face as a result of our current situation, we Americans have a job to do, and we need to get started.

Summary of a Clean Government Amendment Creation and Ratification Process

1. Conduct a relatively low-cost diagnostic public opinion survey to establish the feasibility of a true bipartisan movement to reform the American political system. Answer the question: Is there a bipartisan consensus or potential consensus for political reform, and what is it?
2. Launch a nationwide Left-Right dialogue about political reform through city, town and country resolutions, reading groups, and online. Target the progressive and

conservative activist class. On the web, vote on the *objectives* (ends rather than means) to be achieved in a Clean Government Amendment to the US Constitution. Test the popularity of various commonsense, or "no brainer," reforms that can be passed legislatively. This process will take one to two years.

3. A Clean Government Leadership Committee will draft a constitutional amendment based on the *objectives* revealed through the popular process in step #2, above. The draft will be submitted to the American people via the internet for bipartisan approval. Approval of the amendment language will require the participation of one million citizens and the approval of at least 67% of all progressives and 67% of all conservatives. If these thresholds are not achieved, the amendment will be returned to the Clean Government Leadership Committee for changes and re-voted on, until at least 67% of voters on both the Left and Right approve the final draft. Pursue commonsense, "no brainer" reforms that can be passed legislatively at the same time.

4. Deploy the Clean Government Amendment in elections throughout the United States. Remove status quo politicians – both Republicans and Democrats – who do not support the Clean Government Amendment.

5. Send the amendment on to the states either by first:
   a. Passing the amendment in Congress (two-thirds from each chamber required), *or*
   b. Holding a Constitutional Convention called by the states as permitted under Article V, and pass the amendment in convention.

6. Ratify the amendment by approving it in three-fourths of the nation's state legislatures or possibly in state conventions

10: Answering the Question

S o, what would Madison Do? The question can be answered in one sentence:

James Madison would have us remove every incentive in the American political system that encourages service to narrow, special, and selfish interests at the expense of the common good.

Here is the essential and uncontroversial principle around which James Madison would construct all political reform. Less generally, in chapters three and four, we saw that Madison would call for a system of congressional term limits, to reduce or even eliminate the desire for re-election that causes elected officials to cater to narrow and short-term interests at the expense of the nation. Madison would also think it madness that we permit elected officials to accept money or other rewards from the same interests they regulate; he would insist upon a clean elections system for the United States. To these, he would add other reforms and mechanisms, to make our government far more judicious than it is today.

Beyond the general principles, it's up to us to create the reforms and mechanism necessary to revive Madison's vision, which leaves us with many questions and choices. I am going to suggest two reform programs, either of which could be incorporated into a Clean Government Amendment to the US Constitution. Please note that these are only *suggestions*. One person will not have all the answers. The best solutions will appear as a product of a negotiation balanced between the Left and Right, and processed up and down, between policy wonks and people, along the lines described in the previous chapter.

The first solution I call the "Minimum Madison Amendment;" it's the least James Madison would have us do and is consistent with what I believe is the current popular consensus on political reform. The second program I'll call the "Maximum Madison Amendment," which is a far more radical application of Madisonian principles.

◊◊◊

The Minimum Madison Amendment

Minimum Madison starts with congressional term limits and a new clean elections system for the United States. Congressional term limits, a concept Madison supported in the Virginia Plan and at the founding Constitutional Convention, is the most straightforward.

As pointed out earlier, today public support for term limits is clearer and stronger than for any other reform. Supermajorities support congressional term limits, with the most reluctant group, Democrats, 55% in favor even when their party controls Congress. The debate about the proper length of the limits has ranged from three terms to six terms (6-12 years) in the US House of Representatives. For the Senate, most everyone seems to believe that a two-term limit (12 years) is appropriate. Some critics think six years is too little in the House and others are alarmed that a House member who turns around and runs for the Senate might have an eighteen to twenty-four-year career in Congress, which is too much. A good and sensible alternative that addresses both concerns is an overall twelve-year limit in Congress, which could all be spent in one chamber or split between the two. It's easy to imagine this as the consensus opinion on term limits.

Term limits are relatively easy to write into a constitutional amendment, but not so a new clean elections system for the United States. Recall all the different possible clean election solutions mentioned in Chapter 4: 1) a small dollar-matching system, 2) a system in which every voter receives a voucher worth a given sum to be spent on candidates of the voter's choosing, 3) a blind trust through which private campaign contributions must pass, 4) free media for candidates, 5) public funding of political parties, or 6) some combination of the above.

Which solution(s) should we choose? With each solution come more questions. In the case of a matching system, how do we adjust for districts with more expensive media markets? In the case of vouchers, how much should they be, how are they redeemed, and can the voter spend the entire voucher on one candidate or must it be spread around? If a blind trust, how will it operate so we can trust it? If free media, how is it distributed, how is it paid for, and which media are required to participate? If parties are to be funded, would there be regulation on how they can spend the public money they are given, and who writes these regulations?

Reasonable answers might be developed for all of these questions, and still more questions, but how can the new and necessarily complicated clean elections system ever be written into the Constitution? The amendment would have to go on and on like no other.

And what if we choose the wrong clean elections system, with some fatal flaw? Or maybe we create a reasonable system today, but circumstances change so that it no longer works fifty or one-hundred-and-fifty years from now? We certainly don't want to lock in a bad system that can only be changed through another amendment. This begs the question: can our solution be flexible?

Finally, one big question haunts the entire discussion. Who can we trust to implement and enforce a new clean elections system for the United States? Surely it is not those who are elected to public office. Self-policing on the part of our elected leaders has clearly not worked up until now and should be a non-starter for any new system. How do we answer all these questions in the context of an amendment to the Constitution?

A single constitutional, structural and authentically Madisonian solution could solve the riddle. To help restore James Madison's vision for judicious lawmaking, the United States requires a powerful independent watchdog and administrative body to ensure that the *objectives* of the proposed amendment are met. We could call it "The Clean Government Commission." Here is a sketch of what it might look like:

The Clean Government Commission, consisting of a bipartisan, or ideologically balanced, group of policy experts and investigators, *would regulate in all instances where Congress has inherent conflicts of interest.* Madison wrote that legislators are necessarily their own judges and juries when they write and pass legislation, but surely they are much more so when that legislation affects them directly and personally, as in cases of establishing rules and systems that involve their own potential re-elections, future employment, congressional salaries, pensions and other benefits. In all these instances, the current authority of self-regulation should be removed from Congress and placed exclusively in the hands of the commission.

The commission should be made up of members in proportion to the ideological tendencies among the people. Today I would argue that there are only two such tendencies: progressive and conservative. We are increasingly a politically bipolar nation. Others might want to add independents or centrists, which would be workable as well. In the future we could conceivably be divided into three or more ideological zones. The essential principle when it comes to governing the commission is that majorities from each ideological grouping on the commission must approve any action or new regulation. A commission of twenty-four could be divided into two to four ideological groups, with no group being too small. For convenience and clarity, I will use word "bipartisan" to describe the commission or any committee with a similar purpose, with the understanding that what I mean is "politically balanced and representative of the major ideological groupings in the country."

Among its duties, the commission would create a clean elections system for the United States. It would be free to choose among the existing clean election models, adopt new models, and make adjustments going forward. It would have the power and flexibility to safeguard the American system of elections for all time, to keep them fair and discourage the influence of special interests.

To avoid the weaknesses of the current Federal Elections Commission, the Clean Government Commission could not be a creature of either of the elected branches of the federal government. That leaves the Supreme Court as the most logical guardian to protect the authority and independence of the new commission. There is precedence for the Supreme Court safeguarding election processes. The Court, after all, enforces the right to vote through the Fifteenth Amendment and the Voting Rights Act.

The Supreme Court, however, is neither universally loved nor trusted by the American people. Very few believe that it is always above politics.[116] While the Clean Government Commission could be part of the judicial branch, the members of the commission itself need not be chosen by the Court. Rather, they could be appointed by a bipartisan jury of ordinary citizens, which we can call the "Clean Government Citizens' Jury." As has been suggested, the American jury is probably the nation's most effective popular deliberative political institution. It can therefore be safely relied upon to choose the commissioners.[117]

The Clean Government Citizens' Jury could itself be chosen by lottery from diverse locations around the United States, with non-voters and those with close connections to politicians and political parties disqualified, to help filter out both the partisan and least civic-minded. The jury, like the commission it appoints, would have to be bipartisan, with balanced representation from every point on the political spectrum. Its principal task would be to carefully select fair-minded and expert representatives balanced from the nation's ideological tendencies to sit on the commission. A new jury would periodically convene to review the work of the old commission and appoint a new one. The mechanics of the selection processes for the jury and the commission would be administered by the Supreme Court.

To be independent of the elected branches of government, the commission's funding cannot be subject to congressional and presidential approval, as is the case with all other government expenditures. A radical but necessary innovation is required. The commission's budget could be subject to approval of the jury of citizens that appoints its members, and would therefore be financially independent of Congress; the legislative and executive branches would simply be constitutionally bound to accept whatever annual expenditure the jury of citizens that chooses the commission approves.

The Clean Government Commission would have deep but narrow powers to ensure that any corrupt government official is removed from office and prosecuted. So that it could never become a menace to the liberty of ordinary citizens, the commission's mandate would be focused not on the interests that naturally flourish in a free society, but almost solely on elected and appointed officeholders and other federal employees who might abuse the public trust. It could protect whistle blowers within the government and police bureaucracies against being captured by political or ideological interests.

Though it would be a significant innovation, the Clean Government Commission, to be effective, must have the power to check a potentially partisan or otherwise corrupt Justice Department in the event that the attorney general is tempted to enforce campaign and ethics laws in a partisan manner, or refuses to honestly investigate partisan or ethical abuses within the bureaucracy.

The Clean Government Commission (along with the Senate) might approve presidential nominations for attorney general, have the authority to monitor the enforcement of campaign and ethics laws within the federal bureaucracy, issue warnings and advisories to the attorney general, appoint special prosecutors, and remove any attorney general or FBI director from office for unequal enforcement of the law. Maybe the president should not be permitted to appoint the attorney general at all. Limiting or eliminating the president's role over the nation's administration of justice may seem like an extreme measure, but it would be a mild and painless reform compared to the prospect of politicized bureaucracy, which if permitted to exist, leads down the road to political repression.

This is of course what many conservatives believe has already happened in the Obama Justice Department in association with the IRS. Progressives who might be prone to dismiss the current accusation against the IRS may recall from history the politicizing of the FBI during the civil rights movement. The capture of a federal bureaucracy by ideological or political interests has happened before and can happen again. Even today progressives and conservatives alike are dismayed by the lack of prosecutions against white-collar criminal suspects associated with the banking crisis of 2008. A powerful bipartisan, or ideologically balanced, citizen-jury-appointed Clean Government Commission could help safeguard the right to equal justice for all citizens for all time.

A jury-like system is currently being utilized in California and Arizona, where the people have outlawed the practice of gerrymandering through a citizens' initiative process. California and Arizona now draw legislative districts using an independent and politically balanced citizens' commission selected though a lottery of applicants and ideologically balanced between Democrats and Republicans. The model, though more narrowly focused, is similar to our concept of a jury-appointed Clean Government Commission.

Before moving on to the subject of gerrymandering, however, the experience with Arizona's districting commission raises a warning flag for our proposed Clean Government Commission. In Arizona, a supposedly non-partisan districting commission is being accused of partisan bias. The US House districts there appear gerrymandered under the new commission system, which was specifically created to avoid just such an outcome.[118] Arizona's experience with its districting commission suggests that our Clean Government Commission will need a fail-safe against its inadvertent or manipulative capture of our supposedly non-partisan Clean Government Commission by partisan or other interests. Therefore, in the event that one-third of the commissioners believe that the commission as a whole is derelict in its duties in some way – perhaps maybe that it is corrupted by an interest or regulating in a partisan manner – then those commission members, consisting of at least one third, may summon the Clean Government Jury that appointed the commission in the first place, or call a new jury. The Clean Government Jury would then hear the case and be empowered to remove individual commissioners, replace the entire commission and/or issue instructions. Giving ordinary citizens ultimate authority over the commission is the best way to safeguard its integrity.

With regard to gerrymandering and districting reform, Californians and Arizonans have chosen to cut their new legislative districts based on "communities of interest," which creates racial, ethnic, and economically homogeneous districts. Madison, while he would probably approve of the jury-like approach of drawing districts by commission, would likely prefer economically and culturally diverse districts to discourage elected officials from representing narrow interests. Any federal gerrymandering reform will run up against civil rights issues and the desire by some to maintain a number of predominantly African-American districts. The Commission could address the questions of how long such districts are necessary or desirable, and what benchmarks need to be achieved before racially-drawn congressional districts are eliminated. Surely this practice should not go on forever.

Though it's never been tried, automation would be a guarantee against human bias in the drawing of congressional districts. Using a mathematical formula (a split-line algorithm), states can be divided into equal-sized legislative districts by repeatedly cutting chunks of population into halves until the desired number of districts is reached.[119]

If the Clean Government Commission is to regulate all instances in which members of Congress have an inherent conflict of interest, then it would obviously establish congressional salaries, pensions and other compensation. Madison advocated that no Congress be permitted to raise its own salary and that pay raises should only be authorized by the previous Congress. This would theoretically give the voters a chance to consider the decision at election time. Today a member's salary is $174,000 (higher for leadership positions), with pay raises on autopilot, though Congress has lately been freezing its pay and thus declining the automatic cost-of-living adjustments. A fundamental question to be considered is whether congressional pay should mirror that of other federal positions with comparable responsibilities or whether congressional pay should be tied to the median salary in the United States, plus compensation for the unique housing and travel expenses associated with the position. If being a member of Congress is a profession, then paying members based on comparable federal salaries is appropriate. But if serving in Congress is a public service in which empathy with the typical citizen is useful, then perhaps tying congressional pay to the median salary of all Americans is a better choice.

Currently most members of Congress are millionaires and the wealth of these members tends to increase while in office.[120] During the last great recession, when median household wealth in the United States dropped 39%, most members of Congress enjoyed a 5% increase in their net wealth.[121] A clean elections system would help people of modest means get elected to Congress. Compelling members to put their investments in a blind trust while in office would end any trading on inside information, and tying salaries to the national median income, or to the median income in their own districts (plus housing and travel expenses) would all help Congress mirror the economic well-being of the people-at-large and discourage any self-dealing while in office. We are all probably better off if citizens unwilling to make such short-term personal sacrifices for their country are discouraged from running for public office. A willingness to make personal sacrifices is a mark of the sort of civic virtue we should want to see in our government.

We should also consider what former members of Congress make once they're out of office. Today congressional pensions vary significantly. A one-term senator today would receive a pension of $16,000 after age 62, but a senator who has been in office for thirty years will receive a pension of $125,000 at age 60. Under the current system of unlimited tenure in Congress, a generous pension might be a reasonable substitute for salaries collected by members who retire from Congress to pursue lucrative lobbying jobs, but today members collect both their pensions and salaries for wielding their influence as former members. Indeed, 50% of all senators become lobbyists, up from 3% in 1974, according to Mark Leibovich, author of the darkly hilarious book, *This Town*, about the insular, self-serving, and power-seeking culture of Washington, DC. Since even most professions no longer offer pensions, it's hard to justify such a reward for a position in Congress that is supposed to be temporary public service.[122]

Regulating the revolving door between industry and elected office is another jurisdiction appropriate to an independent body like our Clean Government Commission. First, it is an area where the conflict of interests is obvious and congressional self-regulation therefore inappropriate. Second, the problem of revolving doors is complicated. On the one hand, government wants and needs people with experience from a variety of backgrounds. On the other hand, perhaps Secretary of the Treasury Jack Lew should not have been paid nearly a million dollars by his former employer Citibank *because*, in keeping with his Citibank contract, he took a "full-time high-level position with the United States government or regulatory body."[123] One might reasonably wonder just who Mr. Lew was actually working for. Getting the regulation of the revolving door between industry and government right requires a flexible agency capable of adjusting the policy over time as it seeks the right balance between attracting accomplished citizens from a variety of backgrounds into public service, yet safeguarding our government from capture by special interests.

An independent and powerful Clean Government Commission could also protect and support inspectors general, their investigations, and whistle blowers within the bureaucracy. In fact, inspectors general might be appointed by, and report to, the commission, rather than by the executive branch, which is currently the case. In 2013 State Department Inspector General Aurelia Fedenisn came forward to report that she was told to "back off" her investigation of possible criminal activity at the State Department involving drugs and prostitution. Since going public, she claims that she has been the subject of attempted intimidation.[124] There have also been charges of a culture of retaliation against whistleblowers at the scandal-prone Veterans Administration.[125] In 2015, the *Atlantic* reported the suspension of a USDA scientist allegedly for publishing a paper hypothesizing that a particular chemical used in commercial agriculture was killing monarch butterflies.[126] Inspectors general and whistleblowers are the public's only defense against corruption in the bureaucracy. Political appointees, who often have a selfish interest in assuring the public that everything is just fine in their various departments, simply cannot be relied upon to protect those professionals in government who expose abuse and risk retaliation in order to serve the public.

In summary, Madison would have government serve the broad and long-term good of the nation and its people rather than the narrow moneyed and political interests, which are guiding principles conservatives and progressives today can agree upon. The current incentive structures in our political system need to be reformed to make government more judicious through 1) congressional term limits, 2) a clean elections system, 3) an end to gerrymandering, 4) a regulation of revolving doors between government and industry, 5) safeguards to prevent the capture of the bureaucracy by corrupt moneyed or political interests.

The above objectives, taken individually, would likely be approved by a majority of citizens on both the Left and Right, with some progressives reluctant about term limits and some conservatives opposed to an end to private campaign financing. If bundled together as a take-it-or-leave-it package in the form of a constitutional amendment, however, public support would probably be near unanimous, which is the sort of political muscle we need to change the current entrenched system. In terms of policy, this combination of reforms represents a comprehensive bulwark against the capture of the system by selfish interests; it is the sort of approach James Madison would approve. The challenge arises in the enforcement of those systems; the foxes cannot be allowed to guard the hen house anymore. To solve the problem, a bipartisan, or ideologically balanced, citizen jury can regularly select a bipartisan, or ideologically balanced, Clean Government Commission of professionals, to serve as a sub-branch to the judiciary, which will actuate and enforce the objectives of the Clean Government Amendment and serve as the citizens' watchdog against those who would abuse the public trust.

The Maximum Madison Amendment

On the final day of the Constitutional Convention in Philadelphia, and for the first time during the entire convention, George Washington rose to speak on a substantive matter. The great hero of the Revolution used his prestige sparingly. A delegate from Massachusetts, Nathanial Gorham, had moved that congressional districts initially be made up of 30,000 inhabitants instead of the 40,000 that the delegates had written into the draft document of the Constitution. Now Washington finally spoke. He declared that he wholeheartedly agreed, arguing that the people, fearing the rise of an aristocracy, would feel more secure in their rights with the lower number of 30,000. James Madison joined with the other delegates to unanimously approve the change. The founders decided that a House district would initially comprise 30,000 people.[127]

The issue remained unresolved, however, because the Constitution did not put an upper limit on the size of congressional districts and left that question to be dealt with by Congress as the nation grew. Delegates called to the state conventions where the Constitution was to be ratified were alarmed that House district sizes might grow to be too large, and the people lose control of their government. To allay the many concerns of the delegates at the ratifying conventions, federalists led by Madison agreed to move to amend the Constitution as soon as it was ratified, including an amendment that would address the issue of district size.

Madison, serving his native Virginia as congressman after the ratification of the Constitution, drew up the first list of amendments that would form the basis of our Bill of Rights. Madison's first amendment was an elegant reminder that government was constituted by the people for their benefit, and that "the people have an indubitable, unalienable, and indefeasible right to reform or change their Government."[iv]

Madison's second amendment would have limited House district sizes to some yet undetermined population. Congress would debate what that proper ceiling was, which would vary from 30,000 to 60,000 inhabitants per district. Madison's second amendment would actually become the first proposed amendment – what we might call the "lost first amendment" – to be passed on to the states.

After the first enumeration required by the first Article of the Constitution, there shall be one Representative for every thirty thousand, until the number shall amount to one hundred, after which, the proportion shall be so regulated by Congress, that there shall be no less than one hundred Representatives, no less than

---

[iv] Madison's entire preamble can be found on pages 8-9.

> *one Representative for every forty thou-*
> *sand persons, until the number of Repre-*
> *sentatives shall amount to two hundred,*
> *after which the proportion shall be so*
> *regulated by Congress, that there shall*
> *not be less than two hundred Representa-*
> *tives, nor more than one Representative*
> *for every fifty thousand persons.*

Everyone understood that the intent in the original first amendment was to limit House district size, keep represen-tation popular, and prevent the lower house from becom-ing overly elitist. Unfortunately, the above language was apparently written in haste just before it emerged from a joint House and Senate conference committee. The word-ing here is nearly identical to the House language except for the underlined fatal difference – maybe the 18th Centu-ry equivalent of a typo – in which "less" became "more," twisting the meaning of the amendment entirely. So a flawed original first amendment that was supposed to limit House district sizes went on to the states. That it was the proposed first amendment suggests its importance.

Although the errant language caused some head-scratching and debate in state legislatures, it nevertheless passed in ten of the eleven states necessary for ratification at the time, but got no further. The faulty language was certainly one reason the amendment failed, but that could have been fixed by starting over. More importantly, there was a demographic time bomb in the whole notion. Ben Franklin had famously calculated a prodigious rise of the American population based on reproduction rates in his own time. Madison had done the math, too. Eventually the population of the United States was going to reach a point at which the House of Representatives was simply going to be too big and unwieldy.

The issue played out as the nation grew. By the 1840s,

congressional districts, then comprising 80,000 people, were already much bigger than the largest ones anticipated by the founders. But the size of the House of Representatives also grew. Congress, as required by the Constitution, reapportioned itself every ten years after the taking of the census, with the House of Representatives increasing each time until after 1910, when the total number of members reached 435. After 1920, the Congress declined to reapportion itself, which appears to be a violation of the Constitution.[128] In 1929 Congress officially locked in the 435 ceiling legislatively. Since that time the population has tripled, so that today each member of Congress represents, on average, about 700,000 constituents. If nothing changes in terms of House size and/or the population growth rate, one member of Congress will represent 1.4 million people by 2100. In *Federalist #52* Madison cautioned that the House of Representatives must always maintain "an immediate dependence on, & an immediate sympathy with the people." But is this possible with a citizens-to-representative ratio of 700,000 or a million to one?

There is no conspiracy here. While some founders, like Pennsylvania's James Wilson, anticipated a large House of Representatives, even one as big as 600 members, at some point either the country would have to split up into several smaller republics or House districts would have to grow to be far larger than the founding generation thought prudent. A House of Representatives consisting of thousands of members was simply impractical. Or at least it was until now, in the Information Age.

The founders started with nothing but their history and their imaginations before writing the U.S. Constitution and the various state constitutions. While they based new forms of government on established concepts, they broke irrational rules and thought outside the box. Do we have the smarts, will and confidence to do the same?

It is well known that modern telecommunications and information technologies are promoting democracy and liberty all over the world. Mostly, the democratic forces being unleashed by the internet are destructive in a literal sense: information is being put in the hands of ordinary people, permitting them to organize in efforts to bring down oppressive regimes. It's conceivably a *useful* destruction, but destruction's usefulness has limits. Positive and constructive use of information technology in politics is much more rare.

Currently, American political interests are using information technology to destroy their opponents and enhance their own political power. Data is mined and voters are micro-targeted with well-tested messages. The precise fundraising pitch is delivered to the precise micro-targeted group at exactly the right time. The well-tested hate messaging, designed to fire up the political base and marginalize political opponents, spreads like partisan infernos across the internet via social media. "Fake news" thrives and partisan talking points dominate the public discussion. It's all very effective politics but damages the nation's sense of civility and dumbs-down public understanding by making everyone more narrowminded and ideologically isolated. Information technology has also strengthened entrenched political interests by turning gerrymandering into a science, with voting tendencies measured city block by city block, creating the safest seat possible. None of this is constructive unless you are a politician set on maintaining or increasing your own power.

Does it have to be this way? Couldn't ordinary citizens use technology, not only to reform the system but to base part of a new system on that technology? The lost first amendment may point the way forward. Doesn't the information revolution, and technologies like video conferencing that put people together in the room virtually, permit us to return, radically, to our more democratic roots? Couldn't we once again have legislative districts of 30,000 inhabitants each? What would this mean for us and our republic?

The idea of reviving Madison's lost first amendment is not mine; it is the brainchild of another citizen activist, Jeff Quidam, with a website: thirty-thousand.org.[129] I have never met or spoken to Jeff, but we have exchanged e-mails and messages on Facebook. His work on this issue is evidence of the talent, creativity and civic-mindedness among the American people that could and should be harnessed for the public good in our government.

Limiting House district size to 30,000 inhabitants would be consistent with republican theory, which holds that the lower house in a bicameral system should be a mirror image of the people at large. What better way to accomplish this goal than to increase the House of Representatives to 10,000 (300 million divided by 30,000) and base them at home with their constituents? For the first time in the history of humanity, we could have this kind of democracy.

What are the implications? In theory, there'd be many advantages to a radical reform like this:

Very little money would be needed to run competitively for office. The entire district could be covered door-to-door on foot. Most of the importance of campaign fund-raising would be removed from the process.

Lobbyists would have a hard time establishing enough relationships to get anything done.

Incumbents would lose most of their advantages. Ordinary people – meaning people who are not rich, celebrities, or politicians themselves – would have an even chance of defeating an incumbent in such a small district.

Members of the lower house of Congress would continue to live among those they govern and be influenced by them instead of special and hopelessly partisan interests. The perils of Washington "groupthink" would be nearly eliminated.

Civic virtue and optimism among the American people would increase as a result of seeing government so much closer to home. It would be easy to talk with your member of Congress, rather than some congressional staff paid to make the member look good.

That's a pretty impressive list of pluses. What are the potential minuses?

Even with the use of information technology, collaboration among legislators won't be as easy as it is in person.

It might be difficult to organize so many members.

In theory, at least, the positives far outweigh the negatives. There is very little collaboration between members of Congress now, when they can easily meet in person. House members regularly speak to an empty chamber – so they speak to the C-Span television camera only. Committee hearings are increasingly pre-arranged partisan demonstrations designed more to score political points than gain real information. We are not losing much by moving all this activity into a virtual meeting space with a more numerous and diverse group of legislators running the show. Organizing members might not be that difficult as long as the parties maintain good leadership structures.

Some members would have to be in Washington frequently, including leadership teams who must negotiate with the president and the Senate. House members from various committees could occasionally gather together in person and meet at conferences, either in Washington or at various locations around the country.

We know that creative ideas emerge naturally from large and diverse groups. In the best-case scenario, with so many members of Congress, it would be possible to dramatically expand committee work. Many Americans have a sense that no one in Congress now really understands the operations of the vast government it is supposed to be overseeing. How could they, given that they spend a majority of their time running for re-election?

Regarding the workings of the US government, there is room for many specialists to learn how programs might function better. Ordinary citizens would roll up their sleeves and do this work eagerly. We know this to be true because volunteer citizen-legislators do this at the local level every day to good effect. Members of a radically expanded and democratized house could specialize like never before, with one an expert on an obscure set of worker safety regulations, like rules for a chemical plant, another on the process by which a certain group of pharmaceuticals, like statins, are approved, others on the situation of particular countries, from Albania to Zambia. Our government could conceivably become much smarter and much better supervised.

In the worst-case scenario, the 10,000-member House might be too unwieldly to produce much positive legislation. Responsibility for producing legislation and budgets might have to move to the Senate. But at a minimum, a radically decentralized and democratized House would likely be a very useful negative check on the foolish policies that regularly emerge from Washington. For example, it's hard to imagine the people acting through their 10,000 representatives approving out-of-balance federal budgets every year, or permitting FDIC-insured banks to gamble in the market, with the taxpayers underwriting any potential losses. A highly democratic House would not suffer from a lack of common sense, which, at the very least, could be applied in the negative to stop the worst ideas produced in Washington. More likely, the people would rise to the occasion, create innovative policies and revive American democracy through the new system.

Surely some scholars will argue that Madison was an elitist who would oppose this kind of radical democracy. Indeed, Madison expected that in sufficiently large districts, the leading citizens with outstanding public reputations would be elected to office. Today, we probably all know of fellow citizens within our towns, cities, and counties with such reputations who would make fine members of Congress, but those citizens who are actually elected are less well-known to us because they are probably not part of our neighborhoods. Going into any given election, most candidates don't really have reputations within our communities, as Madison wished them to have, but rather they have images created by money and media. In a community of 30,000, the degrees of separation are small and a citizen's public reputation through webs of personal relationships is knowable, but in a district of 600,000 to 700,000, we must rely on media-filtered images often shaped by the candidate himself. Yes, Madison wanted the best and brightest in office, but such people can be found in populations of 30,000 in which their public reputations are knowable through personal contact or a degree or two of personal separation.

Madison favored giving each of the two houses of Congress different qualities and temperaments as much as possible. Probably for this reason, he called for term limits in only one house. Therefore, as long as the character and temperament of the Senate contrasts with that of the House, term limits in a radically democratic and decentralized House might not be necessary. Steps could be taken, however, to ensure that House members continue to resemble their constituents. Salaries could be tied to the median income in their district and they should be denied personal staff; Washington-based committee staff would be available to assist with legislative work.

To help give the Senate the characteristics Madison wished it to have – wisdom, prudence, far-sightedness, caution, broadmindedness, dispassion – its members could be term-limited to one ten-year term only, which would result in a 20% turnover in the Senate every two years. Still stronger measures to insure against the baneful effects of government by career politicians could be applied. Would-be Senators might be prohibited from office if they have ever run for public office in the past and they could be prohibited from ever running for public office again after their ten-year term in the Senate expires. In this way, the nation would be guaranteed a Senate comprised of citizen-legislators and not professional politicians. Any type of fundraising would be strictly prohibited. The US Senate would, as closely as possible, resemble a citizen jury, yet still be subject to election. Senators would continue to be situated in Washington, where the old House office buildings could be converted to apartments for Senators and their families, to enhance their camaraderie. Let them work, study and deliberate intensely together, to provide for the Senate what a decentralized House might lack. Capitol Hill might become largely the campus of the Senate.

The Clean Government Commission, and all its potential functions mentioned above, would still have a role under the Maximum Madison plan. It would have many more members to watch over, but with members residing among the people and living normally as citizens, corrupt temptations would certainly be much diminished.

Madison and his fellow founding fathers applied their imaginations to existing and proven models when designing our republic. The Maximum Madison plan is a reflection of one of America's most cherished and respected political institutions: the New England town meeting.

Since puritan times a "board of selectman (now called a "select board" in our less sexist/more politically correct age) would spend months preparing the town warrant, consisting of all of the items to be voted on by the people of the town, who would gather one or more times per year in some public space. This old tradition is still practiced in its pure form in small towns throughout New England. In communities where populations have grown to make the gathering of whole towns impractical, town meeting members are now elected. Under the Maximum Madison Plan, our new US Senate could serve as a reflection of the old New England board of selectman, which could prepare the nation's warrant, and the 30,000 member House would mirror the people together gathered in town meeting. If a radically expanded House turns out to be a more creative and pro-active engine of government, and not just a body to approve or disapprove Senate actions, then so much the better. In either case, the concepts behind the Maximum Madison Plan is deeply rooted in American political tradition.

◊◊◊

If I could wave a magic wand to reform the political system of the United States, I would choose the "Maximum Madison" plan. But there are no magic wands. I hope that the Maximum Madison Plan fires imaginations, but as a first step it is too radical. We must climb the ladder of the possible by grabbing hold of the most realistic objectives first, with each step bringing us nearer to our ultimate objectives.

Conclusions

As someone who has worked for years to unite leaders on the Left and Right to address our decayed political system, I feel like a scout who has surveyed the territory. This book is my report back to you, my fellow citizens.

While it's true that many would-be "reformers" disappointed me, they are not villains. The bad actors were all off stage, or in front of the cameras, manipulating and pulling on the levers of power. And even the worst of these lobbyists, hacks, partisan-media-blowhards and politicians might be forgiven, because in the end they and their actions are all merely the inevitable products of our corrupted system, which encourages selfish behavior at the expense of the common good.

What my experience demonstrates is that America's reform leaders and organizations are plagued by exactly the same cancers that we all wish to see removed from our politics: selfish interests, debilitating partisanship, groupthink, and the controlling influence of money. That's the bad news. The good news is that it doesn't have to be this way if we diagnose the problem correctly and prescribe the right treatment.

I have called on James Madison to be our guide to help us reform our political system. Madison believed there was safety in a large republic, in which no single selfish interest would be powerful enough to become oppressive. Madison reassured his contemporaries that interests would check interests so that none could capture the government. Madison's theory, however, has collapsed under the weight of modernity and a big government capable of serving an endless parade of narrow interests that today serve themselves at the expense of the American people as a whole. Madison's vision for judicious government has been completely reversed.

It's not Madison's fault either. He and his fellow founding fathers could not possibly have foreseen our complex modern world and the powerful nation-state we have built to help manage it.

Amazingly, though, Madison did have prescience to recognize the political problem we now face. To Thomas Jefferson, he once privately revealed the hazard in his argument for a large republic. "As in too small a sphere oppressive combinations may be too easily formed angst. the weaker party," wrote Madison, "so in too extensive a one, *a defensive concert* (emphasis added) may be rendered too difficult against the oppression of those trusted with administration." Madison understood that a large, complex and diverse society could be more easily splintered into factions and manipulated by those in power, and that unified and coordinated measures, no matter how necessary, would be challenging. This is where we find ourselves today, in need of *concerted* action.[130]

The main problem is that too many of us don't see who or what the real enemy is. It would be easier in some ways if the nation were under attack from a foreign power. If that were the case, we'd immediately put aside our philosophical differences and rush to defend the country we love.

But the common enemy we face is more insidious, and

arguably more dangerous, than any foreign threat we have ever confronted. The real enemy is corruption by selfish interests, which destroy our republic a little bit more with each passing year. When the corruption becomes too much, so that the government foments another economic collapse or makes another catastrophic foreign policy blunder, rather than addressing the structural rot, we point our fingers at each other.

Again, this is not to dismiss the serious differences of opinion between the American Left and Right. Our philosophical disagreements about the size and role of government are substantial and important, to say the least.

Some conservatives will argue that if the federal government can be shrunk back down to the size envisioned by Madison, then corruption will correspondingly be reduced also. This notion, however, is wishful thinking. The power of the political class and the power of big government are symbiotic and have increased in tandem. The ability of the political class to raise money from interests and for its members to perpetuate themselves in office inevitably leads to new programs, government debt, tax loopholes, short-term thinking, and market corruptions that promote re-elections and political power at the expense of the long-term well-being of the republic. Reduce the power of the political class, change the incentives, and there's a chance to reduce big government. Keep the system as it is, and government will assuredly continue to grow.

Progressives engage in their own fantasies about reform. Some believe that if only enough progressive Democrats are elected, then these same politicians will reform the system by eliminating their own political advantages and privileges. Or maybe if enough progressive judges are put on the Supreme Court, they will decree a new reformed campaign finance system for the United States. None of this is realistic. Those with power will not willingly give it up and even the most activist judges imaginable cannot make the necessary changes. Meanwhile, a political system that caters to interests and not people undermines public faith in government and progressivism in general.

Neither progressives nor conservatives can achieve their goals as things stand now, which is why the system itself is the first thing that must be changed. And that means grassroots progressives and conservatives must form a provisional alliance against the status quo political establishment and the corrupt system on which it thrives.

The activity of progressives and conservatives working together will be good for its own sake. It will promote healing and civility in our communities and undermine the partisan interests whose first priority is serving themselves by demonizing others.

When it comes to reforming the system, I have argued that we should let James Madison point the way forward. Madison would have us remove each and every incentive in our political system that favors selfish interests over the common good. It is a simple, uncontroversial and yet profound guiding principle.

Next, what objectives must we achieve along the way? It should be obvious that we must remove the corrupting influence of money from our politics and discourage political careerism. It's hard to imagine us getting where we need to go without a new clean elections system for the United States and congressional term limits. These major reforms require a constitutional amendment. To follow Madison's advice will also mean many other changes, including a credible enforcement mechanism so that those who benefit from the system may no longer regulate it.

Even these seemingly obvious conclusions must be confirmed as a result of a national deliberation among our people. A successful political reform movement will itself model some of the qualities we wish to incorporate into our political system. It will be both democratic and bipartisan. We need both balanced bipartisan leadership and the active participation of the American people to overcome the formidable obstacles in our path.

Regardless of the hurdles we face, we can't stand pat on the rotting platform of our crumbling political system. We have a journey to make, together, so that government of, by and for the people − and not selfish interests − shall not perish, but be renewed in the spirit on which the United States of America was founded.

Postscript

O n January 20, 2017, Donald J. Trump was sworn in as the 45th President of the United States. It was – to say the least – a remarkable development.

In a blunt inaugural address, President Trump declared, "For too long, a small group in our nation's Capital has reaped the rewards of government while the people have borne the cost."

A *Wall Street Journal*/NBC poll later found that an overwhelming 86% of respondents from across the political spectrum agreed with Trump's assertion. Such a data point goes a long way to explain Trump's victory over Hillary Clinton, the consummate political insider whose tangle of dubious dealings reeked of corruption.[131]

But even if President Trump truly wants to "drain the swamp," as he says, he is such a divisive figure that it's nearly impossible to imagine Democrats supporting any of his initiatives.

Rather the Left's "resistance" will focus on the potential abuse of executive power by President Trump in the same way that the Right believes that President Obama unconstitutionally exceeded his authority. The great danger is that each side will refuse to police its own president and that presidents will become increasingly authoritarian, with each one playing a game of "pay back" against its predecessor of the other party. Indeed, progressives clearly have no more faith in President Trump's Justice Department than conservatives had in President Obama's. The result is a crisis of justice, as well as one of politics.

The abuse of executive authority involving such issues as selective prosecutions based on partisanship, executive orders, NSA surveillance, and war powers, are areas where citizens on the Left and Right generally agree in theory, but where extreme political polarization makes hypocrites of most everyone. And unlawful abuse of presidential power is yet another byproduct of Congress' abdication of its constitutional responsibility, which is to act as a check on the executive branch. Instead, the perpetual political campaign now takes precedence over virtually everything.

Is the United States descending into a kind of partisan death spiral? Almost all news has become "fake news," to one side or the other. Political interests and demagogues are heaping fuel on the partisan inferno and driving the sort of popular political passions that Madison most feared, turning friends and neighbors into enemies and debilitating the government we share. It's not what most Americans want, but no one seems to know how to stop it.

The American people cannot fix our system spontaneously. Leaders with political credibility and financial resources must step up, channel their inner James Madisons, in order to lead a great and ideologically balanced movement to reform our political system.

The questions get frequently asked, but seldom acted upon: If not us, who? If not now, when?

Send a message to Stephen Erickson: WhatWouldMadisonDo@gmail.com

NOTES

[1] http://www.gallup.com/poll/5392/trust-government.aspx,
http://www.gallup.com/poll/208472/congress-approval-drops-down-
february-high.aspx

[2] If there is one book every American should read about James Madison and
the American Founding, I believe it's William Lee Miller's, *The Business of
May Next: James Madison and the Founding* (The University of Virginia Press:
Charlottesville, 1992). The best general biography on Madison is Ketchum,
Ralph, *James Madison* (University of Virginia Press: Charlottesville, 1990) first
published in 1971. Other important books about Madison include, Banning,
Lance *the Sacred Fire of Liberty: James Madison and the Founding of the
Federal Republic* (Cornell University Press: Ithaca 1995) and McCoy, Drew,
The Last of the Fathers: James Madison and the Republican Legacy (Cam-
bridge University Press: New York, 1991).

[3] Quoted in Ketchum, Ralph, *James Madison* (University of Virginia Press:
Charlottesville, 1990) 149.

[4] Historian Gordon S. Wood offers a good discussion on the concern about
self-interests run amok during the period in *The Radicalism of the American
Revolution,* (Random House: New York, 1993) 243-270.

[5] Bailyn, Bernard, *The Ideological Origins of the American Revolution* (Belknap
Press: Cambridge MA, 1967), 130.

[6] Ibid, 94-143.

[7] Ibid, 131.

[8] Richards, Leonard*, Shay's Rebellion: The American Revolution's Final Battle*
(Then University of Pennsylvania Press: Philadelphia, 2002)

[9] *Massachusetts Sentinel* quoted in Richards, p. 20-30

[10] Madison, James in *James Madison, Writings*, Jack N. Rackove, Ed. (The
Library of America: New York, 1999), 69-80.

[11] See Miller, William Lee 22-33.

[12] See McCoy, Drew, *The Last of the Fathers: James Madison and the Republican Legacy* (Cambridge Univocity Press: New York: 1989) 39-83.

[13] Madison, *Federalist #10* in *Writings*, 161.

[14] Madison, *Federalist #10* in *Writings*, 161-162.

[15] Douglas Adair, *Fame and the Founding Fathers,* (Liberty Fund: University Park, IL, 1998), 93-106.

[16] Madison, James, *Federalist #51*in Rackove, 298.

[17] Cost, Jay, *A Republic No More: Big Government and the Rise of American Political Corruption* (New York: Encounter Books, 2015) 49-50.

[18] Ibid, 108.

[19] Another good place to get a sense of the vices of our system is in journalist Elizabeth Drew's *The Corruption of American Politics* (Carol Publishing Group: Secaucus, NJ, 1999).

[20] For an excellent and balanced account of the 2008 financial crisis, see Morgenson, Gretchen and Rosner, Joshua, *Reckless Endangerment: How Outsized Ambition, Greed and Corruption Led to Economic Armageddon* (Times Books: New York, 2011). See also Taibbi, Matt, *The Divide: American Injustice in the Age of the Wealth Gap* (Spiegel & Grau: New York, 2014).

[21] Ibid. 40-41.

[22] https://www.opensecrets.org/news/2008/09/money-and-votes-aligned-in-con/

[23] Morgenson and Rosner, 108-109.

[24] http://articles.philly.com/2001-02-05/news/25319863_1_subprime-loans-predatory-loan-predatory-lending

[25] http://www.ajc.com/news/news/local/atlanta-legal-aids-bill-brennan-works-to-avert-for/nQm2h/

[26] http://www.publicintegrity.org/2009/05/06/5452/predatory-lending-decade-warnings

[27] http://www.bloomberg.com/bw/articles/2012-09-14/tallying-the-full-cost-of-the-financial-crisis

[28] http://www.motherjones.com/politics/2008/03/its-deregulation-stupid

[29] Barofsky, Neil, *Bailout: An Inside Account of How Washington Abandoned Main Street While Rescuing Wall Street* (Free Press: New York, 2012).

[30] http://www.rollingstone.com/politics/news/eric-holder-wall-street-double-agent-comes-in-from-the-cold-20150708

[31] The most thorough book on the process that led to "Obamacare" is by Brill, Steven, *America's Bitter Pill: Money, Politics, Backroom Deals, and the Fight to Fix Our Broken Healthcare System.* In terms of solutions and perspective, the book's focus is too narrow. Alternatives, like Wyden -Bennett, are quickly and unnecessarily dismissed. "Romneycare" should not necessarily be considered the "conservative alternative" to "Obamacare." Nothing "conservative" comes out of a Massachusetts legislature completely dominated by Democrats. Romney is on record as preferring Wyden's model.

[32] Quoted in Brill, 50.

[33] *American Prospect* 2/14/2008

[34] Coburn, Tom A, *Breach of Trust: How Washington Turns Outsiders into Insiders* (WND Books: Nashville TN)

[35] Ibid, 52.

[36] https://www.unz.org/Pub/PolicyRev-1993q1-00076

[37] Rakove, 75-76.

[38] See Banning Lance, *The Sacred Fire of Liberty: James Madison and the Founding of the Federal Republic* (Cornell University Press: Ithaca, 1995) 111-137.

[39] Rakove, 326

[40] Madison's notes taken at the federal convention, June 25, 1787, in Smith, Paige, *The Constitution: A Documentary and Narrative History* (Morrow Quill

Paperbacks: New York, 1980) 172.

[41] Gastil, John, Weiser Phillip, and others, *The Jury and Democracy* (Oxford: New York, 2010).

[42] James Suroweicki, *The Wisdom of Crowds: Why the Many Are Smarter than the Few and How Collective Wisdom Shapes Business, Economies, Societies and Nations* (New York: Doubleday, 2004),188-189. See also, Sustein, Cass, *Why Societies Need Dissent* (Cambridge, MA: Harvard University Press, 2003).

[43]https://www.opensecrets.org/resources/dollarocracy/06.php. Abramoff, Jack *Capitol Punishment: The Hard Truth about Washington Corruption from America's Most Notorious Lobbyist* (WND Books: Washington, DC, 2011) 274.

[44] http://www.opposingviews.com/i/politics/majority-americans-favors-term-limits-congress; Fox News http://www.foxnews.com/politics/2010/09/03/fox-news-poll-percent-favor-term-limits-congress.html; http://www.rasmussenreports.com/public_content/politics/general_politics/september_2011/71_favor_term_limits_for_congress; http://www.gallup.com/poll/159881/americans-call-term-limits-end-electoral-college.aspx

[45] Cost, 109-130

[46] Dixon, R.G., *Democratic Representation: Reapportionment in Law and Politics* (Oxford University Press: New York, 1968)

[47]Herrnson, Paul S., Congressional Elections: Campaigning at Home and in Washington (CQ Press: Los Angeles: 2012) 175.

[48] Coburn, 77

[49] https://www.washingtonpost.com/news/wonk/wp/2013/01/14/the-most-depressing-graphic-for-members-of-congress/

[50] Schweizer, Peter *Extortion: How Politicians Extract Your Money, Buy Votes and Line their Own Pockets* (Houghton Mifflin Harcourt: Boston, 2013) *8*.

[51]Ibid. 24-25.

[52] Ibid, *79-100.*

[53] http://www.nytimes.com/interactive/2015/06/02/us/politics/money-in-politics-poll.html

[54] http://www.gallup.com/poll/163208/half-support-publicly-financed-federal-campaigns.aspx

[55] Granite State Poll, 2011.

[56]Miller, Michael G, *Subsidizing Democracy* (Cornell University Press: Ithaca, NY, 2013); http://web.stanford.edu/~neilm/The%20Impact%20of%20Public%20Financing%20on%20Electoral%20Competition.pdf,

[57] Ackerman and Ayers, *Voting with Dollars*

[58] For a good brief description of the legal history that preceded *Citizens United*, including the *Buckley* case and the post-Watergate reforms that preceded it, see Drew, 43-60.

[59] Rakove, 161.

[60] Abramoff, Jack *Capitol Punishment: The Hard Truth about Washington Corruption from America's Most Notorious Lobbyist* (WND Books: Washington, DC, 2011)

[61] Lessig, Larry http://lessig.tumblr.com/post/119367599797/wow-how-many-mistakes-can-you-fit-into-325-words

[62] http://www.nybooks.com/articles/2015/06/04/how-money-runs-our-politics/

[63]
http://www.wsj.com/articles/SB10001424052748704288304576170974226083178

[64] http://www.thedailybeast.com/articles/2014/11/09/here-s-a-reform-even-the-koch-brothers-and-george-soros-can-agree-on.html; http://truthinmedia.com/billionaires-charles-koch-george-soros-to-team-up-on-criminal-justice-reform-in-2015/

[65] http://www.gallup.com/poll/201152/conservative-liberal-gap-continues-narrow-tuesday.aspx

[66] http://www.politico.com/story/2014/06/2014-virginia-primary-wall-street-eric-cantor-loss-107696

[67] http://www.huffingtonpost.com/lawrence-lessig/the-democrats-response-to_b_462412.html

[68] https://www.washingtonpost.com/blogs/liveblog-live/liveblog/live-updates-jury-reaches-verdict-in-mcdonnell-

corruption-trial/; http://www.nytimes.com/2014/09/05/us/bob-mcdonnell-maureen-mcdonnell-virginia-verdict.html?_r=0

[69] Predictably, various sources have tried to create smokescreens and play gotcha' journalism with Schweizer. FactCheck.org claims that Schweizer is wrong when he says that Hillary Clinton had "veto" power over the uranium deal because final authority rested with the president. But how likely is that a president would involve himself with an issue like this and overrule his secretary of state? No, Hillary did not technically have "veto power," but her influence over the decision was enormous. That's the real point, which is obscured by the "Fact Checkers." The larger picture is that by building on Schweizer's research, the *Washington Post, New York Times* and *Associated Press* found Schweizer's work on the Clinton Foundation to be generally credible. http://www.factcheck.org/2015/04/no-veto-power-for-clinton-on-uranium-deal/

[70] Braun, Stephen and Sullivan, Eileen," Many Donors to the Clinton Foundation Met with Her at State," 8/23/16, http://bigstory.ap.org/article/82df550e1ec646098b434f7d5771f625/many-donors-clinton-foundation-met-her-state

[71] Schweizer, *Throw Them All Out*, 40-44. Pelosi also facilitated a mass transit project that benefitted her real estate interests, 55-57.

[72]http://www.realclearpolitics.com/articles/2012/04/21/corzine_amid_scandal_is_among_obamas_top_bundlers.html

[73] *New Republic,* 2/28/2013:
http://www.newrepublic.com/article/112548/jack-lew-confirmed-treasury-

secretary-democrats-gave-him-pass

[74] *WSJ*1/31/2014 http://blogs.wsj.com/law/2014/01/31/dershowitz-says-dsouza-case-smacks-of-selective-prosecution/

[75] http://www.nj.com/politics/index.ssf/2015/08/njs_menendez.html

[76] *McConnell v. United States*, 13.

[77] Nader, Ralph, *Unstoppable: The Emerging Left-Right Alliance to Dismantle the Corporate State*, New York: Nation Books 2014.

[78] Schweizer, *Extortion,* 175-178.

[79] Boren, David, *A letter to America* (University of Oklahoma Press: Norman, OK, 2011).

[80] The transcript of Lerner's remarks was republished at http://electionlawblog.org/?p=50160, posted May 11,2013.

[81] http://www.usatoday.com/story/news/politics/2013/05/14/irs-tea-party-progressive-groups/2158831/

[82] http://www.propublica.org/article/irs-office-that-targeted-tea-party-also-disclosed-confidential-docs

[83] Just how differently the 6 progressive "targeted" organizations were treated from conservative ones became apparent when those cases were examined by Congress. See http://dailycaller.com/2014/04/07/committee-staff-report-no-progressive-groups-were-targeted-by-irs/

[84] http://blogs.wsj.com/washwire/2014/02/11/camp-irs-targeted-conservative-groups-for-audits/

[85] http://thehill.com/policy/finance/282307-irs-targeted-426-groups-report; http://www.washingtonexaminer.com/irs-filing-lists-426-groups-that-may-have-been-targeted/article/2593076

[86]http://www.wsj.com/articles/SB100014241278873245490045790689141922280866

[87] See Fund, John, and Von Spakovsky, Hans, *Who's Counting? How Fraud-*

sters and Bureaucrats Put Your Vote at Risk (New York: Encounter Books, 2012)227-232.

[88] *The Daily Caller,* 5/14/13.

[89] *Washington Times*, 9/23/13.

[90] http://www.breitbart.com/big-government/2015/09/27/hillary-clinton-campaign-apparently-coordinates-super-pac-email-talking-point/

[91] http://news.investors.com/ibd-editorials/060313-658636-lois-lerner-targeted-durbon-opponent-al-salvi.htm?p=2

[92] *Press Release*, Senator Dick Durbin (D-IL), 10/12/10.

[93] https://sharylattkisson.com/what-the-irs-commissioner-said-about-those-lois-lerner-emails-back-in-march/

[94] http://dailycaller.com/2014/09/05/irs-five-more-employees-lost-emails-in-computer-crashes/

[95] http://dailycaller.com/2015/03/02/exposed-department-of-justice-shut-down-search-for-lois-lerners-emails/

[96] http://www.foxbusiness.com/economy-policy/2015/07/13/irs-ignores-deadline-to-hand-over-lerner-emails/

[97] http://www.washingtonpost.com/politics/federal_government/obama-donor-leading-justice-departments-irs-investigation/2014/01/09/980c010a-796a-11e3-8963-b4b654bcc9b2_story.html

[98]http://www.realclearpolitics.com/video/2014/02/02/obama_on_irs_scandal_not_even_a_smidgen_of_corruption.html

[99] http://www.judicialwatch.org/wp-content/uploads/2014/04/JW1559-0001051.pdf

[100] Rather than use armed agents to physically seize Bundy's cattle, and risk physical confrontations, the government should have deployed lawyers to put a lien on Bundy's property, which would have averted the standoff while serving the cause of justice.

[101] http://www.washingtontimes.com/news/2015/jun/15/jerry-delemus-former-marine-plans-draw-muhammad-co/;
http://www.fosters.com/article/20150928/NEWS/150929404

[102] http://www.politico.com/story/2015/07/man-behind-donald-trump-run-lewandowski-120443

[103] *New York Times, 6/3/2016*
http://www.nytimes.com/2016/06/04/us/politics/donald-trump-constitution-power.html?_r=0

[104] *USA Today, 9/26/2016*
http://www.usatoday.com/story/opinion/2016/09/26/hillary-clinton-emails-mills-server-immunity-jonathan-turley/91092182/

[105] http://talkingpointsmemo.com/livewire/jerry-delemus-trump-bundy-oregon-standoff

[106] http://www.businessinsider.com/bundy-ranch-standoff-nevada-jerry-delemus-2014-4; http://www.unionleader.com/Jerry-DeLemus-indictment;
http://www.unionleader.com/Granite-States-libertarian-streak-fuels-support-for-Jerry-DeLemus

[107] Haidt, Jonathan, *The Righteous Mind: Why Good People Are Divided by Politics and Religion* (New York: Random House, 2012) Haidt, Jonathan, *The Righteous Mind: Why Good People Are Divided by Politics and Religion* (New York: Random House, 2012) 97-103.

[108] Ibid, 45-46.

[109] The idea that groups are subject to natural selection is called "social Darwinism." The concept, which Haidt does not explain, has an unattractive history. In the late 19th century Herbert Spencer and other like-minded intellectuals used the notion to justify European and US empire building, and dominance over less-developed nations, as merely a healthy and normal product of the evolutionary process. By 1970, the ideas of the social Darwinists were so socially repulsive that any role for the group in evolutionary theory became discredited. Haidt doesn't say it, but this is a pretty good example of how political identity can lead to closed minds. As Haidt makes clear, admitting a role for the group in the evolutionary process need not inevitably lead to racism.

[110] Zinn, Howard, *A People's History of the United States* (New York: Harper Collins, 2003).

[111] On street interview in Iowa, 2015, https://www.youtube.com/watch?v=IWD9ydyORl4

[112] Suroweicki, 188-189.

[113] Ibid, XVII.

[114] Ibid, 11.

[115] For more on the history and legal intricacies of calling a Constitutional Convention under Article V, see James Kenneth Rogers, "The Other Way to Amend the Constitution: The Article V Amendment Process" in *Harvard Journal of Law and Public Policy*, Summer 2007 (Vol. 30, Number 3).

[116] Public approval of the Supreme Court is on the decline. Gallup reported that its June 2013 study found that only 34% of respondents have "a great deal" or "quite a lot" of confidence in the Supreme Court. By 2015, this figure was down to 32%. http://www.gallup.com/poll/163586/americans-approval-supreme-court-near-time-low.aspx, http://www.gallup.com/poll/1597/confidence-institutions.aspx

[117] Fishkin and Gastril et al. Sunstein points out that small evenly polarized groups will moderate their positions to find common ground, especially when dealing with issues that are non-routine and require creativity, 111-144.

[118] Selous Foundation, 7/29/2015, http://sfppr.org/2015/07/experience-shows-that-there-is-no-such-thing-as-an-independent-redistricting-commission/

[119] An interesting website shows what various states would look like when carved up into congressional districts based on a split-line algorithm: http://www.rangevoting.org/GerryExamples.html

[120] http://www.opensecrets.org/news/2014/01/millionaires-club-for-first-time-most-lawmakers-are-worth-1-million-plus/

[121] https://www.washingtonpost.com/investigations/capitol-assets-congresss-wealthiest-mostly-shielded-in-deep-

recession/2012/10/06/5a70605c-102f-11e2-acc1-e927767f41cd_story.html

[122] Leibovich, Mark, *This Town* (Penguin Group: New York, 2013).

[123] http://www.bloombergview.com/articles/2013-02-21/citigroup-s-man-goes-to-the-treasury-department

[124] http://www.usatoday.com/story/news/world/2013/06/12/state-department-whistle-blower/2413265/,
http://www.cbsnews.com/news/state-department-memo-reveals-possible-cover-ups-halted-investigations/,
http://foreignpolicy.com/2013/06/17/exclusive-whistleblower-says-state-department-trying-to-bully-her-into-silence/.

[125] https://www.washingtonpost.com/news/federal-eye/wp/2015/09/09/justice-for-one-fired-va-whistleblower-but-exposing-problems-is-still-treacherous/

[126]http://www.theatlantic.com/science/archive/2015/11/is-the-usda-silencing-scientists/413803/

[127] The little-known story of the founding generation's attempt to limit US House district sizes is told by Clair W. Keller's article "The Failure to Provide a Constitutional Guarantee on Representation" in *The Journal of the Early Republic,* Vol. 13, No. 1, (Spring, 1993) 23-54.

[128] See Article I, Section 2 of the Constitution.

[129] http://www.thirty-thousand.org/

[130] Quoted in Gabrielson, Jenna. 2009. "James Madison's Psychology of Public Opinion," *Political Research Quarterly*, Vol. 62., 431.

[131] *Wall Street Journal,* 2/26/ 2017. https://www.wsj.com/articles/many-americans-disapprove-of-trump-but-are-open-to-his-agenda-poll-finds-1488117602